Yale French Studies

NUMBER 88

Depositions: Althusser, Balibar, Macherey, and the Labor of Reading

JACQUES LEZRA	1	Editor's Preface: Labors of Reading
JUDITH BUTLER	6	"Conscience Doth Make Subjects of Us All"
THOMAS PEPPER	27	Kneel and You Will Believe
PIERRE MACHEREY	42	A Production of Subjectivity
WARREN MONTAG	53	"The Soul is the Prison of the Body": Althusser and Foucault, 1970–1975
JACQUES LEZRA	78	Spontaneous Labor
ANDRZEJ WARMINSKI	118	Hegel/Marx: Consciousness and Life
ETIENNE BALIBAR	142	The Infinite Contradiction
GERALDINE FRIEDMAN	165	The Spectral Legacy of Althusser: The Symptom and Its Return
ELLEN ROONEY	183	Better Read Than Dead: Althusser and the Fetish of Ideology
MICHAEL SPRINKER	201	The Legacies of Althusser

Yale French Studies

Jacques Lezra, *Special editor for this issue*
Alyson Waters, *Managing editor*
Editorial board: Denis Hollier (Chair), Christopher
 Miller (Acting Chair), Ora Avni, Peter Brooks,
 Benjamin Elwood, Shoshana Felman, Françoise
 Jaouën, Daryl Lee, Charles Porter, Benjamin Semple,
 Allison Tait
Editorial assistant: Noah Guynn
Editorial office: 82-90 Wall Street, Room 308.
Mailing address: P.O. Box 208251, New Haven,
 Connecticut 06520-8251.
Sales and subscription office:
Yale University Press, P.O. Box 209040
New Haven, Connecticut 06520-9040
Published twice annually by Yale University Press

Copyright © 1995 by Yale University
All rights reserved.
This book may not be reproduced, in whole or in part,
 in any form (beyond that copying permitted by
 Sections 107 and 108 of the U.S. Copyright Law and
 except by reviewers for the public press) without
 written permission from the publisher.

Designed by James J. Johnson and set in Trump
 Medieval Roman by The Composing Room of
 Michigan, Inc. Printed in the United States of
 America by the Vail Ballou Press, Binghamton, N.Y.

ISSN 044-0078
ISBN for this issue 0-300-06578-7

JACQUES LEZRA

Editor's Preface: Labors of Reading

"As I was standing at the Venice Biennale," Louis Althusser opens his essay on "Cremonini, Painter of the Abstract," "in which Cremonini had exhibited some fine canvases, two Frenchmen came in, glanced quickly round and left, one saying to the other, 'Uninteresting: expressionism!'"[1] The phrase, itself advanced by a Frenchman, expresses a certain awkwardness about "Frenchmen" viewing these "fine canvases"—and the balance of the essay can easily (if rather superficially) be understood to suggest by way of compensation that the immediate, false (because "gastronomic") reaction of the two tourists can indeed be balanced by the genuine critic's much more meditative one. The anecdote poses starkly a knot of concepts that go well beyond its immediate use: the "quick" glance is indeed always an "interested" one, conditioned and determined by ideologies it cannot speak; the act of naming ("expressionism!") expresses the logic of avoidance and denial often aroused by the esthetic; what we "recognize" cannot be turned into what we "know" without a re-turn or a revolution that also

---

1. Louis Althusser, "Cremonini, Painter of the Abstract," in *Lenin and Philosophy and Other Essays*, trans. Ben Brewster (New York: Monthly Review Press, 1971), 229.
  Shorter versions of some of the essays in this volume were first presented at the Modern Language Association convention in 1991, at a panel treating the topic of ideology. I want to express my gratitude to the panelists and to Andrzej Warminski, who proposed the topic in the first place. James Kavanagh provided invaluable help in planning this volume, as did Warren Montag. Rebecca Lemon, of the Department of English at the University of Wisconsin—Madison, saw me through a number of tricky editorial decisions with panache and intelligence. My thanks and admiration, finally and especially, to Alyson Waters, the managing editor at *Yale French Studies*, for being able to express patience in the imperative mode, and impatience in the optative.

YFS 88, *Depositions*, ed. Lezra, © 1995 by Yale University.

marks a change in the object to be known; the ideological determination of the meditative look differs from the "quick glance" in taking account, as best it can, of its "interestedness"; and so on. The canvas that Althusser *paints* here, at the opening of his essay, invites us to "see" or "identify" ourselves momentarily in the caricature of the Frenchmen's superficial judgment, but reassures us finally (once we have worked through the argument of "Cremonini, Painter of the Abstract") that such narcissistic self-recognition, a mere preliminary moment in an event to which the canvases recall us, reproduces a face we have already learned to deform—that is, to materialize.

The recent spate of critical reengagements with Althusser's essays, as well as the increasing influence in the United States and Britain of Etienne Balibar and Pierre Macherey's work, suggests that something like this evaluative return has become possible on rather a larger scale. Prodded as much by the death of Louis Althusser and the posthumous publication of his controversial autobiographies as by the recent publication in English of collections of Balibar's works on class and nationalism, and of Macherey's *Object of Literature*, the institutions and orthodoxies that had lionized and then rejected the extraordinary project of *Reading "Capital"* and of *Toward a Theory of Literary Production* have indeed sought to take a second look at the texts that, in the decade from 1965 to 1975, shaped the relation between the languages of philosophy, of political practice, of esthetics, and of literary theory. Independently, the epistemological and professional requirement that critical languages legitimate themselves in part by fashioning or discovering genealogies has generated superb, polemically interested readings of those texts in the field of cultural criticism; within doctrines of positional, performative, or strategic subjectivities in queer theory or in postcolonial thought; and as an aspect of the projects of radical democracy and of the affirmative deconstruction of the concepts of "class," "nation," and "race."

As this last point suggests, the project cannot be antiquarian, the mere rediscovery of texts held in dusty storage for fifteen years, canvases produced for effect like spoils of war hoarded in the basement of some notional Hermitage Museum. Instead, the labor of rereading is immediately double. Any return to the work of Althusser, and any reading of Balibar and Macherey's recent essays in that light, must on the one hand seek to describe with the retrospective clarity of thirty years the broad history occluded by particular battles and engagements, or the *tendential* history of the moment of enunciation of those theses. Call this, classically, the *defamiliarization* of concepts we believe we recognize: the concepts of over- and underdetermination of effect in the social field; the interpellation of individuals as subjects; the constitutive *break* between a Hegelian and a Marxist Marx; the unevenness of origins; the insistence on the posing of theses; etc. On the other hand, any reexamination of the Althusserian legacy in terms of its effects must immediately concern itself with the institutional legitimacy of current critical positions. This process might be called the *reinscription* of those concepts or systems of concepts in the field of their effects, as effects of their own effects. This double labor of defamilarization and reinscription need not suppose that the conditions of its present conjuncture are recognizable and expressible, or that it can parse out the massive causal overdetermination that links particular theses to particular discursive effects. Instead, and to avoid becoming disablingly like a biennial trip to a museum, the labor of reading proposes practical filiations between the provisional analysis of contemporary conjunctures and the blindnesses of the Althusserian project with respect to its own.

The essays collected in *Depositions* are instances of this double labor as well as reflections upon it. They draw upon the languages of philosophy and cultural criticism, of psychoanalysis and gender studies, of political and esthetic philosophy, in an effort at a double positioning and a double deforming or defamiliarizing. And they are, for that reason, as technically and as rigorously *difficult* or *complex* as it was and remains, in Althusser's words, to be "a Marxist in philosophy." This complexity does not herald the contrary call for a utopian moment in which thought or the labor of reading would be *easy*, either because the field of Marxism would have become isomorphous with that of philosophy, fully and transparently theorized, or because the field of philosophy would have become the same as a theoretical practice. "Difficulty" and nonsimplicity name what has to persist as the unrecognizable noncoincidence between practices and systems of concepts, or, to put it a little differently, as the condition of possibility of action, and the condition of impossibility of determining in advance and conceptually what "action" is *for*.

For. To speak or write, or to act "for" another: the extraordinary period stretching from the publication of *For Marx* to the murder of Hélène Althusser, from 1965 to the current attacks in the United States on the National Endowments for the Humanities and the Arts, can indeed be marked by the questions that the preposition "for" opens. It is in large part due to the project set out in *Reading "Capital"* that it is no longer possible to pose, either theoretically or practically, the vestigial Lukácsian and Leninist theses that the intellectual speaks in the first instance "for" the working class. No text advances more complexly, more tormentedly, the need to decide, in the terms of contemporary pragmatism, what intellectuals are "for," what speech is "for," what and how speech-acts can affirm or affect. More: it hardly matters whether we understand this "for" spatially or phenomenologically, indicating the direction of a thought or project, or of an intention; or economically, to designate the person who receives a gift, a grant, or a transaction; or adversatively, "for" in contrast to "against" one position or one institution ("for the Humanities") or another; or substitutively, reading "for Marx" as "in the place of Marx." The matter that the essays in *Depositions* doubly treat, as instances and as reflections, is the overdetermination—the permanent deposings—of the position and languages that a subject can assume today in the field of politics and in the legitimation of discourses that reflect upon and seek to change hegemonies. These essays understand the labor of reading in the wake of the work of Althusser, Macherey, and Balibar as a double deposing, a double incompleting or a double defacement: of what we had thought we recognized, of what a "quick glance" at the familiar canvas of our history told us that certain names and determining concepts had *stood for*; and of what we had thought we knew to be ourselves, the rule of such recognitions and substitutions, a transcendental synthesis, a face.

Or the face we produce *for* something else, the substitute or symptom of a ghostly and deforming *figure*. Althusser's essay on Cremonini reflects at last upon this difficult, doubly absent figure, precisely the figure that keeps his project and the work of Balibar and Macherey from simply eliding the discontinuous labor of reading either with the act of a recognizable "human *subject*," or with the easy schizophrenia of labor's postmodern simulacra. Invisible, it haunts the painter's canvases as it does Althusser's writing, and in its most polemical shape—as the possibility of *history*—it constitutes the ground of inquiry for the essays in this volume:

> The humanist-religious ideological function of the human face is to be the seat of the "soul," of subjectivity, and therefore the visible proof of the existence of the human *subject*, with all the ideological force of the concept of the subject. . . . Cremonini's human faces are such that they cannot be *seen*, i.e., identified as bearers of the ideological func-

tion of the expression of *subjects*. That is why they are so "badly" represented, hardly outlined, as if instead of being the authors of their gestures, they were merely their *trace*. They are haunted by an absence: a purely negative absence, that of the humanist function which is refused them, and which they refuse; and a positive, determinate absence, that of the *structure* of the world which determines them, which makes them the anonymous beings they are, the structural effects of the real relations which govern them. ["Cremonini," 239]

JUDITH BUTLER

"Conscience Doth Make Subjects of Us All"[1]

Althusser's doctrine of interpellation continues to structure contemporary debate on subject formation, offering a way to account for how a subject comes into being after language, but always within its terms. The theory of interpellation appears to stage a social scene in which a subject is hailed, the subject turns around, and then accepts the terms by which he or she is hailed. This is, no doubt, a scene both punitive and reduced, for the call is made by an officer of "the Law" and this officer is cast as singular and speaking. Clearly we might object that the "call" arrives severally and in implicit and unspoken ways, that the scene is never quite as dyadic as Althusser claims, but these objections have been rehearsed, and "interpellation" as a doctrine continues to survive its critique. If we accept that the scene is exemplary and allegorical, then it never needs to happen for its effectivity to be presumed. Indeed, if it is allegorical in Benjamin's sense, then the process literalized by the allegory is precisely that which resists narration, that is, that exceeds the narrativizability of events.[2] Interpellation, in this account, is not an event, but a certain way of *staging the call*, where the call, as staged, becomes deliteralized in the course of its exposition or *Darstellung*. The call itself is also figured as a demand to align oneself with the law, a turning around (to face the law, to find a face for the law?), and an entrance into the language of self-ascription—"Here I am"—through the appropriation of guilt.

Why is it that subject formation appears to take place only upon the

---

1. Shakespeare, *Hamlet*, act 3, scene 1.
2. See Walter Benjamin, *On the Origins of German Tragic Drama*, trans. Peter Osborne (Cambridge: MIT Press, 1987).

YFS 88, *Depositions*, ed. Lezra, © 1995 by Yale University.

acceptance of guilt, that there is no "I" who might ascribe a place to itself, who might be announced in speech, without first a self-attribution of guilt, a submission to the law through an acceptance of its demand for conformity? The one who turns around in response to the call does not respond to a demand to turn around. The turning around is an act that is, as it were, conditioned both by the "voice" of the law and by the responsiveness of the one hailed by the law. The "turning around" is a strange sort of middle-ground (taking place, perhaps, in a strange sort of "middle-voice"[3]) that is determined both by the law and the addressee, but by neither unilaterally or exhaustively. Although there would be no turning around without first having been hailed, neither would there be a turning around without some readiness to turn. But where and when does the calling of the name solicit the turning around, the anticipatory move toward identity? How and why does the subject turn, anticipating the conferral of identity through the self-ascription of guilt? What kind of relation already binds these two such that the subject knows to turn, knows that something is to be gained from such a turn? How might we think of this "turn" as prior to subject formation, a prior complicity with the law without which no subject emerges? The turn toward the law is thus at once a turn against oneself, the turning back on oneself that constitutes the movement of conscience. But how is it that the reflex of conscience is precisely what paralyzes the critical interrogation of the law at the same time that it figures the subject's uncritical relation to the law as a condition of subjectivation? The one addressed is compelled to turn toward the law prior to any possibility of asking a set of critical questions: Who is speaking? Why should I turn around? Why should I accept the terms by which I am hailed? This means that, prior to any possibility of a critical understanding of the law, there is an openness or vulnerability to the law, exemplified in the turn toward the law, in the anticipation of culling an identity through identifying with the one who has broken the law. Indeed, the law is broken prior to any possibility of having access to it, and so, "guilt" is prior to knowledge of the law and is, in this sense, always strangely innocent. The possibility of a critical view of the law is thus limited by what might be understood as a prior desire for the law, a passionate complicity with law, without which no subject can exist. For the "I" to launch its critique, it must first understand that the "I" itself is dependent upon

3. I thank Hayden White for this suggestion.

its complicitous desire for the law for the possibility of its own existence. A critical review of the law will not, therefore, undo the force of conscience unless the one who offers that critique is willing, as it were, to be undone by the critique that he or she performs.

It is important to remember that the turn toward the law is not necessitated by the hailing; it is compelling, in a less than logical sense, because it promises identity. If the law speaks in the name of a self-identical subject (Althusser cites the utterance of the Hebrew God: "I am that I am"), how is it that conscience might deliver or restore a self to oneness with itself, to the postulation of self-identity that becomes the precondition of that linguistic consolidation: "Here I am"?

On the other hand, how might we site the vulnerability of subjectivation precisely in that turn (toward the law, against the self) which precedes and anticipates the acceptance of guilt, a turn that eludes subjectivation even as it conditions it? How is it that this "turn" figures a conscience that might be rendered less conscientious than Althusser would render it? And how is it that Althusser's sanctification of the scene of interpellation makes the possibility of becoming a "bad" subject more remote and less incendiary than it might very well be?

The doctrine of interpellation appears to presuppose a prior and unelaborated doctrine of conscience, a turning back upon oneself in the sense that Nietzsche described in *On the Genealogy of Morals*.[4] And this readiness to accept guilt to gain a purchase on identity is linked to a highly religious scenario of a nominating call that comes from God and that constitutes the subject through appealing to a need for the law, an original guilt that the law promises to assuage through the conferral of identity. How is it that this religious figuration of interpellation restrains in advance any possibility of a critical inter-

---

4. Nietzsche distinguished between conscience and bad conscience in *On the Genealogy of Morals*, linking the first with the capacity to promise and the second to the problem of internalization and of debt. The distinction appears not to be sustained as it becomes apparent that the promising being can only stand for his/her future through first becoming regular, that is, through the process of internalizing the law or, to be precise, "burning it into the will." Internalization, introduced in the second essay, section 16, involves the turning of the will (or instincts) against itself. In section 15, he introduces freedom as that which turns against itself in the making of bad conscience: "This instinct for freedom forcibly made latent... this instinct for freedom pushed back and repressed, incarcerated within and finally able to discharge and vent itself only on itself: that, and that alone, is what the *bad conscience* is in its beginnings" (Friedrich Nietzsche, *On the Genealogy of Morals*, trans. Walter Kaufmann [New York: Vintage, 1969], 87).

vention in the workings of the law, the undoing of the subject without which the law cannot proceed?

The mention of conscience in Althusser's "Ideology and Ideological State Apparatuses"[5] has received little critical attention, even though the term, taken together with the example of religious authority to illustrate the force of ideology, suggests that the theory of ideology is supported by a complicated set of theological metaphors. Although Althusser explicitly introduces "the Church" merely as an *example* of ideological interpellation, it appears that ideology in his terms cannot be thought except through the metaphorics of religious authority. The final section of "Ideology. . ." is entitled "An Example: The Christian Religious Ideology" and makes explicit the exemplary status that religious institutions have occupied in the preceding section of the essay. Those examples include: the putative "eternity" of ideology; the explicit analogy between the "obviousness of ideology" and St Paul's notion of the "Logos" in which we are said to "live, move and have our being"; Pascal's prayer as an instance of ritual in which assuming the posture of kneeling gives rise over time to belief; belief itself as the institutionally reproduced condition of ideology; and the deifying capitalization of "Family," "Church," "School," and "State."

Although the last section of the essay seeks to explicate and expose the example of religious authority, this is not an exposure with the power to defuse the force of ideology. Althusser's own writing, he concedes, invariably enacts what it thematizes,[6] and thus promises no enlightened escape from ideology through this articulation. To illustrate the power of ideology to constitute subjects, Althusser seeks recourse to the example of the divine voice that names, and in naming, brings its subjects into being. In claiming that social ideology operates in an analogous way, Althusser inadvertently assimilates social interpellation to the divine performative. The example of ideology thus

---

5. Louis Althusser, "Idéologie et appareils idéologiques d'état," in *Positions* (Paris: Editions Sociales, 1976), 67–126; or in English, "Ideology and Ideological State Apparatuses (Notes Toward an Investigation)," in *Lenin and Philosophy and Other Essays*, trans. Ben Brewster (New York: Monthly Review Press, 1971), 127–88.

6. Althusser implicates his own writing in the version of ideological interpellation that he explains: "It is essential to realize that both he who is writing these lines and the reader who reads them are themselves subjects, and therefore ideological subjects (a tautological proposition), i.e. that the author and the reader of these lines both live 'spontaneously' or 'naturally' in ideology" ("Ideology and Ideological State Apparatuses," 171). This remark is especially noteworthy insofar as Althusser presumes the authoritative capacities of the voice, and insists that his writing, to the extent that it is ideological, addresses its reader as would a voice.

assumes the status of a paradigm for thinking ideology as such, whereby the inevitable structures of ideology are established textually through religious metaphor: the authority of the "voice" of ideology, the "voice" of interpellation, is figured as a voice almost impossible to refuse. The force of interpellation in Althusser is derived from the examples by which it is ostensibly illustrated, most notably, God's voice in the naming of Peter (and Moses) and its secularization in the postulated voice of the representative of state authority: the policeman's voice in the hailing of the wayward pedestrian with "Hey you there!"

In other words, the divine power of naming structures the theory of interpellation that accounts for the ideological constitution of the subject. Baptism exemplifies the linguistic means by which the subject is compelled into social being. God names "Peter," and this address establishes God as the origin of Peter ("Ideology," 177); the name remains attached to Peter permanently by virtue of the implied and continuous presence in the name of the one who names him. Within the terms of Althusser's examples, however, this naming cannot be accomplished without a certain readiness or anticipatory desire on the part of the one addressed. To the extent that the naming is an address, there is already an addressee, prior to the address; but given that the address is a name that creates what it names, there appears to be no "Peter" without the name, "Peter." Indeed, "Peter" does not exist without the name that supplies that linguistic guarantee of existence. In this sense, as a prior and essential condition of the formation of the subject, there is a certain readiness to be compelled by the authoritative interpellation, a readiness that suggests that one is, as it were, already in relation to the voice before the response, already implicated in the terms of the animating misrecognition by an authority to which one subsequently yields. Or perhaps one has already yielded before one turns around, and that turning is nothing other than a sign of an inevitable submission by which one is established as a subject positioned in language as a possible addressee. In this sense, the scene with the police is a belated and redoubled scene, one that renders explicit a founding submission for which no such scene would prove adequate. For if that submission is what brings the subject into being, then the narrative that seeks to tell the story of that submission can proceed only through exploiting grammar for its fictional effects. The narrative that seeks to account for how the subject comes into being presumes the grammatical "subject" prior to the account of its genesis. And yet, the founding submission that has not yet resolved into the subject would be precisely that nonnarrativizable prehistory of the subject, a paradox that calls the very narrative of subject formation into question. If there is no subject except as a consequence of this subjection, the narrative that would explain this requires that the temporality not be true, for the grammar of that narrative presupposes that there is no subjection without a subject who undergoes it.

Is this founding submission a kind of yielding prior to any question of psychological motivation? How are we to understand the psychic disposition at work at the moment in which the pedestrian responds to the law—what conditions and informs that response? Why would it be that the person on the street responds to the "Hey you there!" by turning around? What is the significance in turning to face the voice that calls from behind? This turning toward the voice of the law is a sign of a certain desire to be beheld by and perhaps also to behold the face of authority, a visual rendering of an auditory scene—a mirror stage or, perhaps more appropriately, an "acoustic mirror"[7]—that allows that misrecognition without which the sociality of the subject cannot be achieved. This subjectivation is, according to Althusser, a *mis*recognition, a false and provisional totalization. What precipitates this desire for the law, this lure of misrecognition offered in the reprimand that establishes subordination as the price of subjectivation? This account appears to imply that social existence, existence as a subject, can be purchased only through a guilty embrace of the law, where guilt guarantees the intervention of the law and, hence, the continuation of the subject's existence. If the subject can only assure his/her existence in terms of the law, and the law requires subjection for subjectivation, then it may be, perversely, that one (always already) yields to the law in order to continue to assure one's own existence. The yielding to the law might then be read as the compelled consequence of a narcissistic attachment to one's continuing existence.

Althusser takes up guilt explicitly in the narrative, however reli-

---

7. See Kaja Silverman, *The Acoustic Mirror: The Female Voice in Psychoanalysis and Cinema* (Bloomington: Indiana University Press, 1988). Silverman notes the "theological" dimension of the "voice-over" in film that always escapes the viewer's gaze (49). Silverman also makes clear that the voice recognized in the cinematic presentation of voice is not only the maternal voice, but a repudiated dimension of the masculine subject's own voice (80–81). Silverman's analysis sheds light on the "voice" of ideology insofar as the subject who turns around already knows the voice to which he responds, suggesting an irreducible ambiguity between the "voice" of conscience and the "voice" of the law.

able, of his murder of his wife Hélène, in which he recounts, in a telling reversal of the police scene in "Ideology," how he rushed into the street calling for the police in order to deliver himself up to the law.[8] This calling for the police is a peculiar inversion of hailing, which "Ideology" presupposes without explicitly thematizing. Without exploiting the biographical, I want to pursue the theoretical importance of this reversal of the scene with the police in which the man on the street calls for the police rather than responding to the police's call. In "Ideology," guilt and conscience operate implicitly in relation to an ideological demand, an animating reprimand, in the account of subject formation. What follows here is an attempt to reread that essay in order to understand how interpellation is essentially figured through the religious example. The exemplary status of religious authority underscores the paradox of how the very possibility of subject formation depends upon a passionate pursuit of a recognition which, within the terms of the religious example, is inseparable from a condemnation.

Another way of posing this question is as follows: How is Althusser's text implicated in the "conscience" that it seeks to explain? And to what extent is the persistence of the theological model a symptom, one that compels a symptomatic reading? In his introductory essay to *Lire le Capital,* Althusser suggests that every text must be read for the "invisible" that appears within the world that theory renders visible.[9] In a recent consideration of Althusser's notion of "symptomatic reading," Jean-Marie Vincent remarks that "a text is not only interesting because it organizes logically, by the arguments it develops in an apparently rigorous fashion, but also because of everything that disorganizes its order, because of everything that weakens it."[10] Neither Althusser nor Vincent considers the possibility that the exemplary status of certain metaphors may become occasions for a symptomatic reading that "weakens" rigorous argument. But it seems that in relation to Althusser's own text, a reconsideration of the central religious tropes of the voice of the law and conscience provides a way to question what has become, within recent literary studies, an unnecessary tension between the reading of metaphor and the reading of ideology. To the

---

8. See section one in Althusser, *L'avenir dure longtemps, suivi de les faits* (Paris: Editions STOCK/IMEC, 1992).

9. Althusser and Etienne Balibar, *Lire le Capital* (Paris: François Maspero, 1968), vol. 1, 26; or in English, *Reading "Capital,"* trans. Ben Brewster (London: Verso, 1970), 26.

10. Jean-Marie Vincent, "La lecture symptomale chez Althusser," in *Sur Althusser: Passages* (Paris: Editions L'Harmattan, collection Futur Antérieur, 1993), 97.

extent that Althusser's religious analogies are understood as merely illustrative, they are set apart from the rigorous argumentation of the text itself, offered in pedagogical paraphrasis. And yet, the performative force of the voice of religious authority becomes exemplary for the theory of interpellation, thus extending through example the putative force of divine naming to those social authorities by which the subject is hailed into social being. This argument does not mean to suggest that the "truth" of Althusser's text can be discovered in the disruptive effects of the figural on its "rigorous" conceptualization. Such an approach romanticizes the figural as essentially disruptive, where it may well be the case that figures compound and intensify conceptual claims. The concern here has a more specific textual aim, namely, to show how the figures—the examples and the analogies—inform and extend the conceptualizations, implicating the text in an ideological sanctification of religious authority which it can expose only through its reenactment.

For Althusser, the efficacy of ideology consists in part in the formation of *conscience*, where the notion of conscience is understood to place restrictions on what is speakable or, more generally, representable. Conscience cannot be conceptualized as a self-restriction, if that relation is construed as a pregiven reflexivity, a turning back upon itself performed by a ready-made subject, but designates a kind of turning back—a reflexivity—which constitutes the conditions for the possibility of the subject's formation. In this sense, reflexivity is constituted through this moment of conscience, this turning back upon oneself, one which is simultaneous with a turning toward the law. This self-restriction is something other than the internalization of an external law: the model of internalization takes for granted the "internal" and the "external" as already formed. This self-restriction is prior to the subject, constituting the inaugurating reflexive turn of the subject, enacted in anticipation of the law and, hence, determined in relation to that law, with a prejudicative foreknowledge of the law. Conscience is fundamental to the production and regulation of the citizen-subject, for it is conscience that turns the individual around to make itself available to that subjectivating reprimand, but the law will represent the redoubling of the reprimand: a turning back and a turning toward. How are these turns to be thought together, without reducing the one to the other?

Before the police or the church authorities arrive on the Althusserian scene, there is a reference to prohibition which, in a Lacanian vein, is linked with the very possibility of speech. Althusser links the emergence of a consciousness—and a conscience—[*la conscience civique et professionelle*]—with the problem of speaking properly [*bien parler*] ("Ideology," 132). "Speaking properly" appears to be an instance of the ideological work of skill acquisition, a process central to the formation of the subject. The "diverse skills" of labor power have to be reproduced. This reproduction of the skills of labor power happens more and more often "outside the firm" and *in school*, that is, outside production and in educational institutions. The skills to be learned are, in the first instance, *the skills of speech*. The first mention of "conscience," which will turn out to be quite central to the success or efficacy of interpellation, is linked to the acquisition of mastery, learning how to "speak properly." The reproduction of the subject takes place through the reproduction of linguistic skills, constituting, as it were, the rules and attitudes observed "by every agent in the division of labour." In this sense the rules of proper speech are also the rules by which *respect* is proferred or withheld. Workers are taught to *speak* properly and managers learn to speak to workers "in the right way" [*bien commander*] (131–32).

Language skills are said to be mastered and masterable, and yet, this mastery is figured by Althusser quite clearly as a kind of submission: ". . . the reproduction of labour power requires not only a reproduction of (the labourer's) skills, but also, at the same time, a reproduction of its submission to the rules of the established order [*soumission à l'idéologie dominante*]" (132). This submission to the rules of dominant ideology leads in the next paragraph to the problematic of *subjection*, which carries the double meaning of having submitted to these rules, and becoming constituted within sociality by virtue of this submission.

He writes that "the school teaches 'know-how' (skills) [*des 'savoir-faire'*]. . . in forms which ensure *subjection* to the ruling ideology [*l'assujetissement à l'idéologie dominante*] or the mastery of its 'practice.'"[11] Consider the logical effect of this disjunctive "or" [*ou*] in the middle of this formulation: "subjection *to* the ruling ideology or—put in different, yet equivalent terms—the mastery *of* its 'practice'" (my emphases). The more a practice is mastered, the more fully subjection is achieved. Submission and mastery take place simultaneously, and it is this paradoxical simultaneity that constitutes the ambivalence of

11. Althusser, *Positions*, 73; *Lenin and Philosophy*, 133.

subjection. Where one might expect submission to consist in a yielding to an externally imposed dominant order, and to be marked by a loss of control and mastery, it is paradoxically marked by mastery itself. The binary frame of mastery/submission is forfeited by Althusser as he recasts submission precisely and paradoxically as a kind of mastery. In this view, neither submission nor mastery is *performed by a subject;* the lived simultaneity of submission as mastery, and mastery as submission, is the condition of possibility for the emergence of the subject itself.

The conceptual problem here is underscored by a grammatical one in which there can be no subject prior to a submission, and yet there is a grammatically induced "need to know" *who* undergoes this submission in order to become a subject. Althusser introduces the term "individual" as a place-holder to satisfy provisionally this grammatical need, but what might ultimately fit the grammatical requirement will not be a static grammatical subject. The grammar of the subject emerges only as a consequence of the very process we are trying to describe. Because we are, as it were, trapped within the grammatical time of the subject [e.g., "we are trying to describe," "we are trapped"], it is almost impossible to ask about the genealogy of its construction without presupposing that construction for the asking of the question itself.

What is there, then, prior to the subject that accounts for its formation? Althusser begins the "Ideology and Ideological State Apparatuses" essay by referring to the reproduction of social relations; he then specifies this reproduction of social relations as the reproduction of social skills and distinguishes between those skills reproduced in the firm, and those reproduced in education. With respect to these latter, the subject is formed. In a sense, this reproduction of relations is prior to the subject who is formed in the course of this reproduction. And yet, the two cannot, strictly speaking, be thought without each other.

The reproduction of social relations, the reproduction of skills, is the reproduction of subjection, but here it is not the reproduction of labor that is central, but a reproduction proper to the subject, one that takes place in relation to *language* and to the formation of *conscience.* For Althusser, to perform tasks "conscientiously" is to perform them, as it were, again and again, to reproduce those skills and, in reproducing them, acquire mastery. "Conscientiously" is placed in quotation marks by Althusser ("pour s'acquitter 'consciencieusement' de leur tâche"), thus bringing into relief the way in which labor is moralized. Significant here, however, is the moral sense of "s'acquitter" lost in its translation as "to perform": if the mastery of a set of skills is to be construed as *an acquitting of oneself*, then this mastery of "savoir-faire" will constitute a defense of oneself against an accusation or, quite literally, a declaring of innocence on the part of the accused. To acquit oneself "conscientiously" of one's task is, then, to construe labor as a confession of innocence, a display or proof of guiltlessness in the face of the demand for confession implied by an insistent accusation.

The "submission" to the rules of dominant ideology might then be understood as a submission to the necessity to prove innocence in the face of accusation, a submission to the demand for proof, an execution of that proof, and the acquisition of the status of the subject in and through a compliance with the terms of the interrogative law. To become a "subject" is, thus, to have been presumed guilty, then tried and declared innocent. And because this declaration is not a single act, but a status incessantly *reproduced*, to become a "subject" is to be continuously in the process of acquitting oneself of the accusation of guilt. It is to have become an emblem of lawfulness, a citizen in good standing, but one for whom that status is tenuous, indeed, one who has known—somehow, somewhere—what it is *not* to have that standing and, hence, to have been cast out as guilty. And yet, because this guilt conditions the subject, it constitutes the prehistory of that subjection to the law by which the subject is produced. Here one might usefully conjecture that the reason there are so few references to "bad subjects" in Althusser is that the term tends toward the oxymoronic within the terms of his text. To be "bad" is not yet to be a subject, not yet to have acquitted oneself of the allegation of guilt.[12]

And yet this performance is not simply *in accord* with these skills, for there is no subject prior to the performing of those skills; it is the performing of the skills that laboriously works the subject into its status as a social being, a guilt, and then a repetitive practice by which skills are acquired, and then and only then the assumption of the grammatical place within the social as a subject.

Yet the subject may be said to perform according to a set of skills, that is, as it were, to take grammar at its word: first there is a subject

12. One might usefully compare Weber's *The Protestant Ethic* with Althusser on this point in which labor is effectively guaranteed through a Protestant ethic, although in Althusser the religious inflection appears to be more Catholic.

who encounters a set of skills to be learned, learns them or fails to learn them, and then and only then can be said either to have mastered those skills or not. To master a set of skills is not simply to accept a set of skills, but to reproduce them in and as one's own activity; this is not simply an acting according to a set of rules, but the embodying of rules in the course of action, and the reproduction of those rules in embodied rituals of action.[13]

What leads to this reproduction? Clearly, it is not merely a mechanistic appropriation of norms, and neither is it a voluntaristic appropriation. It would be as wrong to account for this reproduction in terms of a simple behaviorism as it would to account for it in terms of a deliberate project. To the extent that it precedes the formation of the subject, it is not yet of the order of consciousness, and yet this involuntary compulsion is not the same as a mechanistically induced effect. The notion of ritual suggests that it is performed, and that in the repetition of performance a belief is spawned, which is then incorporated into the performance in its subsequent operations. But inherent to any performance is a compulsion to "acquit oneself," and so prior to any performance is an anxiety and a knowingness that becomes articulate and animating only on the occasion of the reprimand.

Is it possible here to separate the psychic dimension of this ritualistic repetition from the "acts" by which it is animated and reanimated? The very notion of ritual is meant to render belief and practice insepar-

---

13. Pierre Bourdieu elaborates the conception of the *habitus* in *The Logic of Practice* (Stanford: Stanford University Press, 1990), 66–79. He analyzes the embodied rituals of everydayness by which a given culture produces and sustains belief in its own "obviousness." In this way, Bourdieu underscores the place of the body, its gestures, its stylistics, its unconscious "knowingness" as the site for the reconstitution of a practical sense without which social reality would not be constituted as such.

Bourdieu's notion of the *habitus* might well be read as a reformulation of Althusser's notion of ideology. Whereas Althusser will write that ideology constitutes the "obviousness" of the subject, but that this obviousness is the effect of a *dispositif*, that same term reemerges in Bourdieu to describe the way in which a *habitus* generates certain beliefs. For Bourdieu, dispositions are generative and transposable. Note in Althusser's "Ideology and Ideological State Apparatuses" the inception of this latter reappropriation: "An individual believes in God, or Duty, or Justice, etc. This belief derives (for everyone, i.e. for all those who live in an ideological representation of ideology, which reduces ideology to ideas endowed by definition with a spiritual existence) from the ideas of the individual concerned, i.e. from him as a subject with a consciousness which contains the ideas of his belief. In this way, i.e. by means of the absolutely ideological 'conceptual' device (*dispositif*) thus set up (a subject endowed with a consciousness in which he freely forms or freely recognizes ideas in which he believes), the (material) attitude of the subject concerned naturally follows" ("Ideology," 167).

able. And yet, here is where the Slovenian critic Mladen Dolar will argue that Althusser fails to account for the psyche as a separate dimension. Dolar counsels a return to Lacan, much in the same way that Slavoj Žižek suggests a necessary complementarity between Althusser and Lacan.[14] To insist on the separability of the psyche from social practice is to intensify the religious metaphorics in Althusser, that is, to figure the psyche as a pure ideality, not unlike the ideality of the soul. I turn, then, to Dolar's reading of Althusser in order to consider the tension between the putative ideality of subjectivity and the claim that ideology, including psychic reality, is part of the expanded domain of materiality in the Althusserian sense.

Mladen Dolar's essay, "Beyond Interpellation,"[15] suggests that Althusser, despite his occasional use of Lacan's theory of the imaginary, failed to appreciate the disruptive potential of psychoanalysis, in particular, the notion of the Real as designating that which never becomes available to subjectivation. Dolar writes, "To put it the simplest way, there is a part of the individual that cannot successfully pass into the subject, an element of 'pre-ideological' and 'presubjective' *materia prima* that comes to haunt subjectivity once it is constituted as such" (75). The use of "materia prima" here is significant, for with this phrase Dolar explicitly contests the social account of materiality that Althusser provides. In fact, this "materia prima" never *materializes* in the Althusserian sense, never emerges as a practice, a ritual, or a social relation; from the point of view of the social, the "materia prima" is radically *immaterial*. Dolar thus criticizes Althusser for eliding that dimension of subjectivity that remains radically immaterial, barred from an appearance within materiality. According to Dolar, interpellation can only explain the formation of the subject in a partial way: "For Althusser, the subject is what makes ideology work; for psychoanalysis, the subject emerges where ideology fails. . . . The remainder produced by subjectivation is also invisible from the point of view of interpellation." "Interpellation," he writes, "is a way of avoiding [that remainder]" (76). At stake for Dolar is the need to strengthen the distinction between the domain of the symbolic, understood as communicable speech and social bonds, and that of the psychic, which is

---

14. See Slavoj Žižek, *The Sublime Object of Ideology* (London: Verso, 1989), 1–2.
15. Published in English in *Qui Parle* 6/2 (Spring/Summer, 1993): 73–96. The English version is a revision of the original, published in German as "Jenseits der Anrufung," in *Gestalten der Autorität*, ed. Slavoj Žižek (Vienna: Hora Verlag, 1991).

ontologically distinct from the social, defined as that remainder of which the notion of the social cannot take account.

Dolar offers a distinction between materiality and interiority which he loosely aligns with the Althusserian division between the materiality of the state apparatus and the putative ideality of subjectivity. In a formulation with strong Cartesian resonance, Dolar defines subjectivity through the notion of interiority, and identifies as material the domain of exteriority (exterior to the subject). Presupposed here is the notion that subjectivity consists in both interiority and ideality, whereas materiality belongs to its opposite, the countervailing exterior world.

This manner of distinguishing interior from exterior may well seem strange as a characterization or extrapolation of Althusser's position. It was, after all, Althusser's distinctive contribution to undermine the ontological dualism presupposed by the conventional Marxist distinction between a material base and an ideal or ideological superstructure. This undermining took place by asserting the materiality *of* the ideological: "An ideology always exists in an apparatus, and its practice, or practices. This existence is material" ("Ideology," 166).

The constitution of the subject is *material* to the extent that this constitution takes place through *rituals*, and these rituals materialize "the ideas of the subject" (169). What is called "subjectivity," understood as the lived and imaginary experience of the subject, is itself derived from the material rituals by which subjects are constituted. Pascal's believer kneels more than once, necessarily repeating the gesture by which belief is conjured. To understand, more broadly, "the rituals of ideological recognition" (173) by which the subject is constituted is central to the very notion of ideology. But if belief follows from the posture of prayer, if that posture conditions and reiterates belief, then how are we to separate the ideational sphere from those ritual practices by which it is incessantly reinstituted?

Although the question of the subject is not the same as the question of subjectivity, in Dolar's essay it nevertheless remains unclear how precisely those two notions are to be thought together. The notion of "subjectivity" does not have much play in Althusser, except perhaps in the critique of subjectivism, and it is unclear how that term might be transposed onto the terms he does use. This may well be precisely Dolar's critical point, namely, that there is not enough of a place for subjectivity in Althusser's text. Dolar's primary critical concern is that Althusser cannot fully take into account the "remainder" produced by subjectivation (76), the nonphenomenal "kernel of interiority." In fact, Dolar will argue that the distinction between the interior and the exterior is produced through "the introjection of the object" (79). Hence, a primary object is introjected, and that introjection becomes the condition of possibility for the subject. The irrecoverability of that object is, thus, not only the supporting condition of the subject but the persistent threat to its coherence. The Lacanian notion of the Real is cast as the first act of introjection as well as the subject's radical limit.

In Dolar, the ideality of this kernel of interiority sets the limit to both materialization and subjectivation; it constitutes the constitutive lack or the nonsymbolizable Real. As foreclosed or introjected, the primary object is lost and idealized at once; the ideality acquired by this object through introjection constitutes the founding ideality of subjectivity. This insight is the one that Althusser appears to miss, and yet Dolar seems to attribute to him the very distinction between materiality and ideality that is insufficiently realized in Althusser's theory:

> There is a step in the emergence of both the subject and the Other that Althusser leaves out and that can perhaps be best illustrated by Althusser's own example. To elucidate the transition between the external materiality of state apparatuses (institutions, practices, rituals, etc.) and the interiority of ideological subjectivity, Althusser borrows a famous suggestion from Pascal, namely his scandalous piece of advice that the best way to become a believer is to follow the religious rituals. [88]

Dolar refers to this as a "senseless ritual," and then reverses the Althusserian account in order to establish that the creed and the ritual are *the effects* of "a supposition," that ritual *follows* belief, but is not—in the first instance—its condition of production. Dolar underscores the inability of Althusser's theory of ritual practice to account for the motivation to pray: "What made him follow the ritual? Why did he/she consent to repeat a series of senseless gestures?" (89).

Dolar's questions are impossible to satisfy in Althusser's terms, but the very presuppositions of Dolar's questions are countered through an Althusserian explanation. That Dolar presumes a consenting subject prior to the performance of a ritual suggests that he already presumes that a volitional subject must first be in place to give an account of motivation. But how does this consenting subject come to be? This subject appears to be a supposing and consenting one who precedes and conditions the "entrance" into the symbolic and, hence, the becoming of a subject. The circularity is clear, but how is it to be understood? Is it a failing of Althusser's that he did not provide the subject prior to the formation of the subject, or does his "failure" indicate only that the grammatical requirements of the narrative work against the account of subject formation that the narrative attempts to provide? To literalize or to ascribe an ontological status to the grammatical requirement of "the subject" is to presume a mimetic relation between grammar and ontology that misses the point, both Althusserian and Lacanian, that the anticipations of grammar are always and only retroactively installed. The grammar that governs the narration of subject formation is one that presumes that the grammatical place for the subject has already been established. In an important sense, then, the grammar that the narrative requires is a result of the narrative itself. The account of subject formation is thus a double fiction at cross-purposes with itself, symptomatizing repeatedly what resists narration.

If, as Wittgenstein has remarked, "we speak, we utter words, and only later get a sense of their life," then the sense of that "empty" ritual which is speech is anticipated, and that anticipation governs its iterability. In this sense, then, we must neither first believe before we kneel nor know the sense of words before we speak. On the contrary, both are performed "on faith" that sense will arrive in and by the articulation itself—an anticipation that is not for that reason governed by a guarantee of noematic satisfaction. If supposing and consenting are unthinkable outside of the language of supposing and consenting, and this language is itself a sedimentation of ritual forms—the rituals of Cartesianism—then the act by which we might "consent" to kneel is no more and no less ritualistic than the kneeling itself.

Dolar makes his objection explicitly theological by suggesting that Althusser's reformulation of the notion of materiality to include the domain of ideology is too inclusive, that it makes no room for a nonmaterializable ideality: the lost and introjected object that inaugurates the formation of the subject. It remains unclear, however, how precisely Dolar reads "materiality" in Althusser, and whether the ritual and, hence, *temporal dimension* of materiality in Althusser is effaced in favor of a reduction of materiality to the empirically or socially given:

This is also why Althusser's ardent insistence on materiality is insufficient: the Other that emerges here, the Other of the symbolic order, is not material, and Althusser covers up this non-materiality by talking about the materiality of institutions and practices. If subjectivity can spring up from materially following certain rituals, it is only insofar as those rituals function as a symbolic automatism, that is, insofar as they are governed by an "immaterial" logic supported by the Other. That Other cannot be discovered by scrutinizing materiality. . . what counts is ultimately not that they are material, but that they are ruled by a code and by a repetition. [89]

This last remark formulates an opposition between materiality and repetition that appears in a direct tension with Althusser's own argumentation. If ideology is material to the extent that it consists in a set of practices, and practices are governed by rituals, then materiality is defined as much by ritual and repetition as it is by more narrowly empiricist conceptions. Moreover, the rituals of ideology are material to the extent that they acquire a *productive* capacity and, in Althusser's text, what rituals produce are subjects.

Dolar explains that rituals can produce not subjects, but subjectivity only to the extent that they are themselves governed by a symbolic or reiterative logic, a logic that is immaterial. Subjectivity for Dolar is said to "spring up from materially following certain rituals," where the "springing up" is not itself material, but where the notion of "following" a ritual does have a material dimension. Subjectivity arises immaterially from a material ritual performance, but this can happen only on the condition that a logic precedes and supports this ritual performance, an immaterial logic, one that encodes and reenacts the idealizing effects of introjection. But how are we to distinguish the repetition proper to ritual and the repetition proper to the "symbolic autonomatism"?

Consider the inseparability of those two repetitions in Althusser's description of the materiality of ideas and the ideal in ideology:

Ideas have disappeared as such (insofar as they are endowed with an ideal or spiritual existence), to the precise extent that it has emerged that their existence is inscribed in the actions of practices governed by rituals defined in the last instance by an ideological apparatus. It therefore appears that the subject acts insofar as he is acted by the following system (set out in the order of its real determination): ideology existing in a material ideological apparatus, prescribing material practices governed by a material ritual, which practices exist in the material actions of a subject acting in all consciousness according to his belief. ["Ideology," 169–70]

It appears that ideas have their existence as what is "inscribed" in those acts which are part of practices regulated by rituals. Can they appear any other way, and can they have an "existence" outside of ritual? And what might it mean to rethink the material not only as a regulated repetition, but as one which produces a subject acting in full consciousness according to his belief? The subject's belief is no different from Pascal's; they are both the result of that repetitious conjuring that Althusser calls "materiality."

Dolar argues that Althusser fails to take into account the distinction between materiality and the symbolic, but where would we place "interpellation" on this mapping of the divide? Is it the voice of the symbolic or is it the ritualized voice of the state, or is the problem precisely that the two have become indissoluble? If, to use Dolar's term, the symbolic acquires its "existence" only in ritual, then what is to establish the ideality of that symbolic domain apart from the various modes of its appearance and iterability? Ritual takes place through repetition, and repetition implies the discontinuity of the material, and the irreducibility of materiality to phenomenality. The interval by which any repetition takes place does not, strictly speaking, *appear*; it is, as it were, the absence by which the phenomenal is articulated. But, this nonappearance or absence is not for that reason an "ideality," for it is bound to the articulation as its constitutive and absent necessity.

If the theological resistance to materialism is exemplified in Dolar's explicit defense of Lacan's Cartesian inheritance (78), insisting upon the pure ideality of the soul, the theological impulse structures Althusser's work in the figure of the punitive Law. Over and against the law that successfully regulates its subjects, Dolar suggests that the law cannot touch a certain interior register of love: "There is a remainder involved in the mechanism of interpellation, the left-over of the clean cut, and... this remainder can be pinpointed in the experience of love" (85). A bit further on, he asks, "Could one say that love is what we find beyond interpellation?"

Here love is, in his words, a "forced choice," suggesting that what Dolar expected from the notion of a subject who "consents" to kneel and pray is an account of a "forced consent" of some kind. Love is beyond interpellation precisely because it is understood to be compelled by an immaterial law—the symbolic—over and above the ritualistic Laws that govern the various practices of love: "The Other that emerges here, the Other of the symbolic order, is not material, and Althusser covers up this nonmateriality by talking about the materiality of institutions and practices" (89). The Other who is lost, introjected, who is said to become the immaterial condition of the subject, inaugurates, as it were, the repetition specific to the symbolic, the punctuated fantasy of a return that is never completed or completable.

Let us provisionally accept this psychoanalytic account of subject formation, and concede that the subject cannot form except through a barred relation to the Other, and even consider that this barred Other reappears as the introjected condition of subject formation, splitting that subject at its inception. Are there other forms of "losing" the Other that are not introjection, and are there various ways of introjecting that Other? Are these terms not culturally elaborated, indeed, ritualized, to such a degree that no metascheme of the symbolic logic escapes the hermeneutics of social description?

Significantly, where social interpellations are described by Dolar as always "failing" fully to constitute subjects, it seems that no such "failure" is at work in the compulsory character of love. To the extent that primary introjection is an act of love, it is, I would suggest, not an act performed only once, but a reiterated and, indeed, ritual affair. But what is to keep us from making the analogy that we fall in love in much the same way we kneel and pray or that we may well be doing one when we think we are doing the other?

And yet, Dolar's suggestion that love might be what is "beyond" interpellation is an important one. And it seems that Althusser himself would have benefited from a better understanding of how the law itself becomes the object of passionate attachment, a strange scene of love. For the conscience that compels the wayward pedestrian to turn around upon hearing the policeman's address, or the one that ushers the murderer into the streets in search of the police, appears to be driven by a love of the law that can be satisfied only by ritual punishment. To the extent that Althusser gestures toward this analysis, he begins to explain how a subject is formed through the passionate pursuit of the reprimanding recognition of the state. That the subject turns round or rushes toward the law suggests that the subject lives in passionate expectation of the law. This would be a kind of love not beyond interpellation, but, rather, one that forms the passionate circle by which the subject becomes ensnared by its own state.

The failure of interpellation is clearly to be valued, but to figure that failure in terms that rehabilitate a structure of love outside the domain of the social is to risk the reification of particular social forms of love as eternal psychic facts. It is also to leave unexplained the passion that precedes and forms conscience, that precedes and forms the possibility of love, one that accounts for the failure of interpellation fully to constitute the subject it names. Interpellation is "barred" from success not by a structurally permanent form of prohibition (or foreclosure), but by its inability to determine the constitutive field of the human. If conscience is one form that the passionate attachment to existence takes, then the failure of interpellation is to be found in precisely the passionate attachment that also lets it work. According to the logic of conscience, one in which Althusser appeared fully constrained, that passionate attachment to the law is that without which the linguistic guarantee of existence for the subject proves impossible. This complicity at once conditions and limits the viability of a critical interrogation of the law. One cannot criticize too far the very terms by which one's existence is secured.

But what if the discursive possibilities for existence exceed the reprimand voiced by the law, would that not lessen the need to confirm one's guilt and embark on a path of conscientiousness as a way to gain a purchase on identity? What are the conditions under which our very sense of linguistic survival depends upon our willingness to turn back upon ourselves, that is, in which attaining recognizable being requires self-negation, requires existing as a self-negating being in order to attain to and preserve a status as "being" at all?

It may be, in a Nietzschean vein, that such a slave morality is predicated upon that sober calculation that it is better to "be" enslaved in such a way than not "to be" at all. But the terms that constrain the option to "being" and "not being" are precisely those that "call for" another kind of response. Under what conditions does a law monopolize the terms of existence in quite so thorough a way? Or is this a theological fantasy of the law? Perhaps there is a possibility of being elsewhere or otherwise, without denying our complicity in the law that we oppose. Such knowledge will only be answered through a different kind of turn, one that, enabled by the law, turns away from the law, resisting its lure of identity; an agency that outruns and counters the conditions of its existence. Such a turn demands a willingness *not* "to be"—a critical desubjectivation—in order to expose the law as less powerful than it seems. What forms might linguistic survival take in this desubjectivized domain? How would one know one's existence?

Through what terms would it be recognized and recognizable? Such questions cannot be answered here, but they do indicate a direction for thinking that is perhaps prior to the question of conscience, namely, the question that preoccupied Spinoza, Nietzsche, and most recently, Giorgio Agamben: how are we to understand the desire to be as a constitutive desire? Resituating conscience and interpellation within such an account, we might then add to this question another: how is such a desire exploited not only by a law in the singular, but by laws of various kinds?

In conclusion, Agamben offers us one direction for rethinking ethics along the lines of the desire to be and, hence, at a distance from any particular formation of conscience:

> If human beings were or had to be this or that substance, this or that destiny, no ethical experience would be possible. . . . This does not mean, however, that humans are not, and do not have to be, something, that they are simply consigned to nothingness and therefore can freely decide whether to be or not to be, to adopt or not to adopt this or that destiny (nihilism and decisionism coincide at this point). There is in effect something that humans are and have to be, but this is not an essence nor properly a thing: *It is the simple fact of one's own existence as possibility or potentiality.* . . .[16]

Agamben might be read as claiming that this is a possibility that must resolve itself into something, but that cannot undo its own status as possibility through such a resolution. Or, rather, we might reread "being" as precisely that potentiality that remains unexhausted by any particular interpellation. Such a failure of interpellation might well undermine the capacity of the subject to "be" in a self-identical sense, but it may well mark the path toward a more open, even more ethical, kind of being, one of or for the future.

---

16. Giorgio Agamben, *The Coming Community*, trans. Michael Hardt (Minneapolis: University of Minnesota Press, 1993), section 11 (no pagination in text).

THOMAS PEPPER

Kneel and You Will Believe

> Writing and triumph. Nietzsche: *"To write in order to triumph.* Writing should always mark a triumph.". . . . See what he says further on of the triumph (*Überwindung*) over oneself, that is to say, he claims, without any exercise of power (*Gewalt*) over anyone. . . . But we know that "triumph" corresponds, according to Freud, to a phase, and to one of a manic type, in the process of mourning. All the difficulties recognized by Freud in *Trauer und Melancholie:* mania and melancholia have the same "content," and the states of "joy," of "jubilation," of "triumph" (*Freude, Jubel, Triumph*) that characterize mania have the same "economic" conditions as melancholia, etc. Passage from *Überwindung* to *Triumphieren*. . . [1]

ATTACK: ON JUBILATION

In order to come to an adequate discussion of the moment of ideological interpellation in Althusser's writings on the "Ideological State Apparatus," it is necessary to recur to two words, "Liturgy" and "Materiality," that traverse not only Althusser's own writings, but also those of others, not necessarily of his generation, who were also writing their own central texts over the course of the 1960s and who were producing, without knowing it and without the intention of doing so, the corpus of what was to become High Theory in its American context and instance. Furthermore, an analysis of the registers of these words might help us to understand what has taken place, on the American scene, in the supercession of High Theory by Cultural Studies. That is to say, such an analysis might help us more thoughtfully to understand where we find ourselves now, in the scholasticism of the new middle ages, replete with wars, plagues, and identity politics—or else to move.

But before we—and in order to—move on to our words of choice, let us begin, for no other reason than the fact that the word itself marks a beginning, with "jubilation." The topos appears in Lacan's writings

---

1. Jacques Derrida, "Journal de bord," in his *Parages* (Paris: Galilée, 1986), 151–55, my translation.

YFS 88, *Depositions,* ed. Lezra, © 1995 by Yale University.

almost from the beginning, we could say, at any rate, from the beginning of Lacan's Lacan. It is the tonal marker that describes the child's miscovery (*méconnaissance*) of its image in the mirror, where the word "jubilatory" occurs twice on the same page of the final version of the essay, which was first written in the thirties and substantially reworked before its inclusion in the *Écrits* in 1966:

> This event can take place, we have known since Baldwin, from the age of six months, and its repetition has often stopped our meditation before the arresting spectacle of a nursling before the mirror, who doesn't yet have the mastery of walking, or even of the standing position, but who, embraced as he is by some mode of human or artificial support... overcomes the constraints of this mode of support in a jubilatory state, so as to suspend his attitude in a more or less inclined position, so as to bring back, in order to fix it, an instantaneous aspect of the image.

And again, two short paragraphs later:

> The jubilatory taking-on of its specular image by the being still immersed in motor impotence and in dependence upon nursing that is the little man at this *infans* stage, will seem henceforth to manifest in an exemplary situation the symbolic matrix where the *I* hastens in a primordial form, before it is objectivated in the dialectic of identification with the other and before language restores to him his function of subject in the universal.[2]

What is jubilation? It marks, of course, celebration, triumph—and a celebration, moreover, that is linked to the authorities. For a jubilee, in the ancient law of the Jews, was an occasion, every fifty years, when all debts were absolved and when slaves were released from servitude. This became, in Catholicism, a power of the Pope to grant indulgences in return for the observance of pious acts. We also know the military version of the jubilee, that is to say, the triumph, which is a particularly labile and dangerous moment for the regime that grants it to its armed forces: these last can always use the occasion, since they are "all there," for their own purposes.

At the moment of its grasping of its image, of its being grasped, held in narcissistic fascination by its image, the child experiences a jubilatory assumption, its accession to the status of subject. But there is another side to this coin; for jubilation is also, of course, part of the manic cycle. And the gaining of the position of subjecthood is also,

2. Jacques Lacan, *Écrits* (Paris: Seuil, 1966), 94, my translation.

immediately thereupon, the realization that, as subject, one is subjected. One is become a bondsman who must realize that his majesty the ego, who also likes to think he's "all there," as Freud was fond of saying, is not at all as sovereign as he thinks, but is immediately engaged in a war of all against all for recognition by all the other little subjects. And this is only one side of a two-front war: endopsychically, on the inside, the child will of course have to confront the fact that its new-found status is secondary, and that it will ever have to fight the conflicting tendencies of its disparate and more primary and constant drives. The enemy from within will have to be subjugated, in the long run, with more subtle means.

For an instant, in an instant, there is jubilation. But then there is also what Melanie Klein calls the Depressive Position (and, following upon it, for the rest of life, the Manic Defense).[3] And the procession from the one stage to the other, in this allegory of psychoanalysis (to stick with Lacan and to leave Klein), is the procession from the satisfactions of the maternal relation to oedipal war.

Mania becomes our subject, Althusser.

Without going into psychobiography, or into the puritanism of holier-than-thou judgment, it is time to remark the jubilatory character of Althusser's writing, which is always a sketch, always prefatory, never a tractate, always an essay, always, we could say, radically provisional. Its point of departure is always polemical, at war, written in haste, like unleavened bread, the matter of the Paschal or Pascalian Host of future religious ritual and liturgy. It says: Love me while you can, for the future lasts a long time.

We will claim that this mania of beginnings is not at all contingent, but rather essential. It is essential for Althusser, just as it is essential for his student, Derrida, whose long apprenticeship with his teacher is marked, perhaps more than anywhere else, not thematically, but in a compulsive gesture that repeats itself for Derrida the essayist. This gesture says: "If I had the time, I would. . . " And, alas, there is never time; for time lasts a long time, and is always up. But Derrida is not our subject here.

Everything is always a note, and, needless to say, there is always a postscript. The mania of writing gives way to the mourning of reading, or of rereading. Writing is triumph, committing an act, madness, jubi-

---

3. See Donald Woods Winnicott, *Through Paediatrics to Psychoanalysis* (London: Hogarth Press, 1987), 129–44.

lation, leaving a mark; reading is despair, rage, horror at what cannot be undone. We shall return to jubilation, to beginnings, and to the provisional, in and as our end. But before we do so, we shall have to make some investigations into the modes of the aforementioned internal policing mechanisms.

LEVINAS: THE SENSES OF LITURGY

For an instructive point of departure in the discussion of the word "liturgy," I turn to Lévinas's writings of the early sixties, where this word undergoes an astonishing peripety. It is astonishing because, in the work of this anti-Hegelian thinker, the feeling- or thinking-tone of the word goes from a minus to a plus.[4]

"Liturgy" is condemned in *Totalité et infini* as merely sterile repetition, dead repetition, like the unanimated repetition of a sign that brings about the Husserlian Crisis:

> The ethical relation, the face to face, cuts as well across every relation that might be called mystical and where events other than that of the presentation of the original being come to overturn or to sublimate the pure sincerity of this presentation, where inebriated equivocations come to enrich the original univocity of expression, where discourse becomes prayer in the manner of prayer become rite and liturgy, in which the interlocutors are found to be playing a role in a drama that has started outside them.[5]

But by the time of the publication of the essay "The Trace of the Other," in 1963, the same word is given the highest possible meaning, for it is the name given to the highest form, the true form of work, that of movement without return toward the other:

> The work of the Same inasmuch as movement without return of the Same toward the Other—I would like to fix it with a Greek term which, in its primary signification, indicates the performing of an office that is not only completely free or gratuitous, but that requires, on the part of

---

4. I became aware of this reversal during Jill Robbins's discussion (at the annual meetings of the International Association for Philosophy and Literature, Duquesne University, in May 1993) of the use of "liturgy" in *Totalité et infini* in a paper on Lévinas's neutralization of the literary. Without her provocation, my own argument would be poorer. I would like to thank her for having set my thoughts for the kernel of this essay in motion.

5. Emmanuel Lévinas, *Totalité et infini* (Paris: Livre de Poche, 1971), 221–22, my translation. My thanks to Hent de Vries for having suggested the use of this passage to me.

the one who performs it, the putting out of funds at a loss. I would like to attach to it the name liturgy. For the moment we must estrange all religious signification from this term, even if a certain idea of God should appear as a trace at the end of our analysis. Furthermore, as an absolutely patient action, liturgy is not to be ranked as a cult beside works and ethics. It is ethics itself.[6]

Whether the word is praised or blamed, ambivalence always reveals a strong investment. And it is perhaps especially significant that this reversal takes place in "The Trace of the Other," for this essay has, from the moment of its publication, been taken as an abstract of *Totalité et infini*. It behooves us therefore to pay special, hovering attention to a moment when the abstract not only deviates from the argument of the work, but says, in fact, the opposite.

The fact that we must be so careful, in our performance of the office of using the word "liturgy," indicates that things can turn out badly, that there is a bad liturgy, the religious one, that repeats and repeats and (a third time) repeats, and a good liturgy, the Greek one, that gives and gives and gives. Good repetition is opposed to bad repetition. The good one exceeds the limits of my finitude, because it works for the time after my own death; the bad one repeats a movement that always comes back to the same, to the self, to the ego. Liturgy here is the forward-looking face of the *Rückfrage*. It is not dead.

It must not be dead—this is an ethical commandment and this is what makes it liturgy. But at the same time, the tightness of Lévinas's text leads to a paradox: for the animation of the liturgy is not the *Rückfrage* of the subject performing the liturgical office. This would be to remain within all the stuttering and tautological egoisms of being. And it is precisely from this place that Lévinas wishes to depart on his journey, a journey to Mount Moriah, and not home to Ithaca. The animation must come from the other. The animation of my work—so that my work may be written in the Book of Life—must come from the other. My work comes back from the future. Or better yet, it goes into the future, never to come back.

This is a crucial problem, for it is precisely in the text of Lévinas's essay that we cannot speak of a crisis of animation, in respect to liturgy, if we wish to maintain it in its good offices, and to remain in Lévinas's good offices as well. For, if "liturgy" is the very name assigned to the

6. Lévinas, "La Trace de l'autre," in his *En découvrant l'existence avec Husserl et Heidegger* (Paris: Vrin, 1982), 192, my translation.

32 *Yale French Studies*

work which is one precisely because it goes unto the other, then, by the strength of Lévinas's entire argument, it cannot perform its function if it is animated by the intention of its performer, or officer, at all. Or better, if it performs its office, it will do so in a way that can only be entirely indifferent to the intentions of its agent. For the work, conceived by Lévinas as that which is for the time after my time, after my own death, cannot be, in order to do its work, animated by my intention. This is the only way for it to accede unto the time of the other, to escape from my time. It can only survive, not as my sign, but as trace.

If all deadness, all risk of mere repetition, is subtracted from "liturgy," in and by virtue of this return to its origins in the Greek, then liturgy can be this jubilation of ethics itself, but of an ethics, in fact of a *subject* that must exist prior to—or after—the stigmatization of subjectivity. This is the way we can understand what "an absolutely patient action" is, an action located in the middle register, before the stigmatization of the voices into active and passive.[7]

Therefore, "liturgy" is the very name for the moment when Lévinas, responding to the crisis of animation such as it is thought by Husserl, as necessitating a return to the origins of intentionality, a *Rückfrage*, takes the opposite path and says: back to the future. The origin cannot, must not matter. Ontology—or the need to leave it behind—translates most directly into ethics *here*.[8] But all this leaves

---

7. To see what becomes of "patient action," where it ends up, see Derrida, "Différance," in his *Margins of Philosophy*, trans. Alan Bass (Chicago: University of Chicago Press, 1982): "[T]hat which lets itself be designated *différance* is neither simply active nor simply passive, announcing or recalling something like the middle voice, saying an operation that is not an operation, an operation that cannot be conceived either as passion or as the action of a subject on an object, or on the categories of agent or patient, neither on the basis of nor moving toward any of these *terms*. For the middle voice, a certain nontransitivity, may be what philosophy, at its outset, distributed into an active and a passive voice, thereby constituting itself by means of this repression" (8–9).

8. For the same gesture in the opposite direction, I take this opportunity to note that much of the weirdness that has been overlooked in Derrida's "Signature événement contexte" (*Marges de la philosophie*, [Paris: Minuit, 1972]), in order to turn this essay into one of the cornerstones of the Derrida industry, has to do, not with Austin, the essay's ostensible subject, but with the fact that the hypotext of the essay is "The Trace of the Other," and that what Derrida does in this essay is to translate Lévinas's ethical *must* into the logical *must* of language-ontological terms. Lévinas says, it *must* be so, for a movement toward the other to happen. Derrida says, it *must* be so, since the graphematic structure of language dictates it, will have it no other way. This very precise point of comparison between Lévinas and Derrida merits an essay of its own. But it is also necessary that I recall it here. As much as Derrida's famous essay is an essay about Austin, it is an essay in which this problem in Lévinas is worked out—even if Lévinas is

Lévinas in a predicament: for if the sender of the message in the bottle, the one who performs work, must disappear from this work for it to do its work, if the intention of the doer must be irrelevant to the accomplishment of the deed, then how are we to know if the liturgy is bad or good? Obviously, the answer here must be: we cannot, at least not in our time.

As a final word in this all too brief discussion, we must also speak for a moment about the matter of the trace itself: Of what does the trace consist? Clearly, by virtue of what has already been said, it cannot have an ideal or an intentional content. But it must also exceed the ontological opposition between the ideal and the material. It cannot simply be material, for then it is truly dead, unanimated matter. It must, in order to escape, exceed the order of the ontological distinction. And so we do not really have a *word*, in the strongest metaphysical sense, for it. There can be no word for it. But if it is not material, in the discourses that have proliferated around it, it has found itself, somehow, perhaps polemically, more tendentially close to the material than to the intentional. Often, then, the character of the trace has been conceived under the name *materiality*, even if all sense of "matter" has to be subtracted from this "materiality." What remains, though, is the matter of the word itself. And this is no coincidence. "Materiality" may be a provisional and dangerous word, a radically provisional word; but it may also be a word we cannot do without, and for reasons shortly to appear.

ALTHUSSER: LITURGY BECOME MATERIALITY

It may appear to go without saying that "material" and "materiality" are words that are important, nay essential, for Louis Althusser, but it should not. And the matter, the how of the intercalation of these words has much to do with their crucial character. In order to appreciate this, and its implications for Althusser's text, let us look closely at a crucial passage in the provisional *and* canonical "Ideology and Ideological State Apparatuses (Notes toward an Investigation)"[9]:

---

not mentioned—in language-ontological terms. And if only, once again, so as to leave ontology behind.

9. "Ideology and Ideological State Apparatus, (Notes toward an Investigation)," in Louis Althusser, *Lenin and Philosophy and Other Essays,* trans. Ben Brewster (New York and London: Monthly Review Press, 1971).

In every case, the ideology of ideology thus recognizes, despite its imaginary distortion, that the "ideas" of a human subject exist in his actions, or ought to exist in his actions, and if that is not the case, it lends him other ideas corresponding to his actions (however perverse) that he does perform. This ideology talks of actions: I shall talk of actions inserted into *practices*. And I shall point out that these practices are governed by the *rituals* in which these practices are inscribed, within the *material existence of an ideological apparatus*, be it only a small part of that apparatus: a small mass in a small church, a funeral, a minor match at a sports club, a school day, a political party meeting, etc.

Besides, we are indebted to Pascal's defensive "dialectic" for the wonderful formula which will enable us to invert the order of the notional scheme of ideology. Pascal says more or less: "Kneel down, move your lips in prayer, and you will believe." He thus scandalously inverts the order of things, bringing, like Christ, not peace but strife, and in addition something hardly Christian (for woe to him who brings scandal into the world!)—scandal itself. A fortunate scandal which makes him stick with Jansenist defiance to a language that directly names the reality.

I will be allowed to leave Pascal to the arguments of his ideological struggle with the religious ideological State apparatus of his day. And I shall be expected to use a more directly Marxist vocabulary, if that is possible, for we are advancing in still poorly explored domains. [168–9]

Before I begin to explore this preamble to all of the "matters" about to arrive on the scene, I must interrupt my exposition to insist, from the beginning of this analysis, on the wonderful *brio* of Althusser's polemical tone, on the joy one feels in reading this writing. Allow me, for a moment, to praise Althusser—not only for his writing, which is wonderful to read and wonderful to teach; but also in order to remember that it was this voice and this person who taught an entire generation of French philosophers how to think, at the heart of the most centralized Ideological State Apparatus in what we used to call the western world, the École normale supérieure, rue d'Ulm, of which Althusser was the director.

Say what one will about the massive and overwhelming problems, many of them still remaining, of this institution, which was all male even after Althusser's exit. (I withhold from using the hideously pathetic adjectives that have become *de rigueur* at this point: they are all too sentimental and too warm; they cannot bear witness to the coldness necessary to an adequate description of this milieu; and furthermore, they betray the lucidity of Althusser's thinking with their false character.) It was there that Althusser, who spent his entire career at this institution—a very rare fact indeed—served for a long time as *the only* tutor in philosophy.

When Slavoj Žižek writes that the Derrida-Foucault debate is merely the epiphenomenon, a screen memory for the Lacan-Althusser debate, in order to perform a corrective gesture for the American scene in its ignorance of its origins, what is he saying if not that, for the generation that came of age in the 1960s (when Foucault was already, for all intents and purposes, gone from the E.N.S., but no matter[10]); Lacan and Althusser were The Teachers, the ones who counted?[11] One must also recall the name of the Cercle d'épistémologie de l'E.N.S. here, and that of its organ, *Les Cahiers pour l'analyse;* one must recall the names—and there are many others—of Alain Badiou, Jean-Claude Milner, Jacques-Alain Miller, Jean-Michel Rey. Let us speak, then, in praise of a teacher who, by his energy and in his polemical and provisional mode, left his traces in his students. May his name be praised!

In truth, then, we have not left off—even if we have not started—commenting the passage at hand. Topos: Pascal. Subtopic: inversion. The Pascalian dialectic is the dialectic that, in its very acuteness, lasts a very short time.[12] It is an instantaneous and ironic dialectic. It is the dialectic of the name of the one who speaks in his name, Pascal, whose name incarnates the Passover, the miracle of the transubstantiation. Pascal repeats his name: "Two, Four, Six, Eight, time to transubstantiate!"[13] Pascal is the name that materializes itself, the Word become

---

10. I need only mention the words "discursive practice," "clinic," and "prison" in the context of a discussion of Ideological State Apparatuses to point out how much Foucault owes to Althusser. Of course, there are differences of exclusion and inclusion between the lists of the Ideological State Apparatuses and the various discursive practices that create subjects of knowledge for the human sciences. But it is interesting to note that the hospital does not figure in Althusser's list. It would be important, on this point, to compare both Althusser and Foucault with Erving Goffmann's account of the "Total Institution" in his *Asylums: Essays on the Social Situation of Mental Patients and Other Inmates* (Garden City, New York: Anchor Books, 1961). Perhaps in the university need Goffmann's lucidity now more than ever. Goffmann is the kind of American whose eye was cold enough to make a difference, as opposed, say, to Rorty whom I discuss below.

11. See the opening pages of Slavoj Žižek, *The Sublime Object of Ideology* (London: Verso, 1987).

12. See, on the matter of this as an explanation of the aphoristic form of the *Pensées,* Paul de Man, "Pascal's Allegory of Persuasion," in Stephen Greenblatt, ed., *Allegory and Representation* (Baltimore: The Johns Hopkins University Press, 1981).

13. Tom Lehrer, "The Vatican Rag," on his *That Was the Year that Was* (Warner/Reprise Records, 1964).

Flesh.[14] Althusser repeats not only what he learned in school, but what inscribed itself upon his heart in prison:

> I think that idealist and materialist elements can be found in every philosophy, with the dominance of one or the other tendency in any given philosophy. In other words, there exists no radical and brutal division because, in a philosophy called idealist, materialist elements can be found, and vice versa. What is certain is that there is no absolutely pure philosophy. What there are are tendencies. . . .
>
> Pascal is an interesting, because paradoxical, example. Traversing the religious problems he exposes, there also appear epistemological problems, problems in the theory of the history of the sciences, and a theory of social relations, in such a way that we can affirm that he exhibits profoundly materialist traits. I was surprised, while rereading Pascal during these past years, to see how deeply, and without knowing it, I had borrowed philosophical ideas from him: the entire theory of ideology, of miscovery and of recognition, is already to be found in him. I asked myself whence this encounter with Pascal came about, at which point I remarked that the only work I read during the five years I had to spend in a prisoner of war camp in Germany was Pascal's *Pensées*. In the mean time, I had completely forgotten this memory.[15]

What is ideology, if not that which is repeated without knowing it, automatically, we might say, liturgically? So we can say now, Pascal is the ideology of ideology; and furthermore, Pascal's name means ideology, the translation of idea into material practice. Now we can move into a discussion of the next paragraph in Althusser's text on Ideological State Apparatuses, where we shall find the materials necessary to our further construction:

> I shall therefore say that, where only a single subject (such and such an individual) is concerned, the existence of the ideas of his belief is material in that *his ideas are his material actions inserted into material practices governed by material rituals which are themselves defined by the material apparatus from which derive the ideas of that subject.* Naturally, the four inscriptions of the adjective "material" in my proposition must be affected by different modalities: the materialities for

---

14. See also Maurice Merleau-Ponty, *Le Visible et l'invisible* (Paris: Gallimard, 1964), and particularly the last chapter, "L'Entrelacs, le chiasme." I discuss the topos of transubstantiation in regard to this text in "Das Fleisch und das Vergessen des Blickes: Über Merleau-Ponty und Lacan," in Hinderk M. Emrich and Gary Smith, eds., *Vom Nutzen des Vergessens* (Berlin: Akademie Verlag, 1994).

15. Althusser, *Sur la philosophie* (Paris: Gallimard, 1994), 52–53, my translation.

going to mass, of kneeling down, of the gesture of the sign of the cross, or of the *mea culpa*, of a sentence, of a prayer, of an act of contrition, of a penitence, of a gaze, of a hand-shake, of an external verbal discourse or an "internal" verbal discourse (consciousness), are not one and the same materiality. I shall leave on one side the problem of a theory of the differences between the modalities of materiality.

It remains that in this inverted presentation of things, we are not dealing with an "inversion" at all, since it is clear that certain notions have purely and simply disappeared from our presentation, whereas others on the contrary survive, and new terms appear.

Disappeared: the term *ideas.*

Survive: the terms *subject, consciousness, belief, actions.*

Appear: the terms *practices, rituals, ideological apparatus.* It is therefore not an inversion or overturning. . . . [169]

Now we can see: the "materials" are all necessary in order to get rid of the "ideas," but still to be left with the subject. And, along with ideas, "interiority" has been bracketed with the help of scare quotes. Althusser is jubilant, for ideas have been disappeared, with the help of the hypotactic jubilation of the "materials." I use the verb "disappeared" quite consciously in the passive sense, without agent, in order to call attention to a certain subreption or surreptitiousness to which we have been accustomed by a world of very material facts: the disappearance and torturing and killing of bodies, documents, governments, works.

The other side of the coin, of course, of this act of making disappear, of this jubilation at disappearing, is the readiness to assume the Depressive Position.[16] For, as Winnicott points out, the child is ready to get on with the achievement of this phase when it is capable of playing at dropping, at disappearing things. His own reference here is to the *fort-da* account in Sigmund Freud's *Beyond the Pleasure Principle* (Winnicott, 263). I have made ideas disappear! And no doubt I can do it again! I can get rid of the ideas, I can disappear them—*fort!*—and I can keep the subject.

But then why do I have to insist that this is not merely an overturn-

16. Once again, I find myself alluding to Winnicott, and to his glosses on Klein. This time, I am referring to the paper "The Depressive Position in Normal Emotional Development," in Winnicott, 262–77. Here, Winnicott stresses the Depressive Position as an "achievement," the word "depressive" being held back from its common and pathological acceptation. In fact, this paper and the previously mentioned "The Manic Defense" are crucially linked, despite the almost twenty years that separate them. I am indebted to Janet Malcolm for having called my attention to them years ago.

ing, but, as our subject says here, a reshuffling?[17] It must not be *merely* an inversion, for that would be to stay with Pascal, not to have achieved a truly *materialist* dialectic. And how does Althusser do this? He does it by this anamorphic spreading out of the *materials*. If I can subsume everything, all the senses of the different "materials," into one grapheme, then I can make the ideas disappear: "I shall leave on one side the problem of a theory of the difference between modalities of materiality."

The proliferation of the "materials," of course, attests to the wildness of a desire. It is here that we touch upon a real of Althusser's text. This is a dialectic of the "materials." For it is the material of the various "materials" that serves as what Lacan, who is ever present in this text and in the text of Althusser, would call the obturator, the plug or node that serves the stability of the subject's relation to reality.[18]

This is not to indict Althusser, nor to psychoanalyze him. We are dealing with his text. Rather it is to congratulate him for his achievement in showing and in knowing where the moment of gathering—or of scattering—the "materials" has to come. Althusser is to be praised for being so aware of his unthought here. Less honest people would gloss over it. Althusser points to it. He knows that, rather than vitiating what he says is his discourse's status as science, this fact of obturation is the condition of possibility of his discourse being scientific, as opposed to psychotic.

It is this moment of knowledge of what he is doing with his materials that makes him, in fact, into a materialist, and not into a psychotic idealist. And furthermore, to come back to an unfinished motif of our beginning, it is the honesty that leaves the jubilant scattering of the "materials" unquestioned that serves the motif, answers for what we have called above the radical provisionality of the text, of Althusser's

---

17. No doubt Derrida would say "displacement," and he does.

18. De Man chooses the same word in his last essays. In de Man, the senses of "materiality" glide between the Jakobsonian sense of "the materiality of the signifier" and the more difficult sense of the act or fact of positing (*Setzung*) an inscription. It is by pushing "materiality" toward this second sense that de Man made it into the hidden god of his text. Like "god," it is difficult to define, but one always knows where to use it, where it is being used correctly. Up to this time, one's attitude toward the word "materiality" has served as an index of discipleship, because it serves as an index of "rigor." The best discussion of this to have appeared thus far is that of John Guillory, in his *Cultural Capital* (Chicago: University of Chicago Press, 1993). I myself came upon the same crux, from a different path, in "Absolute Constructions," forthcoming in my *Singularities* (Cambridge: Cambridge University Press).

text.[19] By refusing to go into a discussion of the spreading out of the "materials" over several senses, covering matter, states of affairs, acts, repetitions, and the materiality of the signifier, Althusser can hail the subject, he can drag his subject as the subject of ideological interpellation into being. And this hails back to Lacan's hailing, and more specifically to his hailing of Spinoza, one of both Althusser's and Lacan's favorite thinkers[20]:

> Let us see how the *Wiederholen* is introduced. *Wiederholen* is related to *Erinnerung*, recollection. The subject at home, the rememorialization of biography—all that only goes or works up to a certain point, which is called the real. If I wanted to forge before you a Spinozistic formula concerning what's at issue, I would say: *cogitatio adaequata semper vitat eamdem rem*. A thought that is adequate as thought—at the level where we are—always avoids—even if only so as to be found afterwards, in the end—the same thing. The real, here, is what always returns to the same place—to that place where the subject, in as much as it cogitates, where the *res cogitans* does not encounter it. [Lacan, *Les Quatre concepts*, 59; my translation]

This remark takes place only a few moments before Lacan discusses *Widerholen* as coming from *haler, tirer*, that which hails the subject onto a road from which it can never exit. So we now can see why the child likes to see itself in the mirror so much, why this action is so jubilatory: It sees itself, is captured by its image, and says, joyfully, here I am! It will not be until later that this joy is interrupted, and will forever be capable of being interrupted, by someone yelling at me from behind, "Hey, you!"

CONCLUSION (PROVISIONAL)

Identity politics, in its blustering and false jubilation, trapped as it is in a series of false images, will never be able to take up the question of its own setting in place. It will reenact a series of bad-liturgical bedtime

---

19. The same choice of materiality as obturator has the same effect in de Man—that of making the discourse essayistic, provisional. And, just as in the case of Althusser, there the self-proclamation of the text as occasional, provisional, makes its reception canonical.

20. Lacan opens and closes his seminar of 1963–64 on *Les Quatre concepts fondamentaux de la psychanalyse* (Paris: Seuil, 1973) with key references to Spinoza, just as Althusser, in *Sur la philosophie*, refers to him and to the Greek Atomists as being the necessary precursors to what he wants to mean by materialism. My citation from Lacan is from the Collection Points edition (1990).

rituals, which serve only to reinforce a compulsion to repeat, and not to work through. No one will get anywhere by talking about images. And all the little subjects running around will not get anywhere by thinking they have gone beyond the subject, when all the materiality of their motions does is to placate its very form.

Perhaps one of the worst of these little subjects is the homunculus of postideology, the one who believes that he has had the last word on a discourse called "Marxism." (He will only cause it to be reinvented.) Let us look at a recent piece of journalism by Richard Rorty, published on the *New York Times* op-ed page on 13 February 1994 under the title "The Unpatriotic Academy":

> Most of us, despite the outrage we may feel... and despite our despair over what is being done to the weakest and poorest among us, still identify with our country....
>
> Many of the exceptions to this rule are found in colleges and universities, in the academic departments that have become sanctuaries for left-wing political views. I am glad there are such sanctuaries, even though I wish we had a left more broadly based, less self-involved and less jargon-ridden than our present one. But any left is better than none, and this one is doing a great deal of good for people who have gotten a raw deal in our society: women, African-Americans, gay men and lesbians. This focus on marginalized groups will, in the long run, help to make our country much more decent, more tolerant and more civilized.
>
> But there is a problem with this left: it is unpatriotic. In the name of "the politics of difference," it refuses to rejoice in the country it inhabits....

So, in addition to life as it is, in the intimate evasion of all the obscene forms of violence of everyday life in the postmodern world, we are supposed to be—joyful. Never has the typically meliorist, social-democratic point of view seemed so capable of self-parody and fatuousness. But I would like to concentrate on the relation between joy and identification that is repeated several times throughout this article, ripe as it is with the dangerous silliness of sentimental nationalism. It is all a matter of rejoicing in identification. It sounds so much like the forms of American ego-psychology Lacan spent so much time criticizing in the 1950s, because it is the continuation of precisely the strand of American liturgical practice, that is to say liturgy, to which Lacan refers when he speaks of "the American way of life." It takes identification as a kind of stable structure without pitfalls, a processing machinery we should all undergo so that we can be *better.* No god can save us should this joy decide to be compulsory.

This is the proclamation of nationalism as that which transcends ideology. In other words, it is the truth of liberalism. It does not have the cold eye of an Althusser, for it is too young. And what if, in growing older, it should be less tolerant of the sanctuaries?

The last word is: we cannot replace identity politics with the politics of an ever larger, and more coercive and more powerful identification. This is foolish. Nor can we say that Althusser's "material" subreptions, to which he himself calls attention, disqualify his theory of ideology. There is always an obturator, a blind spot in the field of theory, a navel. To think that one can do without it is to believe that one can identify with something nice and whole, with an image, an imaginary fiction. It is not a question of which fiction one identifies with—or it should not be. There are liberal fictions and there are fascist fictions. It is the structure of this act of identification that must be interrogated. It cannot be a matter of the substitution of one idol for another.

Let us hail you, Althusser, to praise you. Jubilantly, we praise you, for the office of the liturgy, of the teaching you performed, and in the taking up of which, in our repetition, we, your children, find ourselves called in being hailed by the materials of your text, that which you have left us.

May this liturgy not have been a dead repetition.

PIERRE MACHEREY

A Production of Subjectivity

I would like to broach here the question of subjectivity, not frontally but laterally, obliquely, as it were, in order to bring to the fore, instead of what is traditionally called a theory of the subject—with the realist prejudice it entails (that *the* subject as such exists)—the concept of a subjectivity without subject. And, in order to do this, I am first simply going to tell a story about the subject to show how it reveals effects of subjectivity.

Someone is speaking, about whom we can say that he holds, from a certain point of view, the position of subject without being, strictly speaking, a subject. In order to begin, it is necessary to allow his voice to unfold nakedly, in its raw state, only specifying that the remarks that are going to be reported are real: not that they really were made, which is something else entirely, but real because they are being given here just as they were already recorded in a context that will be identified later.

> How can we allow young ladies to look at half-naked athletes? Swimming contests should be prohibited, the licentiousness of certain posters should be repressed, severe laws against nudity should be passed.

> Practicing forbidden acts in private rooms knowing that it is prohibited, risking punishment or at least the contempt of respectable people, that is all well and good. But that nudity should be shown and sexual pleasure [*jouissance*] should be desired simply by seeing a public spectacle —all this without risk of punishment, with the consent of parents, and while pretending to remain chaste, *that* is inadmissible. Everything concerning love must remain forbidden and inaccessible; for a young

YFS 88, *Depositions*, ed. Lezra, © 1995 by Yale University.

lady, to see a naked man should be an extraordinary stroke of luck, not the banal exposure of a hospital, or an artist's studio. If women's breasts are shown in public, there will no longer be any pleasure in catching a glimpse of them. We should not take away the charm of the forbidden fruit and relinquish the cult of the secret garden. This is devaluation through debasement.

Airplanes have made it to Geneva in three hours; it is going to be possible to go to India in three days; how horrible! Trips to Italy were reserved for the wealthy; going to America was costly and difficult; luxury is being cheapened, vulgarized. The petty bourgeois have bathrooms; on trains sleeping berths are being installed in third class; can we imagine such abomination! Being king of France used to mean something marvelous; it was the privilege of special families chosen by the heavens; today any lawyer can become President of the Republic and believe himself to be Louis XIV; this takes away any value from governing.

Having arrived at a hotel in New York, I want to take a bath; I learn that there are three thousand bathrooms and that three thousand travelers can take their baths at the same time as I, and my pleasure falls flat: one only has pleasure [*jouissance*] if one is the only one to win first prize; the happiness of others makes me suffer.

The absence of respect for privilege is horrible; in my eyes, a single detractor is stronger than three million admirers: in order to be at peace, I require unanimity.

Etc., etc. One would think we've heard these foolish and sordid words, which could have come out of the mouth of any prudish father nostalgic for convention and privilege, a thousand times before, if indeed third class railroad carriages still existed. However, one detail causes these words to stand out. The one who is uttering them was labeled—at the time these words were being spoken, and in the context in which they were recorded—by a term no longer in use today, an "invert" [*un "inverti"*]. From this point of view his concern for removing the sight of male nakedness from the eyes of young women, and his disgust at the display of women's breasts take on a slightly different sense. Isn't it in this particularity itself that we should begin to look for an effect of subjectivity?

There words belonged, in any case, and to use a label that is still current today, to a "patient": at least he saw himself as such, to the point of entrusting his "health" to the care of a man of the profession, a scholar as well as a practitioner, a "specialist" who, from what we can gather, did not do much to relieve him, but turned him into a "case" for his own personal use: and this is how the comments reproduced above were recorded, published in the context of what is indeed called a case study. It is worthwhile to acknowledge, as if echoing the patient's words, the interpretation proposed by the doctor for what was perceived at the time as a pathogenic ailment, and accordingly placed in the category of "obsessions."

> Obsessions originate in a deficiency, in weaknesses of certain mental functions. M's obsession is the result of a feeling that may not be very worthy but is nevertheless quite common in psychic depressions: the need for exclusivity and a mania for privilege. He has a mistress [this detail is true; however, the good doctor, as we shall see, was not completely privy to its mystery], he is a man of wealth, he takes a few beautiful trips, these are his privileges, they must be preserved, others must not be allowed to encroach on his rights. It does not occur to him that he too could benefit from progress, take longer and more beautiful trips by plane, for example, because he hates future acts and especially new acts. Like all psychasthenics, he wants to preserve the benefits of former acts and of acquired privilege. In order for him to experience the value of the things he possesses, they must be forbidden to others. . . . Let us not consider these ideas from a moral standpoint, but only from a psychological one. They already reflect a weakness and an instability in feelings of pleasure [*sentiments de jouissance*]: the patient needs to add the spice of privilege to things in order to derive pleasure from them; his sexual pleasure [*jouissance*] is diminished, or he believes it to be diminished if he thinks it is banal. This is already an aspect of the devalorization of pleasure that we will observe in cases of morose inactivity, and which can lead to asceticism. In any case, M displays this weakness of feeling [*faiblesse des sentiments*]. . . . The continuation of brooding also depends on another weakness. This type of thinking in a normal mind would quickly result in a simple solution, either in the name of morality, or in the name of experience that shows that pleasure continues to exist in spite of its popularization [*vulgarisation*]. A decision would quickly be made, or at the very least an act of resignation would occur, and all thinking about these occurrences would quickly cease. But our patient can reach no conclusion, and cannot resign himself; he is aware of the objections, but he indefinitely uncovers subtle responses to them. He can talk for hours about the devalorization of sexual pleasure [*jouissance*] through the exhibition of women's breasts in music halls, but he cannot conclude: this is a deficiency in self-

reflection [*la croyance réfléchie*]. The appearance of obsessions in all cases where this weakness of feelings and this deficiency of self-reflection exist is quite obvious. This is the point on which I have focused in my book on obsessions.

The emphatic reference to the patient's mental "deficiency," defined in passing with a reference to the notion of "psychasthenia," allows us immediately to identify the doctor, who is made recognizable by his own theoretical obsessions. He is Pierre Janet, Freud's rival and critic. Janet countered Freud with his own "psychological analysis," founded on a method of inquiry whose fundamental rules are the following: examination of the patient, one on one, and without witnesses; rigorous documenting of the words spoken (we have just seen an example of this); and an examination of the patient's history.[1] Janet had developed a theory of "psychological automatism" (the title of one of his first works), the inferior, "weak" form of psychic thought, against the background of a hierarchial conception of the mental field, which allowed him to interpret the illness as a deficiency, related more or less to organic lesions: here we find a type of medical discourse that is clearly symptomatic of a certain state of knowledge. The case cited, and the interpretation that was proposed, were taken from one of the last works published by Janet, *De l'angoisse à l'extase*.[2]

The "patient" evoked in these pages of Janet's book and presented there under the pseudonym of "Martial" is in reality Raymond Roussel, who did in fact undergo treatment with Janet for a few years, without the latter having ever become aware—despite applying his "method" to an investigation of the case—of what his patient apparently made it a point not to reveal to him: Roussel regularly paid a good-looking and well-mannered young woman for the right to show himself with her in public; he lived with her, so that appearances could be saved, since a man of his age and social class owed it to himself to have a mistress (whose uncovered breasts he may well never once have looked at, even in private).[3]

Raymond Roussel, the author of *Impressions d'Afrique* and *Locus Solus*, who had scrupulously regulated the smallest detail of his dandy's

1. For more details, see Elisabeth Roudinesco, *La Bataille de cent ans*, vol. 1 (Paris: Editions Ramsay, 1982), 247ff.
2. Pierre Janet, *De l'angoisse à l'extase* in *Les sentiments fondamentaux*, vol. 2 (Paris: Editions Alcan, 1928), 146–48.
3. On this and many other aspects of Roussel's life, see François Caradec's *Vie de Raymond Roussel* (Paris: Editions J. J. Pauvert, 1972).

life[4] and who could have come straight out of Proust's universe, constructed his texts with the same precision and a sense of humor linked similarly to spontaneous practical joking or mystification. It is as if, wittingly or not, he had made fun of the great specialist who cost him as much as his "mistress," so that he would *not* cure him, so that he would *not* make him live and think like everyone else, and to whom, in any case, Roussel had not revealed the secret of his sex life, which he must have deliberately hidden behind very closed doors, up to the day he met his rather sad end in one of the rooms of a luxury hotel in Palermo, a suspicious suicide, which could also have been a sordid crime.[5] In his book of posthumous revelations, *Comment j'ai écrit certains de mes livres,* Roussel no doubt took some pleasure [*jouissance*] in citing the passages from the first volume of Janet's *De l'angoisse à l'extase* devoted to Martial's literary madness, gathered around the extraordinary, quasi-Schreberian formula recorded in shorthand by Janet: "I have the sun within me and I could not prevent this awesome blazing of myself"; but he avoided repeating his "obsessional" statements on the need for decency and the continuation of privileges reserved for the elites, which appear in the second volume of Janet's work, and which I have just cited.

We know that Foucault devoted a whole book, published in 1963, to Raymond Roussel: it is in fact the only one of his works whose title is a proper name, the name of a subject.[6] At that time Foucault was still classified as a specialist in psychology, a label he would begin to shed only after the publication of *Les Mots et les choses.* While doing research for his book on Roussel, he encountered and must have read in its entirety Janet's *De l'angoisse à l'extase:* he did not know Martial's words only in the expurgated version appropriated and republished by Roussel himself. In the very last pages of his book, he quotes, without giving the reference, one of the statements we have cited above:

> This is how he stated it for Dr. Janet: "Practicing forbidden acts in private rooms knowing that it is prohibited, risking punishment or at least the contempt of respectable people, that is all well and good. But

---

4. In Caradec's book, we can see, for example, the extraordinary manner in which he took his meals.

5. On this subject, see the investigation made at the scene by L. Sciascia thirty years later.

6. Michel Foucault, *Death and the Labyrinth: The World of Raymond Roussel,* trans. Charles Raus, with an introduction by John Ashbery (New York: Doubleday, 1986). Original French title: *Raymond Roussel* (Paris: Editions Gallimard, 1963).

that nudity should be shown and that sexual pleasure should be desired simply from seeing a public spectacle—all this without risk of punishment, with the consent of parents, and while pretending to remain chaste and virtuous, *that* is inadmissible. Everything concerning love must remain forbidden and inaccessible." . . . Fundamental to Roussel's experience of language, there seems to be a place where birth is hidden, the unique and illegitimate impediment, but it can also be a repetition that is always anticipating itself. . . . Birth, which is excluded from the basic possibility of language, must also be removed from everyday meaning. [161–62]

Janet had limited himself to recording Martial's words; but Foucault tried to listen to what Roussel had said and, in a way, he heard it. The following may be an indication of this: rather than the proposed attempt to build an interpretation around a theme, we have the obliteration of sexuality (designated by the term "birth") in language, a cutting out that causes an isolated sequence to stand out from the mechanical flow of "obsessional" words, as if unmoored from the rest. This sequence is ordered around an interdiction [*l'Interdit*]: "Everything concerning love must remain forbidden and inaccessible."

Here, a true subject utterance [*parole de sujet*] begins to be heard (we are not saying the utterance of *the* subject or of *a* subject): we now have something that has little to do with the sort of banality that Janet was able to document, little to do with tartufism ("Cover those breasts I should not see. . . " the better to show them to me when we're alone). This utterance expresses the very truth of pleasure and *jouissance:* one experiences sexual pleasure [*jouissance*] not in the absence of prohibition, or in spite of it, but with it and, in a way, through it, even if it is by making it deviate from its meaning, thus, by exploiting it. Children know this without needing to be told: games that are not forbidden are not really fun. From this principle, Sade made a terrifying story-telling machine, and Roussel, in his work as a writer, can be said to have followed in Sade's footsteps.

This is precisely the point at which a production of subjectivity begins to occur: it is the moment when Foucault considers Roussel's words as words of truth, and causes a subtle discrepancy to arise between what in these words is simply said—the level at which Janet had, of course, remained—and what is being expressed. We are no longer, then, dealing with insignificant statements, but with a subject utterance [*une parole de sujet*], and it is as such that it can also be considered to be a word of truth [*une parole de vérité*].

How can we not hear in these words, taken from what Martial had said to his doctor, a sort of prefigurement of what Foucault himself, thirteen years after having published his book on Roussel, begins to explain in *La Volonté de savoir*?[7]

> Calling sex by its name... became more difficult and more costly. As if in order to gain mastery over it in reality, it had first been necessary to subjugate it at the level of language, control its free circulation in speech, expunge it from the things that were said, and extinguish the words that rendered it too visibly present.... Yet when one looks back over these last three centuries with their continual transformations, things appear in a very different light: around and apropos of sex, one sees a veritable discursive explosion.... But more important was the multiplication of discourses concerning sex in the field of the exercise of power itself: an institutional incitement to speak about it, and to do so more and more; a determination on the part of the agencies of power to hear it spoken about, and to cause it to speak through explicit articulation and endlessly accumulated detail. [*The History of Sexuality*, 17–18]

In other words, what defines the form power assumes in modern times, as bio-power, is its action upon sexuality, and upon the effects of subjectivity that are related to it, not by repressing it through censorship but, on the contrary, by ensuring its free circulation and thus by taking charge of it: more specifically, by popularizing and trivializing it like a mass or population phenomenon whose particular characteristics, linked to a subject position, are tendentially erased. This was something Martial had already been saying to his psychiatrist, talking to him for hours without succeeding in making himself heard, and asserting the need to enclose the acts of pleasure within exclusive chambers where they could continue to provoke the disapproval of respectable people. This subject utterance is indeed the utterance of someone whom Foucault, in another text, called a "vile man": we could also say that it is the utterance of a writer, whose activity implies the withholding of certain techniques.

Almost thirty years later, then, Foucault seems to have heard the subject utterance made by Martial and which, up to then, had remained a dead letter in Janet's book: Foucault shows this by incorporating these words in his own book. This sheds light retrospectively on the space he had allotted to Roussel's subject position in the

---

7. Foucault, *La Volonté de savoir* (Paris: Gallimard, 1976). Published in English as *The History of Sexuality, Volume 1: An Introduction*, trans. Robert Hurley (New York: Pantheon, 1978), 17–18.

last chapter of his 1963 book, organized entirely around Martial's other great utterance, "I have the sun within me": this chapter is entitled "The Enclosed Sun" [*Le Soleil enfermé*], and it is written in dialogue form, Foucault conversing with himself about a third party who is Roussel:

> Apropos of the "I" which speaks in *How I Wrote Certain of My Books*, it is true that a disproportionate detachment at the heart of the sentences he pronounces makes him as remote as the third-person "he." They become confused in the distance, where self-effacement brings out this third person who has been speaking at all times and who always remains the same. [*Death and the Labyrinth*, 155–56]

If there is any production of subjectivity here, it is not in the sense of the subject and of his simple self-reflection through which he recognizes and makes his identity recognized, with both being the same; instead, it is in the sense, and from the point of view of the other, who poses as a third party, not centrally, but at the margin, at the margins defined by the central position of rules (the forbidden, the law), in relation to which he posits himself through opposition.

This is the position Roussel himself adopted in his oeuvre, the position through which he carried out what, later in the same book, Foucault calls "a radical experience of language": this consists in experiencing the definitive gap that inserts itself between words and things, a fatal void where "there is a space" for a subject position, through a vertigo that, in Roussel's case, was the experience of madness, itself a radical experiencing of the gap. This is what is explained in the last pages of *Death and the Labyrinth*:

> Things, words, vision and death, the sun and language make a unique form, the very someone that we are. Roussel in some way has defined its geometry. He has opened to our literary language a strange space that could be defined as linguistic if it were not its mirror image, its dreamy usage, enchanted and mythic. If Roussel's work is separated from this space (which is ours), then it can only be seen as the haphazard marvels of the absurd, or the baroque play of an esoteric language which means "something else." If on the contrary his work is placed there, Roussel appears as he defined himself: the inventor of a language which only speaks about itself, a language absolutely simple in its duplicated being, a language about language, enclosing its own sun in its sovereign and central flow. [166]

The slender, radiant subject-figure [*figure de sujet*] identified by Foucault in this book published in 1963, between *Historie de la folie* and *Les Mots et les choses*, is the one we could call a subject of language, not in the sense of a subject who possesses language, but as what exposes itself to the risk of language and, in the process, occupies the place defined by its supreme lapse [*défaillance*] that no rule has the power to fill. It is truly remarkable that that same year, 1963, Foucault proceeded to study another figure of subjectivity that can be seen as parallel to and complementing the previous one: the figure embodied in the "clinical" reality of the suffering body. *Birth of the Clinic* is posited on a rather simple idea that can be summarized as follows: the modern positivity of medical knowledge is linked to the formation of a new figure of man, one in which man no longer appears as a subject who is essentially alive, altered more or less by illness— an independent entity that attacks him from the outside—but as a body as such, haunted by the inevitability of its own death, a death that possesses him and constitutes him as "alive." In the conclusion to this book, this idea is presented in the following terms:

> This structure, in which space, language, and death are articulated— what is known, in fact, as the anatomo-clinical method—constitutes the historical condition of a medicine that is given and accepted as positive. Positive here should be taken in the strong sense. Disease breaks away from the metaphysic of evil, to which it had been related for centuries; and it finds in the visibility of death the full form in which its content appears in positive terms. Conceived in relation to nature, disease was the non-assignable negative of which the causes, forms, and manifestations were offered indirectly and against an ever-receding background; seen in relation to death, disease becomes exhaustively legible, open without remainder to the sovereign dissection of language and of the gaze. It is when death becomes the concrete a priori of medical experience that death could detach itself from counter-nature and become *embodied* in the *living bodies* of individuals.[8]

This "structure" thus precedes the development of medical knowledge and techniques, which are only effects derived from it: it makes this knowledge and these techniques possible but cannot be defined at their level.

The position of suffering subject thus corresponds to a certain "experience" of man, as Foucault goes on to explain:

---

8. Foucault, *Birth of the Clinic: An Archaeology of Medical Perception*, trans. A. M. Sheridan Smith (New York: Pantheon, 1973), 196.

It will no doubt remain a decisive fact about our culture that its first scientific discourse concerning the individual had to pass through this stage of death. Western man could constitute himself in his own eyes as an object of science, he grasped himself within his language, and gave himself, in himself and by himself, a discursive existence, only in the opening created by his own elimination: from the experience of Unreason was born psychology; from the integration of death into medical thought is born a medicine that is given as a science of the individual. And, generally speaking, the experience of individuality in modern culture is bound up with that of death: from Hölderlin's Empodocles to Nietzsche's Zarathustra, and on to Freudian man, an obstinate relation to death prescribes to the universal its singular face, and lends to each individual the power of being heard forever; the individual owes to death a meaning that does not cease with him. The division that it traces and the finitude whose mark it imposes link, paradoxically, the universality of language and the precarious, irreplaceable form of the individual. (197)

We should note that, here again, we are facing an experience of language: it is in Hölderlin that we should look for the secret of Bichet's enterprise.

What do the singular experience of language carried out by the "I-he" that was Roussel and the appropriation by medical practice of bodies that are alive and that it treats like cadavers, at least potential ones, have in common? The fact that both belong to the same historical ontology of closure or finitude from which is produced "a tight, coherent, unique figure, the one where we now find ourselves" (*Death and the Labyrinth*). This is how the conditions that determine our access to the being-subject are established, these conditions being those of the present moment that nothing forces us to consider as eternal. In this sense, it is against a background of closure or finitude and death that a production of subjectivity can occur today, in a precarious form that remains that of the event.

In a text on Boulez, Foucault uses a phrase that comes closest to defining this subject position: "to provide the strength with which the rules can be broken in the very act that brings them into play."[9] This strength is the one that Martial had displayed by shutting himself behind closed doors to perform unspeakable acts, the same

---

9. Foucault, "Pierre Boulez ou l'écran traversé," an interview published in *Le Nouvel Observateur* in 1982, and used as the preface to *Pierre Boulez: Jalons pour une décennie* (Paris: Christian Bourgois, 1989).

strength he used to achieve a body of work in which the secrets of language, at least of our language, and our limits as historical subjects, are simultaneously exposed and contained.

In conclusion, we should note that the effects of subjectivity that can be drawn from the story we have just told do indeed belong to a process without subject and without subjects. Roussel should not be considered an exemplary figure of the subject, good or bad: if he appears as this I-he, capable once in a while of uttering words of truth [*une parole de vérité*], it is not in the definitive withdrawal, the doubling back upon itself, of a whole identity complete unto itself, which would be enough to identify him as "himself"; instead, it is through the—ultimately accidental—reworking of what he had said, thematized at that point as an utterance [*un énoncé*], a reworking by Foucault some years later, without which it would have been impossible to speak of an effect of subjectivity. It then becomes quite obvious that subjectivity becomes manifest only in the process that makes its circulation possible. But doesn't this talk of a circulation of subjectivity lead us back to intersubjectivity, that other classic figure of the theory of the subject? No, for the issue is not a relation between constituted subjects whose reality would be given prior to their entry into a relation: if the act of encountering—and in this particular case, a removed encounter that allows someone who is living to hear the voice of someone who has died—is vital to the production of effects of subjectivity, it is to the extent that this act absolutely precedes the very existence of those executing it. Then, like shimmering reflections on the surface of troubled waters, figures of the subject—unhindered by any and all necessity—allow themselves to be fleetingly glimpsed.

—Translated by Roger Celestin

WARREN MONTAG

"The Soul is the Prison of the Body": Althusser and Foucault, 1970–1975

> It is impossible to *know* anything about men except on the absolute precondition that the philosophical (theoretical) myth of man is reduced to ashes. So any thought that appeals to Marx for any kind of restoration of a theoretical anthropology or humanism is no more than ashes, *theoretically*. But in practice it could pile up a monument of pre-Marxist ideology that would weigh down on real history and threaten to lead it into blind alleys.
> —Louis Althusser, "Marxism and Humanism"

> Three centuries ago certain fools were astonished because Spinoza wished to see the liberation of man, even though he did not believe in his liberty or even in his particular existence. Today new fools, or even the same ones reincarnated, are astonished because the Foucault who had spoken of the death of man took part in political struggle.
> —Gilles Deleuze, *Foucault*

Not so many years ago it was possible (or perhaps inevitable) to read Althusser's "Ideology and Ideological State Apparatuses"[1] and Foucault's *Discipline and Punish*[2] not only as counterposed texts, but as expressions of opposing systems of thought that might be compared and contrasted, their resemblances and differences noted, but which would remain as ineluctably separate as the men who wrote them. And despite the well-known disposition of both Althusser and Foucault to question, if not reject, the very notion of authorship as exemplary of the myth of the originary subject, it remains very difficult to separate these texts from the subsequent lives and works of their authors. For, while Althusser's text proclaimed its Marxism on every page,

---

1. Louis Althusser, "Ideology and Ideological State Apparatuses," in *Lenin and Philosophy*, trans. Ben Brewster (New York: Monthly Review Press, 1971). Hereafter referred to as "Ideology" in citations in the text.
2. Michel Foucault, *Discipline and Punish*, trans. Alan Sheridan (New York: Vintage, 1977).

Discipline and Punish (in which Marx is cited approvingly on a number of occasions) was nevertheless most often read as a proleptic and hence still obscure manifestation of what would soon become Foucault's open hostility to Marxism (or at least certain kinds of Marxism)[3], and thus as a critique and rejection of the central theses of even Althusser's highly unorthodox remarks on ideology.

Everyone, more or less, has read these texts. The debates that followed their appearance (which admittedly most often took the form of praise or blame) have long since given way to summaries and elucidations that present, in a simplified form, the "essential arguments" of these justly renowned works. And this is precisely the problem: to borrow a phrase from Swift, the original texts often seem buried under mountains of commentary. They appear beyond recovery in the sense that, although the originals are often read, they are always already mediated through other works which, although external to them, appear to have decided their meaning once and for all.

There can be no question, however, of simply putting the seemingly countless commentaries aside to recover the real texts. For it was Althusser himself who wrote that "there is no such thing as an innocent reading."[4] Let us then begin by noting the readings that are imposed upon us, the themes and problems that, as if by a kind of projective identification, appear to arise spontaneously from our encounter with these texts even as they are determined by the way these texts have already been read. To begin to free ourselves from these readings, we must, of course, read the readers and summarize the summarizers, and not simply the best of them, but also those most representative of their genre, namely the mediocre and even the plainly bad. What is remarkable about them is that in their very imprecision and repetitiveness they allow us to speak of these two texts together. For despite the obvious differences between "Ideology and Ideological State Apparatuses" and *Discipline and Punish*, differences in vocabulary and reference points (implicit as well as explicit), the two works have continued

---

3. It is striking to read today Francois Ewald's very influential review of *Discipline and Punish*, "Anatomie et corps politique," which appeared at the end of 1975 in *Critique* (side by side with the first version of Deleuze's "A New Cartographer" from his book *Foucault* [trans. Soéan Hand (Minneapolis: University of Minnesota Press, 1988)]). Ewald projects onto Foucault's text a systematic opposition to Marx and to any conceivable form of Marxism that is utterly absent from the letter of the work, even though Foucault himself later appeared to endorse such a reading.

4. Althusser, *Reading "Capital,"* trans. Ben Brewster (London: New Left Books, 1970), 14.

to provoke remarkably similar criticisms (which, perhaps because of their frequency, no longer appear to be criticisms at all and are taken as "objective" or even sympathetic observations). Thus, to take the two commentaries that have arguably most shaped the reception of these texts, and which exhibit the full range of criticisms (in variety as well as quality), E. P. Thompson's critique of Althusser in *The Poverty of Theory* and Habermas's critique of Foucault in *The Philosophical Discourse of Modernity* (and elsewhere) address quite similar themes. "Ideology and Ideological State Apparatuses" and *Discipline and Punish* were both seen as "limit texts" that took to their logical conclusion certain disturbing and unthinkable notions that had only appeared in mediated form in the earlier work of Althusser and Foucault. Both texts were charged with offering a subtle and perversely persuasive (or even seductive—given that their appeal was said to be literary rather than genuinely philosophical or theoretical) functionalism, a structuralism that denied all that was distinctively human, whether historically invariant needs and natures, the daily "experience" that was said to form the basis of human thought and feeling, or even the irreducible freedom that provided the sole ground of our morality. Such structuralist-functionalism could only result in the evacuation of all historical agency, portraying a world without the possibility of resistance or even change. Althusser and Foucault, despite their differences, produced an analysis of domination that could itself only be a ruse of domination, insofar as the effect of their work was to paralyze individual initiative and to overwhelm critical thought with the idea that ideology or power were inescapable. The program of theoretical antihumanism announced in the pages of Althusser's *For Marx* (1965) and Foucault's *The Order of Things* (1966) was equated with a political or, increasingly, moral indifference to concrete human beings that achieved its fullest expression in the works of the 1970s.

It would of course be possible to respond that these charges are off the mark, inaccurate, or unfair, and to attempt to supply true interpretations in place of the false.[5] And yet, the detractors of Althusser and

5. Although it might be more valuable to trace the political and theoretical trajectory of anti-Althusserianism and anti-Foucauldianism (and, more generally, of what Pierre Macherey has called anti-antihumanism). Within Marxism (that is, taking the work of those who openly identify themselves as Marxists), the case of Althusser is particularly interesting. For apart from cultural studies (in the broad sense), much of Anglo-American Marxism has simply forgotten Althusser (Foucault was always regarded as an enemy). From E. P. Thompson's tirade against Althusser (*The Poverty of Theory and Other Essays* [New York: Monthly Review Press, 1978]) to Perry Anderson's

Foucault have stumbled on a truth that the partisans of these philosophers have often denied: that the two works are not opposed and external to each other, the one an alternative to the other. Rather than feeling compelled to choose between "Ideology and Ideological State Apparatuses" and *Discipline and Punish*, and thus between Althusser and Foucault, to the extent that we take the commentaries in all their unevenness to be objectively determined effects of the works in question, we may read the apparent dilemma, Althusser or Foucault, in the manner of Spinoza, as Althusser *sive* Foucault, Althusser, that is, Foucault. Perhaps it is now (that is, from a certain historical distance) possible to regard Althusser and Foucault (understood as proper names that denote bodies of work) as reciprocal immanent causes, dynamic and inseparable, no longer as creators of systems that must be accepted or rejected *in toto*, but rather as philosophers who sought to problema-

---

In the Tracks of Historical Materialism (London: Verso Press, 1983)—which was less emotional but no less dismissive—until the mid-eighties when he was quietly buried (appearing in Jon Elster's *Making Sense of Marx* [Cambridge: Cambridge University Press, 1985] only in adjectival form as the poisonous "Althusserian" atmosphere at the Ecole Normale Supérieure that Elster found it convenient to avoid), Althusser's theoretical antihumanism was apparently deemed unworthy of refutation. Despite the immense outcry *no one responded to the arguments of "Marxism and Humanism" or "Ideology and Ideological State Apparatuses" point for point.* It was enough, apparently, to say that, because we cannot imagine revolt against domination without the classical concept of the individual as subject, as a center of initiatives, as radical origin of thought, speech, and action, it therefore must exist. Once Althusser's questioning of the category of the subject was forgotten, there was a massive return to essentialism, with Thompson's attempt to save the phenomenon of human experience from dwindling into rational choice individualism. It is quite ironic that the dominant form of Anglophone academic Marxism, far from being the self-contained theoretical realm that Anderson thought it ought to be (in order thus to be preserved from the contagion of an irrevocably foreign poststructuralism), now derives its epistemology from Karl Popper's *The Poverty of Historicism* (New York: Harper and Row, 1964), its theory of class struggle from Mancur Olson's *The Logic of Collective Action* (Cambridge, Mass.: Harvard University Press, 1971), and its political positions from John Rawls's *A Theory of Justice* (Cambridge, Mass.: Belknap Press of Harvard University Press, 1971). While Althusser was once roundly denounced for speaking of the heterogeneity of Marx's texts, it is now a received truth in these quarters that there is little that makes sense in Marx except the moral doctrines that he himself disavowed. It is also highly ironic that Habermas's rationalism and humanism, which, according to Anderson, were the antidote to Althusser's theoretical anarchy and nihilism, were very publicly placed in support of the imperialist forces in the Gulf War (nor was Habermas alone in this among the antiantihumanists). Habermas has continued to defend this "police action" by appealing to the doctrine of human rights (Jürgen Habermas, *The Philosophical Discourse of Modernity*, trans. Frederick Lawrence [Cambridge, Mass.: MIT Press, 1987]). Althusser's critique of the spontaneous philosophy of economic and political liberalism would appear more urgent than ever.

tize certain concepts and notions that many in their time and ours felt could not be questioned. Further, these commentaries, both positive and negative, are useful to us in another way. For it is not only what the critiques of Althusser and Foucault actually say that allows us to link these texts quite closely; it is also what they do not say, the theoretical concerns common to both Althusser and Foucault that are overlooked by their commentators with the regularity of a symptom, the silences and oversights that the commentaries share and that were imposed upon them by the historical conjuncture in which they were written.

It is useful to begin by noting the nature of the theoretical activity of Althusser and Foucault as they themselves defined it: they were neither sociologists nor historians; their objective was not to create theories of society and even less to provide analyses of specific historical moments. They were philosophers, although, again, not in the traditional ("Continental") manner. They did not seek to produce new systems of thought in the sense that we speak of Cartesianism, Kantianism, or Hegelianism. On the contrary, a careful survey of their work shows that their primary concern was to discover how certain concepts functioned in specific historical conjunctures, not from a position outside this history, but rather from within it, in order to allow something new to be thought, to make it possible, as Foucault said, "to learn to what extent the effort to think one's own history can free thought from what it silently thinks, and so enable it to think differently."[6] Such a "philosophical exercise" (ibid.) is at once very limited and extraordinarily ambitious and far-reaching. It is nevertheless absolutely necessary.

Althusser was especially interested in what philosophy "thought silently," or, to use his language, in the "obviousnesses" of philosophy, in philosophy. To insist on this is to appear to move far from the political realm (which Althusser argued was at stake in philosophy) and to a purely theoretical realm of necessarily little interest to the world. We seem to have converted Althusser, not only a Marxist but a Communist, into a pure academician, applying philosophy to itself, tinkering with self-evident concepts in order to produce clever paradoxes *pour épater les bourgeois*. To this charge Althusser responded that "philosophy intervenes in reality only by producing results *within itself.*"[7]

---

6. Michel Foucault, *The History of Sexuality, Vol. 2: The Use of Pleasure*, trans. Robert Hurley (New York: Vintage, 1986), 9.

7. Althusser, *Philosophy and the Spontaneous Philosophy of the Scientists and Other Essays*, ed. Gregory Elliott, trans. Ben Brewster (London: Verso, 1990), 107.

How does philosophy work upon itself? By questioning the tenacious (and properly philosophical) concepts whose obviousness renders them all but unquestionable, like "the 'obviousness' that you and I are subjects. . . . It is indeed a peculiarity of ideology that it imposes (without appearing to do so, since these are 'obviousnesses') obviousnesses as obviousnesses, which we cannot *fail to recognize* and before which we have the inevitable and natural reaction of crying out (aloud or in the 'still, small voice of conscience'): 'That's obvious! That's right! That's true!'" ("Ideology," 172).

Foucault described his own activity in very similar terms: "To give some assistance in wearing away certain self-evidences and commonplaces about madness, normality, illness, crime and punishment; to bring it about, together with many others, that certain phrases can no longer be spoken so lightly, certain acts no longer, or at least no longer so unhesitatingly, performed; to contribute to changing certain things in people's ways of perceiving and doing things; to participate in this difficult displacement of forms of sensibility and thresholds of tolerance—I hardly feel capable of attempting much more than that. If only what I have tried to say might somehow, to some degree, not remain altogether foreign to some such real effects. . . . And yet I realize how much all this can remain precarious, how easily it can all lapse back into somnolence."[8]

All this sounds so modest, too modest, I suspect, for many philosophers today who, not content merely to produce theories of justice (an enterprise so utterly foreign to Althusser and Foucault), would design the blueprint of the well-ordered and fair society of tomorrow. But the modest questioning of certain obviousnesses produced effects of the most explosive kind. Some of the world's most eminent historians, sociologists, and philosophers were moved to "put out the fire." The ferocity of their reactions may today appear surprising or even startling. But we should not be surprised: the ferocity is a sign of how sensitive certain ideological points can be, of how utterly intolerable is the mere questioning of some "certitudes." In this, even the most bitter tirades are valuable indicators.[9] They suggest that the simple, if

---

8. Foucault, "Questions of Method," in *The Foucault Effect: Studies in Governmentality*, ed. Graham Burchell, Colin Gordon, and Peter Miller (Chicago: University of Chicago Press, 1991), 83.

9. The reader will recall the terms of E. P. Thompson's refusal even to criticize this particular work of Althusser's: "'Ideology and Ideological State Apparatuses'. . . is perhaps the ugliest thing he has ever done, the crisis of the idealist delirium. I will spare

unexpected, questions that Althusser and Foucault dared to ask about "certain commonplaces" possess a force that is not nearly exhausted and will likely turn out to be more important than the systems that their opponents and many of their admirers have attributed to them.

The most unforgivable question that Althusser and Foucault asked concerned the subject. Their stubborn insistence that the individual was not given, but constituted or produced as center of initiatives, an effect, not a cause of the conflictual processes of ideology or power (a thesis central to both works) had, as Althusser put it, "everything required to offend . . . common sense."[10] While this notion has received much attention, its theoretical precondition (at least in the sense Althusser defined the interpellated or constituted subject) has nearly been passed over in silence by the controversies of the last two decades. It is a theoretical point (not the only one but one of the most important) where the two works overlap and which, from a certain position, prevents them from being entirely separated, even as it is the point at which the two works might seem most opposed. I refer to Althusser's assertion (which has no formal or explicit counterpart in *Discipline and Punish*), in a language so different from that of Foucault as to appear irrelevant to his project, that ideology has a material existence. It was precisely because such a phrase seemed to Foucault to contain an insurmountable paradox that he, from very early on, rejected the term "ideology." It appeared impossible that "ideology" could be dissociated from some form of ideal or immaterial existence, whether ideas or consciousness:

> I wonder whether, before one poses the question of ideology, it wouldn't be more materialist to study first the question of the body and the effects of power on it. Because what troubles me with these analyses which prioritize ideology is that there is always presupposed a human subject on the lines of the model provided by classical philosophy, endowed with a consciousness which power is then thought to seize on.[11]

And this is precisely the paradox of Althusser's attempt to undermine what he called "the ideological concept of ideology" with the

---

myself the tedium of criticism, since in its naivety, its refusal of all relevant evidence, and its absurd idealist inventions it exposes itself" (174).

10. Althusser, *Essays in Self-Criticism*, trans. Grahame Locke (London: New Left Books, 1976), 94.

11. Foucault, "Body/Power," in *Power/Knowledge: Selected Interviews and Other Writings 1972–1977*, ed. and trans. Colin Gordon (New York: Pantheon, 1980), 58.

notion of "ideology" itself, forcing a word whose ever visible etymology reminds us of its reference to ideas (in the mind and thus endowed with an ideal or spiritual existence), as well as whose use in a variety of Marxist and non-Marxist discourses seemed almost ineluctably to refer to a notion of consciousness, *against* "ideas," *against* "consciousness," and, finally, *against* every form of interiority, leaving nothing recognizable in his conception of ideology but the name. Of course, such a tactic was entirely in keeping with what Foucault himself called "the tactical polyvalence of discourse," the rule that enjoins us to "conceive discourse as a series of discontinuous segments whose tactical function is neither uniform nor stable," and which implies constant "reutilizations of identical formulas for contrary objectives."[12] This is not to say that Althusser's exploitation of this specific theoretical polyvalence entirely prevented his notion of ideology from being read as a continuation of earlier theories, or even as a not very original theory of the indoctrination of preexisting consciousnesses.[13] On the contrary, the evidence of the last two decades confirms that the very use of the term "ideology" (which he nevertheless considered unavoidable given the absence of more effective concepts) tended to obscure the radical originality of Althusser's theses on the nature of human servitude, their irreducibility to preceding theories of ideology.

Althusser approached the central thesis of the "Ideology" essay (ideology interpellates individuals as subjects) through two preliminary theses "one negative, the other positive. The first concerns the object which is 'represented' in the imaginary form of ideology, the second concerns the materiality of ideology" ("Ideology," 162). The conjunction of these two theses perfectly captured the apparently paradoxical nature of Althusser's notion of ideology. For how could ideology be simultaneously imaginary and material, and how could the notion of the "imaginary" be conceived, except in reference to a consciousness whose illusions, whose false ideas, prevent it from knowing or perceiving the real? It is noteworthy that the negative thesis of the imaginary was widely taken up by commentators (and not just those who discerned in it an allusion to the work of Lacan), while the positive thesis of the materiality of ideology went nearly ignored.[14] The "imag-

---

12. Foucault, *The History of Sexuality, Volume 1: An Introduction,* trans. Robert Hurley (New York: Vintage, 1980), 100.

13. See, for instance, Nicholas Abercrombie, Stephen Hill, and Bryan Turner, *The Dominant Ideology Thesis* (London: George Allen & Unwin, 1980), 20–24.

14. To my knowledge, the most extended treatment of the topic of the materiality of

inary form of ideology" appeared to be the *only* link between what had heretofore been understood as ideology and Althusser's often bewildering attempts to separate himself from all the familiar bearings. For many readers ideology was still "false," "illusion," even the false consciousness (why not?) of an interpellated subject, a subject constituted, yes, but constituted as already possessing the false (imaginary) ideas that in turn give rise to actions that tend to the reproduction of (rather than resistance to) the existing relations of production.

Such an interpretation, however, was not simply a misreading projected onto Althusser's text. For how else are we to understand the distinction, seemingly so central to Althusser's notion of ideology (and stated at the very outset, prior to the section "On Ideology"), between the "Repressive State Apparatus" that functions (in the last instance) "by violence" and the "Ideological State Apparatuses" that function "by ideology ("Ideology," 145)? Of course, the statement that Ideological State Apparatuses function by ideology is, formally speaking, an empty tautology (at least until Althusser defines ideology); by opposing it to the violence of the Repressive Apparatuses, however, he appears to endorse a political dualism of force and consent (a term, it should be noted, that is conspicuously absent from the essay and from Althusser's work in general), of a double but asymmetrical domination that exercises force and violence on the body, but only as a last resort, the preferred mode of domination being that which persuades the mind to choose of its own irreducibly free will to subject itself to the powers that be. The servitude that is freely chosen will prove much more durable than that which is forced upon an unwilling subject in that it is lived as legitimate and lawful. Ideology here becomes indoctrination, the inculcation of beliefs (whether true or false) that will inevitably find expression in the actions of the individuals who "possess" them. There thus appears a linear sequence: ideas (the ruling ideas) are communicated to individuals who form beliefs that cause them to act. The fact that such notions are fundamentally incompatible with the elements of Althusser's definition of ideology in the final section of "Ideology and Ideological State Apparatuses" did not prevent many readers from taking the essay as a variant of the traditional theory of ideology. For this very reason, it is worth (re)tracing the line of demarcation that separates what is new and unprecedented in this

---

ideology is that of Paul Hirst in *On Law and Ideology* (London: Macmillan Press, 1979): approximately one and a half pages.

extraordinarily complex and heterogeneous work from the images, words, and even concepts that preserve a continuity with the "tradition" of ideology.

Althusser began his discussion of his second, positive, (but still preliminary) thesis with a warning that ideology, even as it could be said to be imaginary, did not consist of false or illusory ideas "contained" in the minds of individuals (and still less in some collective mind or spirit) that would then cause them to act in certain ways. The entire discussion of ideology here is designed to call radically into question the notion that mental beliefs cause physical bodily actions. It is at this precise point that he lost a large majority of his readers and it is not difficult to see why. The arguments that follow "Thesis Two: Ideology has a material existence" move from paradox to paradox, not forward to new conclusions but backward into Althusser's text itself, contesting and undermining certain formulations (e.g., violence and ideology), or, more precisely, the certitudes, the unquestionable givens upon which such formulations appear to be based.

Althusser begins his discussion of the material existence of ideology with the statement, in certain ways calculated to appeal to a kind of orthodoxy, that the Ideological State Apparatuses, each of them, is the "realization of an ideology" ("Ideology," 166). Now, "realization" in this sense is, for a number of reasons, not a usage we would expect to find in Althusser. It seems that we are to understand that the ideology precedes its expression in the materiality of an apparatus, as an idea precedes (and causes) an action. This would of course mean that ideology has an (ideal?) existence prior to its material incarnation, a notion that is ruled out by the second thesis itself: ideas do not (ever) have a spiritual or ideal existence, only a material one. Without taking up any of these questions, Althusser (in the same paragraph) restates ("returns to") the thesis: "An ideology always exists in an apparatus, and its practice or practices. This existence is material" ("Ideology," 166). The restatement, of course, changes the meaning of the original statement in certain important respects, given that "always exists in" is not the same as "is realized in." The reformulation eliminates the suggestion of the temporal and causal priority of ideology in relation to the apparatuses and thus eliminates any notion that ideology can exist external to its material form.

But while the second formulation solves certain problems associated with the first, it also poses new questions. I refer specifically to the use of the preposition "in": ideology always exists *in* an apparatus. Let us go further and combine the two formulations to achieve the full effect of the paradox: ideology always exists in the apparatus that is its realization. Thus ideology is neither the cause (in any commonly accepted sense of the term) nor the effect of the apparatuses that constitute its material form. This is not, however, the first appearance of this precise paradox in the history of philosophy. Althusser had, as Michel Pêcheux put it, "a real companion in heresy . . . who also knew the art of taking unforgivable questions to extremes."[15] Of course, Althusser was well aware of this companion, whose importance not simply for this essay but for Althusser's work as a whole was notorious. When it comes to the question of ideology, he argued that "to be a Spinozist or a Marxist . . . is to be exactly the same thing" ("Ideology," 175). As is well known, Spinoza questioned the model of every conception of the originary subject (or actor or agent of an action): God. For the relationship of God to the created world cannot be that of an actor separate from his action, which would thus be the expression of a preexisting intention. God can only be an immanent cause whose will and intentions exist solely in an actualized state: "God could not have been prior to his decrees nor can he be without them."[16] Human beings insist on imagining God as a transitive cause, whose will precedes his actions and decrees because they, argues Spinoza, imagine themselves (or their minds) to be the free causes of their actions, whereas in fact mind and body, thought and action are simultaneous and inseparable, and determined by the same causes. Perhaps Althusser deliberately refrained from directly using the Spinozist language that caused such controversy when it appeared at the end of *Reading "Capital,"* but the concept is there: ideology is immanent in its apparatuses and their practices, it has no existence apart from these apparatuses and is entirely coincident with them. Ideas have thus disappeared into their material manifestations, absent causes that "exist" only in their effects (or, to add a Freudian reference that is entirely in keeping with both Spinoza and Althusser, ideas in this sense are causes that are ever only constituted *nachträglich*, retroactively, as the effect of their material effects).

It is certain to be objected at this point that ideas, even those that have disappeared into their material forms, must originate somewhere; and even if we are not methodological individualists who trace all

15. Michel Pêcheux, *Language, Semantics, and Ideology: Stating the Obvious*, trans. Harbans Nagpal (London: Macmillan Press, 1982), 214.
16. Benedict Spinoza, *The Ethics*, trans. Samuel Shirley (Indianapolis: Hackett, 1982), Proposition 33, Scholium 2.

action back to an original actor (or actors) and all thought to an originating "thing that thinks," is it not the case that consciousness or mind retains a place in this scheme if only as a relay point that facilitates the translation of "ideas" and "thought," however instantaneously, into ideological practices that, after all, depend on the corporeal obedience of individuals? Must these individuals not first (be made to) believe in order then to obey? But Althusser denounces even this notion as "an absolutely ideological 'conceptual' device (*dispositif*)" insofar as it separates ideas ("endowed with a spiritual existence") from "(material) behavior" (*comportement*), and institutes the priority of the former over the latter ("Ideology," 167). So, according to this conceptual device, if an individual "believes" in God, then he or she will go to church and pray. If an individual "believes" in the law, then he or she will obey it. What if an individual does not act according to the beliefs that he proclaims openly or "knows" secretly that he holds? He is then either a hypocrite or, more interestingly for our purposes, does not know what he believes. It is probable that Althusser, at this point in the text, had in mind a passage from Descartes's *Discourse on Method*: "In order to ascertain their real opinions, I ought to take cognisance of what they practiced rather than of what they said, not only because, in the corruption of our manners, there are few disposed to speak exactly as they believe, but because very many are not aware of what it is that they really believe, for as the act of mind by which a thing is believed being different from that by which we know we believe it, the one is often found without the other."[17]

Althusser subjects such statements to a symptomatic reading: despite the insistence on separating spiritual ideas from material actions, as internal intentions that are externally realized, this "ideology of ideology," faced with a discrepancy between the ideas and beliefs on the one hand and actions on the other, must, precisely to preserve this conceptual device, posit ideas other than those that the originating subject thinks it has, ideas that "correspond" to the actions the subject performs. The fact that these interpolated ideas do not preexist "their" actions, i.e., the actions that correspond to them, can mean only one thing: "The ideology of ideology thus recognizes, despite its imaginary distortion, that the 'ideas' of the human subject exist in his actions" ("Ideology," 168). The formula is repeated: just as ideology always ex-

---

17. Cited in Pierre Macherey, *A Theory of Literary Production*, trans. Geoffrey Wall (London: Routledge & Kegan Paul, 1978), 82.

ists in an apparatus, so do ideas (of individual subjects) exist in (their) actions. It is at this point that Althusser crosses a certain threshold in his "restatement" of his thesis concerning the ideas and actions of individuals: "His ideas are his material actions" (169). A few lines later, as if to blunt the force of his critique or to obscure the tracks of his theoretical detour (through Spinoza, whose name is not mentioned once in the section "ideology has a material existence," arguably the most Spinozist part of a very Spinozist essay), he tells us that while the term "ideas" has disappeared from further considerations of ideology, the notions of "belief" and "consciousness" survive (169). This is a very revealing moment in that it shows Althusser's desire to preserve or, rather, appear to preserve an entire conceptual vocabulary, with the sole exception of the term "ideas." It is as if it would be too much altogether to eliminate the terms "belief" and, even more, "consciousness" (the importance of which for Marxist thought in all its diversity can hardly be overestimated). But do these terms and, even more importantly, the notions of interiority that they suggest actually survive in Althusser's text? Should we, as so many readers have done, take Althusser at his word?

In fact, the word "consciousness" appears only once in the remainder of the essay. Not only is it placed in quotation marks, but it is immediately qualified in the following way: the reproduction of the relations of production is assured "in the 'consciousness,' i.e., in the behavior" (*dans la conscience, c'est-à-dire, dans le comportement*)[18] of individual subjects. Consciousness, i.e., behavior: the reference here is not only to the content of Spinoza's famous, and equally offhanded, remark (*Deus sive Natura*, God, i.e., nature) but, even more perhaps, to Spinoza's philosophical strategy. Fifteen years after the publication of "Ideology and Ideological State Apparatuses," Althusser wrote:

> What also fascinated me about Spinoza was his philosophical strategy. . . . For Spinoza began with God! He began with God and finally (I believe, in accordance with the tradition of his worst enemies) he was (like Da Costa and so many other Portuguese Jews of his time) an atheist. A supreme strategist, he began by laying siege to the enemy's

---

18. It is essential to note that *comportement* is consistently rendered in the English translation of the essay as "attitude," which suggests an internal, subjective state, whereas the French suggests the opposite, namely external conduct of behavior. Ben Brewster's otherwise accurate and elegant translation has thus unfortunately contributed to a misunderstanding of the materialism proper to the essay.

most vital and most heavily fortified point or rather placed himself there as if he were his own enemy and therefore not under suspicion himself of being the enemy, taking over the enemy's theoretical fortress and turning it against that enemy, as if one were to turn the cannons of a fortress against its occupants.[19]

One scholar has called the procedure Althusser refers to here the "strategy of the *sive*,"[20] the strategy of remaining inside the dominant conceptual regime while carrying out an operation of theoretical transformation and translation: God or nature, right or power, preserving words while changing their meanings and then returning these words against this regime. Althusser has preserved the language of interiority, the words "belief," "consciousness," in the very same sense that Spinoza preserved the concept of God, in order more effectively to subvert it.

To illustrate this point, Althusser takes an example from Pascal, condensing into a single sentence a series of arguments and postulates from the *Pensées:* "Kneel down, move your lips in prayer, and you will believe." This "wonderful formula," he writes, "will enable us to invert the order of the notional schema of ideology" ("Ideology," 168). The order to which he refers is of course the causal order according to which thought precedes action as its cause: if an individual kneels down and prays, such an action is the consequence of that individual's belief in God and his desire to act upon his belief (for he might suffer from "a weakness of will"). Pascal's hypothetical libertine, however, poses more complicated problems. His difficulty concerns belief, not action: convinced that his destiny has been wagered, he wants to believe in God but cannot, he desires to desire God but feels only emptiness where the desire he desires to feel ought to be. Pascal's advice to the libertine is truly "scandalous": what you do is more important than what you believe. Perform the prescribed gestures and utter the prescribed words and your lack of belief will not matter. But perhaps even more scandalously, he reassures the libertine that action or practice, to use Althusser's term (at least, if it is conducted according to rituals performed within the apparatus of the Church), will *produce* belief, thus instituting a tendential primacy of the body over the soul, of matter over spirit. To invert "the notional schema of ideology," however, is not necessarily to call it into question. For Pascal's position

---

19. Althusser, "L'unique tradition matérialiste," *Lignes* 18 (1993): 85–86.
20. André Tosel, *Spinoza ou le crépuscule de la servitude* (Paris: Aubier, 1984), 55.

appears to resemble a kind of behaviorism, a theory of the conditioning of the mind through the body that makes the soul a mere reflection of the body without substance or material form.

Althusser, however, has set for himself the opposite objective: to demonstrate the material existence of ideas, beliefs, and consciousness. Accordingly, he immediately translates Pascal's language into "a more directly Marxist vocabulary" in order to show that "we are not dealing with an inversion at all":

> I shall therefore say that, where only a single subject (such and such an individual) is concerned, the existence of the ideas of his belief is material in that *his ideas are his material actions inserted into material practices governed by material rituals which are themselves defined by the material ideological apparatus from which derive the ideas of that subject.* [169: Althusser's emphasis]

Althusser's translation is again a betrayal of the original in that every notion of a sequence and a separation between the mental and the physical, the soul and the body, spirit and matter has disappeared, and further, the ideas that "are" the actions of an individual no longer transcend physical existence insofar as they are always already "inserted" into practices that are in turn governed by the rituals of an apparatus. The four repetitions of "material" in this passage are important. Words may remain (e.g., "belief," "consciousness"), but Althusser has effectively banished any notion of interiority, or rather, he shows that the internal is always already translated in the Spinozist manner into the external "expression" which it cannot be understood to precede and outside of which it has no existence. There are only exteriorities, not only the materialities of actions and movements but also the materialities of discourse, whether written, spoken, or silent and invisible, but still material, still producing effects as only the material can, not originating "inside" us whether in intentional speech acts or in the unintentional but nevertheless eloquent speech that is spoken to us in the secrecy of sleep, the speech that is ours but is spoken only where we are not. Ideas, beliefs, consciousness are always immanent in the irreducible materiality of discourses, actions, practices.

Here, Althusser plays certain theses from Spinoza's *Ethics* against the "ideology of ideology" that assumed its definitive form during the Enlightenment: "The philosophy of the Enlightenment . . . saw in knowledge and its public diffusion the solution to all personal and social contradictions, including the dissipation of all ideological illusions."[21] When Kant wrote, "Argue as much as you like and about whatever you like, but obey,"[22] he certainly meant to lay the groundwork for an unending but orderly progress presided over by an enlightened monarch who, by simultaneously demanding corporeal obedience and allowing freedom of discussion, would himself be convinced to adjust the law to a constantly developing rationality that, in turn, would never be allowed to threaten social order with its zeal. But, even more, he imagined an intellectual freedom that coexists with but transcends bodily servitude, unconditioned by determinations that would remain of a purely physical order and that would therefore be incapable of affecting the activity of the mind.

Is it possible to think freely in a world of obedience? Spinoza, in the words of Althusser, "was not of this opinion." For him "the soul (the *mens*, the activity of the mind) is in no way separate from the activity of the organic body; on the contrary, the soul only thinks insofar as it is affected by the impressions and movements of the body, therefore it thinks not only with the body but *in it,* consubstantially united to it prior to any separation."[23] Against the entire liberal tradition from Hobbes (who was the immediate object of Spinoza's critique) to Kant (and beyond), which posits a human interiority free and separate from the laws (and forces) that govern the physical world as if it were "a kingdom within a kingdom . . . that has absolute power over its actions and is determined by no other source than itself,"[24] Spinoza argues that whatever decreases or limits the power of the body to act, simultaneously decreases the power of the mind (*mens*) to think (*Ethics*, Proposition 11). Spinoza judged a society not by its consciousness but by its rituals, practices, and institutions. As he explains in the *Tractatus Theologico-Politicus,* the longevity of the Hebrew state was no more a matter of its "collective consciousness" than of its divine election; its longevity was produced and insured by ceremonial rites and sacrifices, by the material and external manifestations of a faith that was less a religion than the ideology of the historical nation-state. Because the life of its people was "one long schooling in obedience . . . no one desired what was forbidden and all desired what was com-

---

21. Althusser, "L'unique tradition matérialiste," 96.
22. Immanuel Kant, "An Answer to the Question: What is Enlightenment?" in *Kant's Political Writings,* ed. Hans Reiss (Cambridge: Cambridge University Press, 1970), 55.
23. Althusser, "L'unique tradition matérialiste," 96.
24. Spinoza, *The Ethics,* preface, 3.

manded."[25] From Spinoza's account of the protodisciplinary society, it may be concluded that there can be no liberation of the mind without a corresponding liberation of the body, no criticism of the existing social order that is not immanent in acts and practices of resistance and revolt.

What are we now to make of the distinction between the violence of the Repressive State Apparatus and the "ideological" functioning of the Ideological State Apparatuses in the light of Althusser's Spinozism? It is certain that Althusser rejects the dualism inherent in Gramsci's formulations on hegemony: the centaur, half beast, half human, inhabiting simultaneously the world of ideas and beliefs (in which consent is shaped), and the world of force and violence. Althusser himself admitted that there was no absolute distinction between the Repressive State Apparatus and the Ideological State Apparatuses, arguing that every apparatus is characterized by a "double functioning" ("Ideology," 145). Even apparently purely ideological apparatuses such as the school or the church "use suitable methods of punishment, expulsion and selection, etc., to 'discipline' not only their shepherds but also their flocks" (145). Here, of course, we are just a step away from "discipline" in Foucault's sense. If we take seriously Althusser's statement that "we think with our bodies," then we can no longer understand the distinction between violence and ideology as a distinction between the external and the internal, between the domination exercised on bodies and the domination exercised on minds. Instead, we are forced to acknowledge the "consubstantiality" of force and persuasion, that there is no persuasion (or activity at all) of minds, except insofar as it is immanent in force that may be overwhelming or subtle, force that inflicts pain, damage, or death, or force that is quietly and unobtrusively physical, managing bodies and spaces with neither pain nor harm.

There remains, of course, Althusser's central thesis: ideology interpellates individuals as subjects. If with Spinoza Althusser holds that "mind and body . . . are one and the same individual thing" (*Ethics*, Part 2, Proposition 21) and consequently that if we think, we think with and in our bodies, there is, strictly speaking, no place for subjectivity in the modern sense. What, then, is this factitious if not fictitious interiority with which we are endowed, which is added to us, a

---

25. Spinoza, *Tractatus Theologico-Politicus*, trans. Samuel Shirley (Leiden: E. J. Brill, 1989), 266.

paradoxical interior that, having no place in us, is constructed around us, outside of us? Interiority and consciousness (and the internal acts that supposedly occur within these unconditioned spaces) function as the supplement of servitude, its supplemental origin, the origin of the origin, the mark of a domination that folds back upon itself to add to its superior force the guarantee of its own legitimacy. The imposition of human servitude through force and fraud is not enough; it must retroactively produce its origins (in the modern epoch at least) in the will of each and every subject, "man by man," as Hobbes would say, a foundation that simultaneously rises upon and buries the violence of its origins, where "conquest, enslavement, robbery, murder, in short, force play the greatest part."[26] In the liberal tradition, this scheme takes the form of the "acts of will," the "intentions" that originate nowhere else but *in* ourselves (it is in this sense that each individual in his or her freedom is a "kingdom within a kingdom"), that found the political order (at least *our* political order) and are the guarantees of its legitimacy. This interiority is thus the site of origins, but origins that were never present: the consent that we have always already given and that "founds" the power that rises against us, the rights that we have always already transferred to the powers that be that, having received our authorization, cannot really be opposed to us. Althusser says it brutally: we are interpellated as subjects so that we will freely choose our own subjection. For Foucault (writing in 1971, one year after the publication of "Ideology and Ideological State Apparatuses"), this was the very historical meaning of humanism, which he defined as "the totality of discourse through which western man is told: 'Even though you don't exercise power, you can still be a ruler. Better yet the more you deny yourself the exercise of power, the more you submit to those in power, then the more this increases your sovereignty.'"[27] But interiority is not an illusory presence to which the materiality of the body (with which we think) might be opposed, for the "interpellated" interior is itself "constituted" and therefore fully real, not opposed to the exterior but its continuation: the figure of the fold, whose importance for Foucault Deleuze has demonstrated at length,[28] is merely another way of understanding the ideological interpellation of individuals as subjects.

26. Karl Marx, *Capital*, vol. 1 (New York: Vintage Press, 1977), 874.
27. Foucault, "Revolutionary Action: 'Until Now,'" in *Language, Counter-Memory, Practice: Selected Essays and Interviews by Michel Foucault*, ed. Donald F. Bouchard (Ithaca: Cornell University Press, 1971), 221.
28. Deleuze, *Foucault*, 94–123.

Despite (or perhaps because of) Althusser's subtle and enormously complex attempts to turn the notion of ideology against the ideological conception of ideology, Foucault expressed suspicion of the term *ideology* from very early in his career, and his suspicions, it must be said, were often directed at Althusser's uses of the term. It was as if Foucault followed with critical attention the successive definitions of ideology offered by Althusser and felt compelled to engage, often polemically, with them. Althusser's early definition of ideology as "the lived relation between men and their world,"[29] which was opposed by "science," was vigorously contested in the pages of *The Archeology of Knowledge*,[30] a number of whose arguments were in turn adopted by Althusser in his self-criticism of 1974. But this strange "dialogue," whose participants did not directly address or even name each other (perhaps it was unnecessary), did not stop there. Almost immediately after the publication of "Ideology and Ideological State Apparatuses" in *La pensée* in 1970, the terms of Foucault's critique of ideology changed, even as he himself renewed his acquaintance with Marxism and became an active participant in the extraparliamentary Left. The problem with the concept of ideology was no longer that it seemed to denote a realm of *doxa*, of belief and opinion in opposition to the sanctified world of scientific knowledge, but rather that ideology seemed logically confined to the realm of consciousness and ideas and therefore destined to remain idealist, diverting our attention from what is at stake in any form of subjection: the body, the body that works and whose power produces value, the body that obeys by acting or by refraining from action. In one sense, this critique of ideology cannot possibly be directed against Althusser's essay, in that its terms, its insistence on the primacy of the body, are exactly those we have just described in Althusser. But in another sense, Foucault may be understood to confront "Ideology and Ideological State Apparatuses" with its contradictions and unevennesses, developing certain of its theses (notably those concerned with the materiality of ideology) in order to show their stark incompatibility with other elements of Althusser's discussion of ideology.

In particular, *Discipline and Punish* underscores the way the arguments that comprise the thesis "ideology has a material existence"

29. Althusser, *For Marx*, trans. Ben Brewster (London: Verso, 1969), 233.
30. Foucault, *The Archaeology of Knowledge*, trans. A. M. Sheridan Smith (New York: Harper, 1972), 184–86.

appear to call into question the distinction between the RSA and the ISAs as a distinction between violence and ideology (understood in turn as an opposition of force and consent). As we have seen, the "citation" from Pascal, the image of the subjected body that is determined to kneel down, move its lips in prayer, and simultaneously to "believe," suggests that, while there is no question of the body being caused to act by a persuaded, indoctrinated, or deceived mind (contrary to some of Althusser's suggestions at the beginning of the essay), neither can "its" acts be understood as the effects of violence or repression (involving the army, the police, or the courts), which would, of course, not exclude a notion of a mind or consciousness that rationally calculates likely outcomes of actions, and decides to choose the wiser, i.e., safer course of obedience (a notion excluded by the essay's central thesis of the interpellated subject). Foucault, unencumbered by the "ideology of ideology," and having no need to turn its language against it, can argue in a directly Spinozist manner that since bodies (and the thinking that takes place in them, with them), and not consciousness or interiority, are at stake in the practices of subjection, and since only bodies determine bodies, it is all the more striking that so little attention has been paid to the physical processes of subjection, processes whose divergent modalities cannot be grasped in the terms of the violence-ideology distinction:

> Subjection is not only obtained by the instruments of violence or ideology; it can also be direct, physical, pitting force against force, bearing on material elements, and yet without involving violence; it may be calculated, organized, technically thought out; it may be subtle, make use of neither weapons nor terror and yet remain of a physical order. [*Discipline and Punish*, 26]

Does this mean then that, as some critics have charged, humans are reduced to the level of brute beasts, not only without consciousness, but without even ideas or words or thought of any kind? Here Foucault's response (which is, as Pierre Macherey has argued in "Towards a Natural History of Norms," more Spinozist than Nietzschean)[31] is as well known as it is controversial: "There is no power relation without the correlative constitution of a field of knowledge, nor any knowledge that does not presuppose and constitute at the same time power rela-

---

31. Macherey, "Towards a Natural History of Norms," in *Michel Foucault, Philosopher*, trans. Timothy J. Armstrong (London: Routledge, 1992), 179.

tions" (27). Knowledge, which is decidedly not the same thing as "consciousness," cannot be said merely to arise, as an effect separate from its cause, from power relations (note the plural, which emphasizes the conflict and antagonism that characterize power as Foucault defines it), which would then form the foundation to which it might be reduced. Knowledges (Foucault's nominalism enjoins us to speak of them in the plural) are in no way exterior to power relations, caused by them only finally to transcend them; rather, they can only be understood as immanent in the materiality of practices and apparatuses. Readers have often asked if *Discipline and Punish* is a history of ideas or a history of institutions, thereby imposing upon it the idealist dilemmas (mind or body, words or things, ideas or reality) that the work refuses from the outset.[32] Foucault, to use Althusser's language (and in this way make it evident that, despite his refusal of the entire problematic of ideology with its paradoxes and impasses, Foucault cannot completely escape the difficulties Althusser faced in speaking of the material existence of ideology), has written a history of ideas that cannot be separated from the physical, material practices in which they are (always already) realized. This, rather than the functionalism and defeatism that are often ascribed to him, would appear to be what is truly scandalous about his work: his refusal to regard the history of psychiatry, medicine, or criminology apart from their practical and institutional forms, namely, the asylum, the hospital, and the prison, the forms of the ordering and distribution of bodies in space in which these knowledges participate, the position that they, in their material incarnations, occupy in a field of conflicting social forces. If to confront the most noble ideas of human freedom with their often sordid materiality is a provocation, then nothing was more provocative than Foucault's observa-

32. It is interesting to note that Deleuze insists on the presence of a dualism (of the visible and the articulable) in Foucault's *oeuvre*, although he later qualifies it as "a preliminary distribution operating at the heart of a pluralism" (*Foucault*, 83). Foucault is thus contrasted to Spinoza, whom Deleuze describes as a "monist," a traditional but highly dubious proposition. See Macherey, "Spinoza est-il moniste?" in *Spinoza: Puissance et Ontologie*, ed. Myriam Revault D'Allunes and Hadi Rizk (Paris: Kimé, 1994). It appears that because Deleuze tends, despite himself, to a dialectical reading of Foucault's work according to which each stage represents the interiorization/resolution of preceding stages, the realm of the articulable as stated in *The Archaeology of Knowledge* combines with its opposite, the realm of the visible, from *Discipline and Punish* and *The History of Sexuality*, to produce a higher unity. It might be argued instead that the (Spinozist) notion of the mutual immanence of knowledge and power developed in the later work marks a decisive break with the dualism of *The Archaeology of Knowledge* (the separation of practices into the discursive and the nondiscursive).

tions on the liberal dreams of Enlightenment thinkers. Thus, what has so offended contemporary readers is not that Foucault neglected the great themes of the seventeenth and eighteenth centuries, the ideas of freedom, right, and law, but rather, that he refused to regard them as disembodied ideals, existing in consciousnesses and representations. Instead he seeks to determine their "dark side," the technologies of power, the forms of struggle and subjection that accompanied and made possible the utterances that constitute these doctrines:

> Historically, the process by which the bourgeoisie became in the course of the eighteenth century the politically dominant class was masked by the establishment of an explicit, coded and formally egalitarian juridical framework, made possible by the organization of a parliamentary, representative regime. But the development and generalization of disciplinary mechanisms constituted the other, dark side of these processes. The general juridical form that guaranteed a system of rights that were egalitarian in principle was supported by these tiny, everyday, physical mechanisms, by all those systems of micro-power that are essentially non-egalitarian and asymmetrical that we call the disciplines. [*Discipline and Punish*, 222]

From this point of view, not only is it impossible any longer to speak of an opposition between ideological apparatuses, on the one hand, whose primary function would be to produce "ideologies" understood in the old sense of ideas and beliefs, and, on the other, the repressive apparatus (always in the singular for Althusser), which would employ force or the threat of force; it is equally impossible to speak of the knowledges linked to an apparatus as being in any way external to (or innocent of) its functioning, like beautiful lies that would conceal or deny the harsh realities of the disciplinary regime. Instead, Foucault shows that the knowledges that took shape in an apparatus such as the army in the seventeenth and eighteenth centuries, knowledges that would be diffused to other seemingly counterposed apparatuses (e.g., the school), had nothing to do with what is usually meant by ideology, the "values," as Althusser suggests, of nationalism and social order. Rather, what was historically important about the army (like the police and the entire penal system) were the ideas, often nothing more than theoretical fantasies or strategic objectives (subject to the contingencies of "the perpetual battle" [*Discipline and Punish*, 26] that characterizes the field of social forces) immanent in its multiform operations. The order that the army attempted to impose on its own ranks was, of course, not secured as much by the inculcation of values and beliefs as by the technologies of the body: the distributions according to which bodies were enclosed and simultaneously partitioned, the investments that sought, by working on bodies, by recomposing and reconfiguring them, to increase both their utility and docility and, finally, the forms of supervision, from perpetual and anonymous surveillance to the examination based on a normalizing judgment.

In fact, Althusser's central thesis (ideology interpellates individuals as subjects) only takes on its full meaning in relation to what we might call Foucault's reading of the materiality of ideology, a notion rewritten as the "physical order" of the disciplines. The phrase "ideology interpellates" is often read as a (tragic) drama of recognition that resembles the dialectic of consciousness and self-consciousness in Hegel's *Phenomenology of Spirit:* the subject exists in itself and for itself only insofar as it is recognized (or hailed). Thus, the interpellation of the subject would itself be a subjective process, unfolding entirely within the realm of consciousness or intersubjectivity, it would thus be ideological in the old sense, a false idea or representation counterposed to reality. While such a reading is all the more surprising given the fact that Althusser called the theme of recognition an "ideological" motif that could not be explained except by abandoning any philosophy of consciousness ("Ideology," 173), it was Foucault who argued that, if we can consider the individual as subject "the fictitious atom of an ideological representation of society," we must regard that fiction correlatively as "a reality fabricated by this specific technology of power that I have called discipline" (*Discipline and Punish,* 194). For Foucault, the individual does not preexist his or her interpellation as a subject but emerges as a result of strategies and practices of individualization.

Foucault allows us to see the regime of individualization (or at least the descending individualization that particularizes and identifies those on whom power is exercised) as a strategy, perhaps the strategy of the disciplinary regime faced with the reality of mass movements, the reality of collective action made possible by the new enclosures of the factory, the prison, and the school:

> It must also master all the forces that are formed from the very constitution of an organized multiplicity; it must neutralize the effects of counter-power that spring from them and which form a resistance to the power that wishes to dominate it: agitations, revolts, spontane-

ous organizations, coalitions—anything that may establish horizontal conjunctions. [221]

The same economic and political imperatives that led to the formation of masses, necessitated strategies that, at the level of knowledge, tended to reduction, segmentation, and serialization, in short, an entire "science of the individual" (191) and, at the level of physical forces, to separation, partitioning, and cellularity. Contrary to an entire tradition that can conceive of domination only as the denial of a natural individuality through forced collectivization, Foucault argues that:

> Instead of bending all its subjects into a single uniform mass, the disciplinary regime separates, analyses, differentiates, carries its procedures of decomposition to the point of necessary and sufficient single units. It "trains" the moving, confused, useless multitudes of bodies and forces into a multiplicity of individual elements—small, separate cells, organic autonomies, generic identities and continuities, comminatory segments. Discipline "makes" individuals; it is the specific technique of a power that regards individuals both as objects and as instruments of its exercise. [170]

The fantasy immanent in the practices of discipline is to abolish "the crowd, a compact mass, a locus of multiple exchanges, individualities merging together, a collective effect," and to replace it "by a collection of separated individualities" (201).

The individual thus abstracted from the mutual entanglements and dependencies, from the "coagulations" proper to social existence is then endowed with a soul, or, depending upon the domain of knowledge and the nature of its apparatuses, a "psyche, subjectivity, personality, [or] consciousness. . . . The man described for us, whom we are invited to free, is already in himself the effect of a subjection more profound than himself. A 'soul' inhabits him and brings him to existence, which is itself a factor in the mastery that power exercises over the body. The soul is the effect and instrument of a political anatomy; the soul is the prison of the body" (29–30).

The soul is the prison of the body: no statement so captures the despair that many readers have claimed to have found in both "Ideology and Ideological State Apparatuses" and *Discipline and Punish*. It is possible, however, to read these works otherwise. For, from the materialist positions that Althusser and Foucault occupy, there can be no total domination or total authority. Only rights and privileges can be transferred, alienated, or appropriated; power, which both Althusser and Foucault conceive in physical terms, "is exercised rather than possessed" (*Discipline and Punish*, 26) and cannot be given or taken away. Only in the juridical imagination can the power of the masses, which is real and material no matter how ineffectual or dispersed its exercise, be taken or given away. If we read Althusser and Foucault to the letter, the dilemma we face is not how to secure greater rights and guarantees of our independence and autonomy, how to prevent the dominant ideology from infiltrating the sanctuary of our interiority, or how to transcend that which dominates us in order to negate through thought the existing state of affairs and imagine its utopian contrary. Our dilemma is rather how to increase our power, how to diminish the forces that individuate and separate us and thus prevent us from uniting with others in order to act and to think more effectively and with greater strength for our liberation. What can liberation mean without transcendence? An old voice reminds us that the materialism of Althusser and Foucault is not quite without precedent: there are "no ideals to realize," only a future consisting of forces already active in the present[33] whose triumph or even persistence nothing guarantees. To identify these forces and to find a way to participate in their struggle: perhaps Althusser and Foucault, in their lives as well as their works, meant nothing more than this.

---

33. Marx, *The Civil War in France* (Peking: The Foreign Language Press, 1970), 73.

JACQUES LEZRA

Spontaneous Labor

For John X. LaPorta

Consider the project outlined in the opening pages of *Reading "Capital"* to "illuminate . . . from within [*Capital*], as the exact measurement of a disconcerting but inevitable absence, the absence of the concept . . . of the *effectivity of a structure on its elements* which is the visible/ invisible, absent/present keystone of [Marx's] whole work."[1] The possibility of illuminating, let alone measuring, agency or effectivity *from within* a text, however broadly defined, is very much in the balance today, as it was between 1963 and 1967, when the "anthropological" Hegelianism current in Europe after the War came into question most severely. The effects of that questioning remain manifest in and as the confrontation of the vocabularies of humanism, culturalism, and strategic essentialism (among others) in discussions of the futures of the Marxian legacy, discussions whose practical means may well prove to have been their most fruitful theoretical end: the constitution of their own incompleteness as a provisional object of knowledge, or as a concept. To put it differently: the work of "measurement" opened by Balibar, Althusser, and Macherey radically *unfinished*, in Balibar's provocative term, the possibility of reflecting upon Marxism as a system of concepts ("life," "class," "history," the "party," "mode of production," and so on), whether subsumed under the notion of practice or under that of theory. It also posed that act of reflection as an unavoidable ethical as well as a theoretical necessity—as a *rule*—in any thought on agency or effectivity.

What follows here is principally descriptive: what is the nature, and what are the determining conditions, of this double task of unfinishing and of posing reflection? The task turns first upon an understanding of

---

1. Louis Althusser and Etienne Balibar, *Reading "Capital,"* trans. Ben Brewster (London: New Left Books, 1970), 29.

YFS 88, *Depositions,* ed. Lezra, © 1995 by Yale University.

the philosophical *concept* at odds with the project of epistemological, functionalist Marxism that Hirst, Hindess, and others outlined and powerfully criticized as early as *Marx's "Capital" and Capitalism Today*. In its roughest form, this is hardly news: the "history" of philosophy, the "history" of the production and constitution of the concept of philosophy, is the "history" of the battles waged over the concept itself (the German *Begriff* differing in important ways from *conceptus* and its declensions). The term holds in postwar philosophical debate the contested place that came to be occupied in the social sciences by the words *structure* and *function;* indeed, the crises of each discipline can be charted in the changing destinies and unhappy marriages of the three terms. I take the contradiction, if it can still be called that, between a functionalist theory of ideology attributed to Althusser (manifest, for instance, in the notoriously misunderstood constitution of the subject as *Träger*, position-marker or carrier of ideological "sense") and an aesthetics of the concept to signal the care with which the possibilities of agency and effectivity begin to be drawn, in these first strong challenges in France to the hegemony of the language of subjective consciousness, *against* and *within* the vocabulary of the concept.[2] For much of what is most disturbing—or "traumatic," to use Slavoj Žižek's word—about the project of *Reading "Capital"* lies in the measurement or the enactment of a profound hesitation in the traditional determination—in the history—of the concept itself.

"A *conceptus*," writes Kant of *Begriff* in the Vienna Logic, "is a *raepresentatio communis*, which is common to many things"—an entirely conventional description of abstraction from the manifold that leaves undecided on what grounds *conceptus* is to be distinguished from "thing," and whether *raepresentatio* is to be taken in one or the other of the classical senses most often associated with it: as mere representation or appearance [*Erscheinung*], or as the appearing of the common essential in the manifold.[3] The discussion in the *First Critique* of the *transcendental* grounds upon which abstraction or synthesis must rest sharply qualifies the unproblematic use and elision of *raepresentatio* and of "things," and ultimately of *anthropos*

---

2. Gregory Elliott's comments on the "deleterious consequences" of Althusser's concept of "structural causality" are especially at issue. See his important *Althusser: The Detour of Theory* (London: Verso, 1987), 179 and *passim*.
3. Immanuel Kant, "The Vienna Logic," in *Lectures on Logic*, trans. J. Michael Young (Cambridge, England: Cambridge University Press, 1992), 348.

and *logos*, characteristic of a certain Enlightenment. The statement in the opening of the "Transcendental Analytic" is well known:

> No knowledge is possible without a concept . . . and a concept is always, with regard to its form, something general, something that can serve as a rule [*Regel*]. Thus the concept of body [*vom Körper*] serves as a rule to our knowledge of external phenomena, according to the unity of the manifold which is thought by it. It can only be such a rule of intuitions because representing, in any given phenomena, the necessary reproduction of their manifold elements, or the synthetical unity in our consciousness of them [daß er bei gegebenen Erscheinungen die notwendige Reproduktion des Mannigfaltigen derselben, mithin die synthetische Einheit in ihrem Bewußtsein, vorstellt].[4]

The movement from the notion of the *communis* to the concept's use here *as a rule* signals the transition from an ontology to an ethics, the language of necessity [*die notwendige Reproduktion*] serving as a straddle between formal or transcendental knowledge and its practical outcome for bodies, or, in other words, as a bridge from the first to the second critiques. The status of the *rule*—which the First Critique describes elsewhere, powerfully, as a riddle [*Rätsel*]—in these lines is equally important for, like the "necessity" with which it is coupled, it is neither empirical nor transcendental. Rather—and Kant's formulation is very precise—the concept is *necessarily* always, as to its form, what *can serve* as a rule [*zur Regel dient*] uniting concrete contents, a servant or handmaiden [*Diener*] that makes the rules. This hesitation helps to explain why the concept, both a self-evidently shared representation and a rule, is perennially at issue in left-Hegelian thought: in the lesser *Logic* as well as in the *Philosophy of Right*, Hegel explicitly draws the connection between this ambiguous "service" performed by the form of the concept, and the "service" or slavery by means of which knowledge of "external phenomena," in Kant's terms, becomes a genuine phenomenology of spirit:

---

4. In the *Critique of Pure Reason*, trans. F. Max Müller (New York: Anchor, 1966), 104 (A106). The German original is from the Suhrkamp edition of *Kritik der reinen Vernunft*, vol. 1 (Frankfurt a.m.: Suhrkamp, 1982), 167. This deduction has provided, at least since its treatment in Hegel, the classical articulation of the relation between "external phenomena," "concepts," and their "synthetical unity in consciousness"—or, as the *Science of Logic* puts it: "It is one of the profoundest and truest insights to be found in the *Critique of Pure Reason* that the *unity* which constitutes the nature of the Concept is recognized as the *original synthetic* unity of *apperception*, as unity of the *I think*, or of self-consciousness." In *Hegel's Science of Logic*, trans. A. V. Miller (London: Unwin, 1969), 584.

If the logical forms of the concept were really dead and inert receptacles [*tote, unwirksame und gleichgültige Behälter*] of conceptions and thoughts, knowledge about them would be an idle curiosity which the truth might dispense with. On the contrary they really are, as forms of the concept, the vital spirit [*lebendige Geist*] of the actual world. That only is true of the actual which is true in virtue of these forms, through them and in them.[5]

The characteristic inversion of "life" and "death" in these lines cannot quite mask the difficulty Hegel takes from Kant: if it is neither empirical nor transcendental, if it is a *raepresentatio* as both mere appearance [*Schein*] and as translucence of the essential, if it is a *rule* that *serves*, how can the opening *formality* of the concept be known as such, and how can this knowledge then affect "life" or the "actual"?

This problematic circularity, which turns upon an elision of "object" and "concept" remarked powerfully by Heidegger, still marks and defines the form as well as the "actual world" of the genealogy of the concept.[6] The passage in the First Critique's brief definition from an extensive sense of body as *res* or *extensio* ("Thus the concept of the body [*Körper*] . . . ") to the restricted, anthropomorphic sense as *corpus* marks one such elision, and the programmatic line from *Reading "Capital"* with which I opened, which proposes to "illuminate . . . from within [*Capital*], as the exact measurement of a disconcerting but

---

5. *Hegel's "Logic*," trans. William Wallace (Oxford: Oxford University Press, 1975), 226. I have modified the translation to reflect the generally accepted terms for the Hegelian originals (from *notion* to *concept*, for instance, and from *constituent functions* to *moments*). The ontologization of logical form in Hegel is a persistent and indeed characteristic maneuver, as the introductory discussion of *Begriff* in the *Science of Logic* makes clear. See also the remark to paragraph 160 of the lesser *Logic*, which also treats the "inferior view" that "generally reckons the concept a mere form of thought" (223ff).

6. The conflation of "object" and "concept" has its own problematic in the *Phenomenology*, as Heidegger shows: see, in his "Hegels Begriff der Erfahrung," the comments on paragraph 12 of the "Introduction" to the *Phenomenology*, which makes clear that for Hegel, object and concept are moments in a dialectical movement, and thus fundamentally nonidentical. Heidegger's role in setting the terms for the critique of this "progressive" notion of the development of the concept in Hegel is notoriously overdetermined: it is no accident that the project of *Being and Time* founders at the point where the discussion of *Begriff* in the *Enzyklopädie* begins. Hirst and Hindess comment that epistemological Marxism "depends on the conception of objects existing independently of knowledge yet in forms appropriate to knowledge itself," and derive from a critique of this epistemology the understanding that "there are no basic concepts" in Marxism or in any other theoretical discourse. In Anthony Cutler, Barry Hindess, Paul Hirst, and Athar Hussain, *Marx's "Capital" and Capitalism Today* (London: Routledge and Kegan Paul, 1977), 217–18.

inevitable absence, the absence of the concept . . . of the *effectivity of a structure on its elements* which is the visible/invisible, absent/present keystone of [Marx's] whole work," marks another. For just as the *production* of the concept has to be distinguished starkly from the *abstraction* of the concept, a dialectical procedure whose roots in idealism Marx quite correctly signaled, the project of "illuminating an absence" has to be distinguished from the project of Husserlian phenomenology, for which "absence" is precisely that which cannot be "illuminated" as such, but only as the determinate absence of something else, of the object of knowledge not-yet-there. The formal difficulty is classical: if judgments about objects or particulars produce (that is, reveal) the concept of the "manifold elements" *in* the object, they also produce (that is, generate or fashion) the concept *as an object*. What will always be excluded from judgment will be the concept of this double proposition, for the "manifold elements" of the concept of "production" cannot themselves be subordinated a priori to the "synthetical unity of our consciousness." If the concept is *produced* (or its absence illuminated), there can be no a priori concept of the production of the concept: and this "absence," which fundamentally unfinishes the *formal* project of reading *Capital* and of *Reading "Capital,"* cannot be "illuminated" in the same sense as one speaks of "illuminating" the absence of a concept of effectivity.

Part of what constitutes the double task of unfinishing and posing reflection is the proposition that the formality of the concept is not materially embodied, not allegorized or figured after its formality is known, but that in some way that formality itself has a material, anthropomorphic status—the sort of project Althusser could well have inherited from Merleau-Ponty, for instance.[7] This anthropomorphism, however, is something other than a common ground or *raepresentatio communis*. The relation between *anthropos* and *morphe* is not the source of a rule of generality, but the spot where any synthetical unity, and hence any subjective sense of agency or effectivity are subordinated to what I can, hastily, call the occurring of a material allegory, or an allegory about the occurring or appearance of matter. This difficulty is soon shown to structure the field of political agency as well, either in

---

7. The interplay of the languages of visibility and reading suggests a close reading of Merleau-Ponty's *Le Visible et l'invisible* (ed. Claude Lefort [Paris: Gallimard, 1964]), published posthumously and based on a series of courses, dating to the mid 1950s, that Althusser knew well. English translation: *The Visible and the Invisible,* trans. Alphonso Lingis (Evanston: Northwestern University Press, 1968).

the shape of a profound crisis of legitimation (the determining representations of an ideology are not only shown to be groundless, but the very form in which such representations *become* determining is shown to lack practical value); or as the necessity of an apocalyptic definition of the "last instance" of determination, a theological horizon posited for the advent of a concept which remains forever not-yet-there. That no conventional, or rather, no *democratic* form of political organization can be derived from either alternative may help to explain Althusser's well-known turn toward the philosophical task of "posing" or positioning theses. This is no help, however, in the second aspect of the question: whether bodies as a result are "objects" or "concepts."

Let me, as I try to tease out Althusser's place in recent attempts to address these questions, return again to a brief review of the terms in which the debate over the concept was posed, the hesitation over the notion of rule was received, and the effort to separate its "regard to form" from the "concept of the body" it concerns was treated. The very familiarity of the terms, of course, is deceptive, since the disguised persistence of "effectivity," or of "metonymic or structural causality," or of the term "concept" itself in contemporary critical discourse cannot be detached from the various narrative forms (of origin, of revolution, of return, of confession) that inflect that persistence. Nevertheless—and setting aside, for the moment, what consequences this inflection might have for our "life," as well as for the work of *Reading "Capital"*—we recall, in a first *formal* approach, that the target of Althusser's first exploration of the relation between epistemology and materialism is not Kant but the "philosophy of the concept" associated most commonly with the Young Hegelians, and against which Marx begins to develop what he hopes will be a genuinely materialist dialectic. Of Hegel's various definitions of the concept, the apodictic passage in the lesser *Logic* is the most notorious, and perhaps the most fruitful, since the assertion that "the Concept is the principle of freedom, the power of substance self-realized" functions both as a definition and as a way of anticipating the ethico-political elaboration of the logic of essence to be found in the *Philosophy of Right*.[8] The attributes of this "principle of freedom" include, among others, its distinction from both the mere representation and from the Idea of a thing, its

---

8. I understand Hegel and Marx's trajectory here quite differently from Lucio Colletti, *Marxism and Hegel*, trans. Lawrence Garner (London: NLB, 1973).

"onward movement" or development from substance to the truth of substance. Still, it is the aspect of self-realization [*die für sie seiende substantielle Macht*] proper to the concept that proved most influential, and most troubling. The being-for-itself of the concept, which the *Logic* describes as "an independence which, though self-repulsive into distinct independent elements, yet in that repulsion is self-identical, and in the movement of reciprocity still at home and conversant only with itself," sketches by means of this "movement" the complex dialectical oscillation between attribution and essence, between *concretum* and *generalia* that is the condition of possibility of judgment and of individuality. This "movement," Hegel argues, constitutes a form of totality "in which each of its moments is the very total which the concept is."[9] The "moment" of individuality, which is embodied in the form of the judgment [*Urteil*] linking subject and predicate, depends upon this relation of mediated identity to the concept of which it is a "moment."

One can see the attraction of the doctrine of the concept for the younger Marx. Because the "individual" judgment in its authentic form bears a relation of mediated identity to the concept (of class, for instance, or party, or historical moment), it becomes possible to describe concrete situations (again, both historical and philosophical) as having a greater or lesser degree of identity with the determinants of that situation. Consciousness in this (primarily Lukàcsian) reading becomes, as in Hegel, both what registers the difference between the concrete situation and the concept, and the resultant of the identity between the two. The unease of this formulation reflects the very impasse upon which Marx will break with the Idealist tradition, and which the well-known lines from Althusser's "On the Materialist Dialectic" express as a critique of Hegel's understanding of the status of the concrete:

> It was absolutely necessary to come this far if we were to recognise that even within the process of knowledge, the "abstract" generality with which the process starts and the "concrete" generality it finishes with, Generality I and Generality III, respectively, are not in essence the same generality, and, in consequence, the "appearance" of the Hegelian concept of the autogenesis of the concept, of the "dialectical" movement whereby the abstract universal produces itself as concrete, depends on a

---

9. *Hegel's "Logic,"* 223 ff. For the original, see G.W.F. Hegel, *Enzyklopädie der philosophischen Wissenschaften im Grundrisse* (1830), ed. F. Nicolin and O. Pöggeler (Hamburg: Felix Meiner Verlag, 1959), 151ff.

confusion of the kinds of "abstraction" or "generality" in action in theoretical practice.[10]

The replacement of self-realization with a fundamental discontinuity [*coupure*] in the arena of "theoretical practice" provides in Althusser's essay an alternative to the logic of definition—of being-in-essence—and also introduces the notion of theoretical practice whose *political* consequences he would deplore almost immediately. At its most powerful, "On the Materialist Dialectic" recognizes between the "moment" and the concept a fundamental discontinuity that threatens the logic of essence: the "real transformation" that takes place between the "abstract generality" and the "concrete generality" requires and produces a *material* transformation in the object and subject of knowledge. But this *coupure* also deepens an apparent hesitation, at issue as early as the *Phenomenology of Spirit*, concerning what Althusser's lines translate as the "autogenesis" of the concept: the concept is at once presented as self-realization (at the level of ontology) and, at the level of history, as itself product, product in particular of the labor [*Arbeit*] and the fear [*Furcht*] of the Slave.[11] By dividing the autogenesis of the concept (its *für sie seiende*) from its moments, Althusser reintroduces not only the category of *matter* into the dialectical, organic "movement" of the concept, but also a form and a condition of *labor* (and of *fear*, let us not forget) that remain *permanently* alien from themselves.

And yet at the same time as they begin to develop this fundamental indeterminacy within the epistemology of the concept, "On the Materialist Dialectic" and, later, Reading "Capital" provide an analogy intended, apparently, to cover and explain the coexistence of a "real transformation" with an epistemological continuity between objects

10. Althusser, *For Marx*, trans. Ben Brewster (London: Verso, 1969), 187–8. For the original, see *Pour Marx* (Paris: Maspero, 1965), 191.

11. Kojève's importance in the understanding of the Hegelian Concept in postwar philosophical thought cannot be stressed enough. His explication of the Master-Slave relation in particular, in *Introduction à la lecture de Hegel* (Paris: Gallimard, 1947; edited in English as Alexandre Kojève, *Introduction to the Reading of Hegel*, assembled by Raymond Queneau, ed. Allan Bloom, trans. James H. Nichols, Jr. [New York: Basic Books, 1969]), was determining for the generation of scholars that included Althusser. On the Concept, see, among other pages, 130–49 of the English translation and, on the part played by *work* in the appearing of the Concept, especially 230ff: "Work, therefore, is the authentic 'appearance' of Negativity or Freedom, for Work is what makes Man a dialectical being, which does not eternally remain the same, but unceasingly becomes other than it really is in the given and as given."

and objects of knowledge. Persistently offered and as persistently disavowed in much argumentation indebted to the cryptic description of *commodity fetishism* in *Capital*, this analogy understands the production of the object of knowledge from the "real" or concrete object to be *like* the ghostly extraction of the commodity-form from the material. In Althusser, famously, this process of "constituting" returns to the Hegelian vocabulary of "determination," adding only a qualifying "in the last instance," which has served, if anything, to exacerbate the sense that the terms mask a strong contradiction. For it is far from clear how a "genuine transformation," a "difference in essence" distinguishing generalities can yield nevertheless to the mediation of the practice of *theory*—an objection that can be made in resolutely Kantian language: the "object" as such is no more accessible to "knowledge" *after* (both logically and temporally) it has "become" an object of knowledge than "knowledge" as such is accessible in the world of objects. Theoretical practice is then required to retain for knowledge the ghostly form of the object as such alongside, or within, the object of knowledge that it has become—although this ghostly form cannot itself be in the same sense an object for knowledge. As "On the Materialist Dialectic" imagines it, theoretical practice is not only fundamentally discontinuous, but also and to the same extent the source of metaphoric vocabularies that function therapeutically or ideologically to mask those very discontinuities.[12]

Around this promise—whose closeness to delusional pathologies affecting individuals no less than political organizations should be noted—turn the strongest recent treatments of the critique of the concept, whether explicitly indebted to Althusser, Macherey, and Balibar or not.[13] In part, the trend toward new versions of psycho-Marxism represents a critical rehabilitation of arguments made by Michel Pêcheux in France, and by the *Screen* group in Britain, in the early

---

12. Marx's description of the "fantastic form" assumed by social relations embodied in commodities pertains here, especially the necessary recourse to "the mist-enveloped regions of the religious world" for a vocabulary on which to base an understanding of the "Fetishism which attaches itself to the products of labour." In *Capital*, vol. 1, trans. Samuel Moore and Edward Aveling (New York: International Publishers, 1967), 77.

13. Much of Macherey's recent work has indeed focused on this question, as does Balibar's examination of the relation between "mass," "class," and "idea." It is upon the problem of the status of the concept in Hegel's language that the Slovenian school has staked its sense that linguistically oriented forms of argumentation are effectively repressing the "traumatic kernel" in the dialectic of essence.

1970s, that pose theoretical thought at the crossing of the question of the unconscious and the possibility of democracy. Beginning in the mid-1980s, the group of scholars and activists surrounding Ernesto Laclau and Chantal Mouffe, but including also Slavoj Žižek, Mladen Dolar, and others, takes for its point of departure in analyzing the field of social relations a critique of an indexical system of psychoanalytic "reading" indebted strongly to the notion of "lecture symptomale" posed in *Reading "Capital."*[14] The disillusionment of Althusser's early proponents (Hindess and Hirst, among others), the argument reads, derives in part either from a misreading or from an effective repression of a "traumatic kernel" in Althusser's work. Whether for one or the other reason, the flight from Althusser's effort to reconstruct the *"effectivity of a structure on its elements"* understood that project finally to privilege either the "structure" (leading to a valorization of a functionalist theory of ideology, and politically to the form of closure associated with Stalinism) or the "elements" (leading to a theoretical humanism in line with Eurocommunism) rather than their relation: the problem of the concept of *effectivity*.[15] The difficulties that attach to determining the place and function of the term "determination" in

14. It is not accidental, though the filiation to Lacan is distorting, that we hear in Dolar and Žižek an echo of Macherey's *Theory of Literary Production:* "A true reading . . . ignores none of this multiplicitiy. Above all it involves—beyond an enumeration of constitutive elements—seeing, rather than linkage, harmony or unity, which are deformations and idealisations, the *reason* of its process. It is not, once again, a question of perceiving a latent structure of which the manifest work is an index, but of constituting the absence around which a real complexitiy knits itself." The argument here is stark: reading understood as "seeing"—*voir*—takes in the first instance the shape of seeing a "reason" rather than a structure or a unity; in the second it becomes divided between mere perception—*percevoir*—and an act of production or constitution. At the same time, the temporal scheme is given with great compression: it is in practice impossible to distinguish whether the complexity of the real "knots itself" [*se noue*] around an "absence" that already knots itself; or whether the constituting of this absence provokes, like the retrospective clustering of symptoms around a trauma, this knitting/knotting. Macherey's language thus suggests the extent to which a vulgarized psychoanalytic model is being rejected. The "manifest" work's connection to its "latent" absence is understood to involve not the semiology of an index [*indice*], whose stability rests upon being a phenomenal representation as well as a material part of what it signifies, but on a process or a procedure: the transposition of the model of "production" or "constitution" of an absence upon the process of analytic recollection of psychic "work" is in question. In Macherey, *A Theory of Literary Production,* trans. Geoffrey Wall (London: Routledge, 1978; 1989), 100–01. I have corrected Wall's translation, which inverts the sense of the paragraph. See Macherey, *Pour une théorie de la production littéraire* (Paris: Maspero, 1966; 1970), 122.

15. The false separation between ideological and aesthetic *effect* is only one aspect of this broader problem.

Althusser's work have themselves in some instances provoked the beginnings of a more developed theoretical inquiry into the nature of "contradiction" in the texts of the middle 1960s.

Theoretical practice, even in this schematic understanding, promises a relation to fiction or fantasy not easily squared with its function in the materialist dialectic.[16] For it is precisely in its connection to *fantasy* that the term "determination" ceases to provide the determinable sense of ideological closure that these critical fictions or critical lives most urgently require. Beginning with *Hegemony and Socialist Strategy*, for example, Laclau and Mouffe narrate compactly the trajectory of Althusser's thought on social relations as a descent or retreat from the possibilities opened by the concept of *overdetermination*. The story is immediately recognizable, and it is especially important for Laclau and Mouffe because it functions as a synecdoche for Marxist thought more generally (with the exception of Gramsci, but including their own work prior to *Hegemony and Socialist Strategy*): as a result of its analytic rigor, Althusser's thought is able to posit the indeterminacy of the category of totality, and of the category itself; but it must retreat from that position for reasons that are not only pragmatic, but also theoretical. Much of the engagement and retreat that Laclau and Mouffe outline suggests the sort of strong but ambivalent reading of Hegel that Colletti had already suggested. I want to linger for a moment, however, on the most economical of their formulations of this scheme:

> [T]he most profound *potential* meaning of Althusser's statement that everything existing in the social is overdetermined, is the assertion that the social constitutes itself as a symbolic order. The symbolic—i.e., overdetermined—character of social relations therefore implies that

---

16. Indeed, for both Althusser and Lacan, as David Macey has recently argued, the notion of the "concept" was tied to a particular moment in the intellectual history of the postwar—and especially to the work of Canguilhem. Macey's argument that Althusser elects to withdraw from the increasingly conceptualized language of the *Cahiers pour l'analyse* group toward the realm of "fantasy" is of interest here, in great part since it suggests a movement contrary to the one Laclau and Mouffe propose: toward a region that is not determinable "in the last instance," but whose temporality remains indeterminate. See David Macey, "Thinking with Borrowed Concepts: Althusser and Lacan," in *Althusser: A Critical Reader*, ed. Gregory Elliott (Oxford: Basil Blackwell, 1994), 142–58, especially 151ff. Rastko Mocnik argues ("Ideology and Fantasy," in *The Althusserian Legacy*, ed. E. Ann Kaplan and Michael Sprinker [London: Verso, 1993], 139–56), in line with Žižek and others, for understanding Althusserian ideology as "'working upon' fantasy. . . . Being a quilting-point, fantasy punctually connects the ideological façade with its specific exterior: so-called social reality" (151–52).

they lack an ultimate literality which would reduce them to necessary moments of an immanent law. . . . This analysis seemed to open up the possibility of elaborating a new concept of articulation, which would start from the overdetermined character of social relations. But this did not occur. The concept of overdetermination tended to disappear from Althusserian discourse, and a growing closure led to the installation of a new variant of essentialism. This process . . . was to culminate in *Reading Capital*.[17]

So, in any case, the story goes.[18] Two things about this description are immediately striking. The stress on *overdetermination* as the defining characteristic of the symbolic does some violence to the elaboration in Althusser of the concept of *underdetermination*, especially as it is described in the "Soutenance d'Amiens." In the second place, the assimilation of the field of the symbolic to the "lack of an ultimate literality" is posed as enabling the undoing of "reduction" to an "immanent law." These tactics significantly, and characteristically, assimilate the concept of "literality" to that of "essence" by means of the term *determination*, which is understood to condense a set of parallel determinations: the semantic determination of the figurative by the literal; of the representation by the concept and ultimately by the referent; of "articulation" (Laclau and Mouffe) by precisely the sort of "articulating subject" that seems banished from Althusser. And yet, as surely as the "literality" of a symbol is not *the same* as its "essence," the horizon of the "ultimate" *lack* of literality of the symbolic does not in itself guarantee that a different order of literality cannot "install" other variants of essentialism (including an essentialism of the figure, for instance). If social relations "lack an ultimate literality," this is to say that the process by which they can be said to stand for something—

17. Ernesto Laclau and Chantal Mouffe, *Hegemony and Socialist Strategy* (London: Verso, 1985), 98.

18. As told in only slightly different terms by Žižek, it is a powerful, convincing story: "In *Hegel ou Spinoza?* Macherey maintains that Spinoza's philosophy must be read as a critique of Hegel—as if Spinoza read Hegel and was able to answer the latter's critique of 'Spinozism'. The same could be said of Hegel in relation to Althusser: Hegel outlines in advance the contours of the Althusserian critique of (what Althusser presents as) 'Hegelianism'. Moreover, Hegel develops the element that is missing in Althusser (the one that had prevented him from thinking through the notion of overdetermination); that is, the element of subjectivity that cannot be reduced to imaginary (mis)recognition qua effect of interpellation—that is to say, the subject as $; the 'empty', barred subject." In his "Identity and Its Vicissitudes: Hegel's 'Logic of Essence' as a Theory of Ideology," in Ernesto Laclau, ed., *The Making of Political Identities* (London: Verso, 1994), 53.

other social relations, relations of power, the effectivity of a structure, etc.—will always be interminable. Thus the project of "elaborating a new concept of articulation" will also always be interminable— unless, that is, the "elaboration" of the new concept occurs independently of (that is, cannot be *determined* on the basis of) the semiotic aspect of social relations. Laclau and Mouffe continue:

> If the concept of overdetermination was unable to produce the totality of its deconstructive effects within Marxist discourse, this was because, from the very beginning, an attempt was made to render it compatible with another central moment in Althusserian discourse that is, strictly speaking, incompatible with the first: namely, determination in the last instance by the economy. [*Hegemony and Socialist Strategy*, 98]

It is here, where the unexpected recourse to the language of totality most clearly suggests a degree of uncertainty, that the originality of Laclau and Mouffe's project becomes evident, and that their distance from Hindess and Hirst is most strongly marked. Associated throughout *Hegemony and Socialist Strategy* with a conceptual Hegelianism that the work regularly links to an occlusive sense of "determination," "totality" is reintroduced as a desirable possibility—the "totality of deconstructive effects." To produce this "totality" of effects requires, presumably, that no effort be made to make the overdetermination of the symbolic "compatible" with the order of determination *in the last instance*, and that the interminability of "elaboration" be understood not as what Idealist philosophy calls a "bad infinity," susceptible to no understanding and to no totalization, but a "good" one: the simplest form of subsumption of "difference" or contradiction into identity, the "simple infinity" also called the "absolute Concept" in the *Phenomenology*.[19] The difficulties that such an effort poses are perhaps too evident: if "the last instance" can be understood to be the horizon of any act of judgment, then assigning it a concrete condition of possibility (determination by the economic) seems to require us to subordi-

---

19. See especially Miller's translation of paragraph 162 of the *Phenomenology*: "This simple infinity, or the absolute Concept, may be called the simple essence of life, the soul of the world. . . . It is self-*identical*, for the differences are tautological; they are differences that are none. This self-identical essence is therefore related only to itself; 'to itself' implies relationship to an 'other', and the *relation-to-self* is rather a *self-sundering*; or, in other words, that very self-identicalness is an inner difference." In G.W.F. Hegel, *Hegel's Phenomenology of Spirit*, trans. A. V. Miller (Oxford: Oxford University Press, 1977), 100.

nate to those conditions what we experience and understand as the present constellation of social relations. The "overdetermination" of these relations is secondary, from the point of view of judgment, to their predetermination. And yet, from the point of view of experience (that is, from the point of view of the phenomenology of the subject), the predetermination of social relations remains (permanently) a matter of hypothesis, their "secondariness" itself "secondary" to an experience of "actually existing" social relations. It is ideology, then, that steps into this sharp disjoining of the conditions of possibility of judgment and of experience, making them "compatible" both *in principle* and *in the last instance.*

"Incompatibility" differs in this way from the more productive sense of a rupture or a contingent judgment that Laclau and Mouffe outline, but any reliance upon the notion will reintroduce categories perhaps best abandoned. "Incompatibility," which becomes merely a first moment in the inevitable production and reproduction of ideology, bears for this reason a most uncomfortable similarity to the organicist determinism of a work like Lukács's *History and Class Consciousness.* For if *Hegemony and Socialist Strategy* is to "elaborate a new concept of articulation" without making that process of "elaboration" into a form of determination or of ideology, it must retain the disruptive force of "incompatibility" without subordinating it to the organicism of a theory of production or reproduction, or to an interminableness that relies finally upon a "good infinity" linked indissociably to the doctrine of "bad" totalities that Laclau and Mouffe seek to avoid. It must retain "incompatibility," then, without dissevering judgment from experience—that is, without abandoning the possibility of the production of the *concept.* Into this knot, and in the place occupied in Althusserian epistemology by the notion of ideology, Laclau and Mouffe introduce the psychoanalytic process of *capitonnage,* quilting or suturing, which Jacques-Alain Miller elaborates, in "Suture (Elements of the Logic of the Signifier)," from the work of Lacan. Statements about suture necessarily bear marks of syntactical strain, since the "elaboration" of its concept takes place only in and as the paradoxical combination of future and perfected past. "Suture," it seems, is not a form of "determination"; it is not "an attempt [by a subject] to make compatible," but a node of fantasy that produces the subject position; and it is not (yet) an "object of knowledge"—that is, a concept. It has, instead, to be understood as the improperly conceived ground upon which a miscognized [*méconnu*] subject is acted and can act, can "affirm" within a contingent, rather than a determined, horizon. For this reason, the marks of "suture" do not make a determined "totality" of the overdetermined field of symbolic social relations. Fantasies or symptoms elaborated at the level of the cultural or social signifier, rather than at the level of an "ultimate literality" that "would reduce them to necessary moments of an immanent law," these points mark the unforeseeable locations at which different, often competing, discourses devoted to describing the field of social relations (the languages of feminism, of cultural materialism, of aesthetics, of epistemology) will suddenly show themselves to have become articulated.[20]

The fullest development of Miller's discussion of suture has until recently been in the arena of psychoanalytic vocabulary.[21] From the point of view of an "unfinishing" of reflection, or of the possibility of elaborating a radically democratic politics or philosophical practice, the concept of suture and its utopian companion, the horizon of an "unsutured" social field, seem equally promising.[22] Always bordering

20. Gramsci is the crucial figure in this, especially at moments when he follows Engels in dismissing the mechanistic sense of historical determination characteristic of "pocket geniuses" who reduce the "infinite variety and multiplicity of history" to economic schemes. Gramscian "philology," the "methodological expression of the importance of ascertaining and precising particular facts in their unique and unrepeatable individuality," operates side by side with "more general 'laws of tendency'" *for practical, not theoretical reasons.* This stress on the *practical* "co-participation" of these schemes radically distinguishes Gramsci's work from the sort of "reduction . . . to necessary moments of an immanent law" that Laclau and Mouffe correctly address. See Antonio Gramsci, "Problems of Marxism," in *Selections from the Prison Notebooks,* ed. and trans. Quintin Hoare and Geoffrey Nowell Smith (New York: International Publishers, 1971), 428–29.

21. Compare, however, Macherey's discussion of the effort to read Hegel in Freud, "Le leurre hégélien," *Le Bloc Note de la Psychanalyse* 5 (1985): 27–50.

22. Laclau and Lilian Zac have more recently clarified the political stakes of the use of suture: "There are signifiers occupying this point of suture in a particular political field. Let us take the case of the policy of disappearance put into effect by many Latin American dictatorships. The signifier '*desaparecidos*' occupies a central place in the political field, where various discursive threads are knotted. On the one hand, the authorities tend to deny the existence of any *desaparecidos*; all government arrests have been executed according to the legal framework. Thus, the *desaparecidos* as a category are excluded from the world of objects. On the other hand, the authorities recognize their existence but deny responsibility for their disappearance. . . . As a result of these two operations, these *desaparecidos* inhabit a space where they are neither dead nor alive; they can reappear, they can also be killed. Their death and their life is suspended, deferred. And by means of this operation fear is installed into that context: the *desaparecidos* point to the existence of another space, a space of suspension, which is both part of, and excluded from, the realm of 'society,' and, in this way, it becomes necessary to define its limits." "Minding the Gap: The Subject of Politics," in Laclau, ed., *The Making of Political Identities,* 33–34.

positions whose concept remains to come [à-venir], understood always in the horizon of apocalyptic rhetoric, suture as a thought *about the possibility of totality* rests upon an elision that is clear in its initial formulation. Miller, opening his influential essay, links his discussion of Frege to the relation between "objects," "concepts," and the process of "determination." In fact, Kant's discussion of the concept is very much at issue as well:

> An object only has existence in so far as it falls under a concept, there being no other determination involved in its logical existence, so that the object takes its meaning from its difference to the thing integrated, by its spatio-temporal localisation, to the real. Whence you can see the disappearance of the thing which must be effected in order for it to appear as object—which is *the thing in so far as it is one*. It is clear that the concept that operates in the system, formed solely through the determination of subsumption, is a redoubled concept: *the concept of identity to a concept.*[23]

Miller goes on to identify this redoubled concept with the zero in Frege's numerical system—the place of a lack, and a lack that is the quilting point at which the subject, or what can be called subject-effects, can appear. The distance from Hegel seems unbreachable: the disappearing of the thing [chose], insofar as it is one, is not the disappearance of the immediate object-for-itself, to be subsumed in a mediate object-for-consciousness; much less does the ex-centricity of the thing with respect to the object become in its turn determinable, thinkable, for a subject.[24] And yet the "determination of subsumption" that Miller describes retains an unmistakable filiation to Hegel's apparent solution to the problem posed by the unknowable formality of the concept. The phenomenological "integration" of the thing to

23. Jacques-Alain Miller, "Notes on Suture," 27. See Laclau and Mouffe's remarks on Miller, by way of Stephen Heath's commentary: "As Stephen Heath points out, 'suture names not just a structure of lack but also an availability of the subject, a certain closure. . . . The stake is clear: the 'I' is a division but joins all the same, the stand-in is the lack in the structure, but nevertheless simultaneously, the possibility of a coherence, of the *filling* in.' It is this double movement that we will attempt to stress in our extension of the concept of suture to the field of politics" (*Hegemony and Socialist Strategy,* 88). The derivation from Frege to some extent obscures the transcendental line: see for instance the discussion of the transcendental apperception [*transzendentale Apperzeption*] in the *First Critique* (A 106–07).

24. The nature of this ex-centricity is of course the subject of Lacan's question: "Is the place that I occupy as the subject of a signifier concentric or excentric, in relation to the place I occupy as subject of the signified?" In his "The Agency of the Letter in the Unconscious," in *Ecrits,* trans. Alan Sheridan (New York: Norton, 1977), 165.

the real erases it *as thing* and produces it *as integer*, but only insofar as this "disappearing" itself is both retained (as producing "meaning": the "meaning" that the object "takes" from its difference to the thing) and erased (the "identity to the concept" of the object requires that the "thing" that the object replaces appear nowhere as an unsubsumed aspect or representation of the object). The complexities and the success of Miller's position derive, again as in the Vienna Logic's definition of the concept, from the ease with which the nature of the "object" shifts—the concrete object that "falls under a concept" is of a different order from the "object" "identity to a concept." This second is only first a "thing" by virtue of the effacement of the difference between "thing" and "object" in its case. For Miller's analysis to proceed, "identity to a concept" has to be both "thing" and "object," both phenomenalized ("localised") and made to "fall under a concept," that is, abstracted. Abstraction and phenomenalization are here elided, principally so that the function of "taking meaning" from a difference both preserved and erased can itself be preserved. The ellipsis, accomplished here upon the *one* signifier that covers *two* concepts, splitting the concept "object" to which the term "object" refers, instances the logic of condensation that the essay goes on to elaborate, but only after making it clear that the "concept of identity to a concept" operates in the "system" as a concept precisely not identical to itself—that is: in a formal sense, identity (to a concept) does not *exist,* although it does *occur.*

The inchoate difficulties in Miller's description of the redoubling of the concept surface acutely when that redoubling is extended to the language of political agency. If suture and the unsutured in *Hegemony and Socialist Strategy* are not forms of determination, they nevertheless remain linked subtly and explicitly to a notion of totality of effects, to the *perfection* (in the verbal sense) of effects in and as the field of the social. This promise of perfection derives in great measure from an analogy between the process of conceptual embodiment and the process of symbolic or social materialization in and as social organizations or institutions—the relation, say, between the will and the law. This is not, of course, just any instance. From Hegel to Althusser, the reach and implications of the analogy between conceptual embodiment and institutionalization will be determined by its association with an impasse dating to Rousseau: whether the concept of the collective will is produced spontaneously from, or preexists, the definition of a collectivity of individual wills.²⁵ The question notoriously and symptomatically bedevils Engels, and Althusser returns to it as early as "Contradiction and Overdetermination" to make his own, and Marx's, distance from a classic understanding of the individual that Engels still embraces depend upon the possibility of learning from a Rousseaunian error. His question forcefully echoes *Reading "Capital"*'s concern with the "effectivity of structures on their parts": "Why is

25. This impasse, expressed with different valence but remarkably similar vocabularies, remains at issue in treatments of the concept of individuality, from Habermas to John Rawls. The *Social Contract* and its consequences are at issue from the first. The distinction between the "fiction" of the "general will" and the mode of "absence of a general content" is powerfully advanced in the *Logic*, precisely at the moment when Hegel considers the passage between individuality and universality. Thus the note [*Zusatz*] to the passage from Hegel's *Logic* cited above, posing that if "the logical forms of the concept were really dead and inert receptacles of conceptions and thoughts, knowledge about them would be an idle curiosity which the truth might dispense with," distinguishes the "real universal" from that which is merely held "in common" in these words: "The distinction . . . between what is merely in common, and what is truly universal, is strikingly expressed by Rousseau in his famous *Contrat social*, when he says that the laws of a state must spring from the universal will (*volonté générale*), but need not on that account be the will of all (*volonté de tous*). Rousseau would have made a sounder contribution towards a theory of the state if he had always kept this distinction in sight. The general will is the notion of the will; and the laws are the special clauses of this will and based upon the notion of it (*Lesser Logic*, 228). The concept is the form of generality itself, and Hegel would seem to need to explain for the region of phenomenology what Rousseau does for that of ethics: the relation between individuality and generality. In the *Zusatz*, as in many of the passages in the *Philosophy of Right*, the weight of the argument is shifted to the relation between the notion of the will and its "special clauses," the laws. That the *Zusatz* should say "springs from" indicates its filiation to the sort of self-generating notion that is developed earlier in the *Logic* and in the *Phenomenology*. Not that the laws are in this case the means by which the concept is understood or becomes transparent: indeed, once the laws are understood to be based upon the concept they will keep it from sight. The law has to be subsumed under a concept of the general will, but also must apply to all. This being for all of the law takes the place of that which is general, and in a certain sense belongs to no one: the concept of the general will. The issue then becomes the way in which basing that which is *de tous* (the exercise of the law) upon what is *general* (the concept of the general will) preserves and records the presence or the effectivity of the notion of the will—but also eliminates it, makes it forgettable—makes one blur into the other. This hiding-forgetting of the notion by the law is the expression of a fantasy of foundation ("based upon . . . " and "springs from") that is the product of that forgetting, and which legitimates it. The state—the Rousseaunian state—can only exist on the basis of this forgetting, which amounts also, we might add, to a forgetting of the very myth told in (for instance) the "Discourse on the Origin of Inequality." The theme is constant in Hegel: "The merit of Rousseau's contribution to the search for this concept [of the Idea of the state] is that, by adducing the will as the principle of the state, he is adducing a principle which has thought both its form and its content, a principle indeed which is thinking itself, not a

everything so clear and harmonious at the level of *individual wills*, whereas *beneath this level* or *beyond it*, all becomes either empty or tautological?" (Contradiction and Overdetermination," 124). Because the very "transparency" of the problem has become the index of its ideological stakes, Althusser concludes that Engels is forced, by the obstacles it poses, into the realm of fiction, "a fiction quite as optimistic as the fiction of bourgeois economics, a fiction closer to Locke and Rousseau than to Marx, . . . [proposing] that the resultant of all the individual wills, and the resultant of these resultants, actually has a general content, really embodies determination in the last instance by the economic (I am thinking of Rousseau, whose dearest wish was that the particular wills, cut off from one another, might come together in a fair vote, producing that miraculous Minerva, the general will!)."[26] As the ironic stress on "actual" and "real" suggests, this formulation marks a moment when Althusser is beginning to shape the contrasting thesis that ideology, that "resultant of these resultants," is their *imaginary* embodiment. The lesson to be derived is indeed that the complex geometry of the social "produces" something other than a concrete content, or that the content produced is not susceptible to embodiment. Engels's naive, optimistic fiction instead retreats from the rigor of Marx's position to the notion that "determination in the last instance" by the economy is actually *embodied* in the "resultant" of the individual wills as their concrete content, an argument that itself crucially links a pedagogical notion of influence to a form of historical

---

principle, like gregarious instinct, for instance, or divine authority, which has thought as its form only. Unfortunately . . . he takes the will only in a determinate form as the individual will, and he regards the universal will not as the absolutely rational element in the will, but only as a 'general' will which proceeds out of this individual will as out of a conscious will. The result is that he reduces the union of individuals in the state to a contract and therefore to something based on their arbitrary wills . . . and abstract reasoning proceeds to draw the logical inferences which destroy the absolutely divine principle of the state, together with its majesty and absolute authority." *Hegel's "Philosophy of Right,"* trans. T. M. Knox (Oxford: Oxford University Press, 1952), 156–57, and 11–18, where this self-realizing power is shown to have implications for the social. See Pierre Méthais's suggestive analysis of the distinctions between Hegel and Rousseau on the question of the generality of the will, "Contrat et volonté générale selon Hegel et Rousseau," in Jacques D'Hondt, ed., *Hegel et le siècle des lumières* (Paris: PUF, 1974), 101–48.

26. "Contradiction and Overdetermination," in *For Marx*, 125. Michael Sprinker's discussion of Althusser's confrontation with Rousseau seems to me especially fruitful: see his *Imaginary Relations: Aesthetics and Ideology in the Theory of Historical Materialism* (London: Verso, 1987), where the *décalage* between individual and general will is defined by analogy to Paul de Man's notion of text.

embodiment or identification, opposing on one side Rousseau and Engels (who does not learn from his teacher's errors) and on the other Marx and Althusser, who do. The error at issue, for Althusser and Marx as for Hegel (who in an important note to the *Logic* comments on Rousseau's incapacity to keep "before his eyes" the distinction between the concept [*volonté générale*] and its particular special clauses [the laws that govern the *volonté de tous*]), has to do with the phenomenology of *embodiment:* the embodying of the concept as concrete content, that is, the "production" of the concept from and within the material, cannot be the same as the "production" of the material—the concrete—from the concept. Within the language provided by the *Social Contract,* the solution to the aporias of production, bordering conceptual embodiment and institutionalization, occurs as the spontaneous work of a miracle—that is, as a fantasy or a delusion, or as a work of literature.[27]

And yet the lesson to be drawn from this observation is far from clear. Althusser, who uses Rousseau here as the exemplary instance of the thinker in whom conceptual embodiment is fundamentally mythic, also suggests approvingly that Rousseau is exceptional among "18th century ideologues" in wanting his wish to be "productive"— that is, to have a material "effect." The production or birth of "marvelous Minerva," martial wisdom fully armed springing from the forehead of Jupiter to defend Genevan republicanism as she had once protected Athenian democracy, itself embodies, with characteristic terseness, the strategic value of the optimistic fiction as both embodiment or figure, and critique of embodiment. If it cannot, it seems, be construed as a *material effect,* the set of determinants or *raepresentationes communes* proposed in the *Social Contract* should nonetheless be construed as an *ideological effect,* with distinct material consequences (the French Revolution, in one reading). The indecision marks a shift both in the understanding of Rousseau, reflected in an ambivalence in the description of the law and of theological language (as an ideological apparatus), and of the notions of *matter, effect,* and *body.* When Althusser takes up again the form that this "dearest wish" has for Rousseau, he does it returning to the status of the "necessary fic-

---

27. Althusser's definition of "spontaneity" in *Philosophy and the Spontaneous Philosophy of the Scientists,* trans. Warren Montag (Verso: London, 1990) is useful, though it requires supplementing: "Convictions" or "beliefs" are *spontaneous* when they "stem from the experience of scientific practice itself in its everyday immediacy" (133).

tion," considering again its possible relation to material effect. In his analysis of the *Social Contract,* "Sur le 'Contrat Social' (les Décalages)" (1966), Althusser suggests that Rousseau builds the theoretical argument about a chain of *décalages,* impasses each of whose solution in turn generates a further, slightly more general impasse. Each of these impasses poses a genuine threat to the possibility of a generalized notion of the social: thus the *décalage* between the "total alienation" of the slave and the "total alienation" required to enter into a social contract is resolved as the difference but also identity between the two parties to the contract, the individual and the social body; this position then reveals a *décalage* between alienation and advantageous exchange, which in turn becomes, again, the problem of the relation between the general will and the particular will, that is, the problem of the law. Rousseau both solves and displaces this last contradiction, as he does the previous ones, by means, Althusser argues, of wordplay—"upon a 'play' of words such that Rousseau calls *by the same name* both the *specific* interest of the individual taken in isolation, and the *specific* interest of the social group" ("Les Décalages," 35). But this "solution" obeys an important imperative: for without solving these problems, the "décalages" become confrontations, descriptions of impasses, in such a way that the act of naming—"Rousseau calls by the same name"—returns again to the originating moment at the heart of the "Discourse on Language," an act of naming that produces what it names.

The dismissal of Rousseau's fictionalizing in "Contradiction and Overdetermination" has by this point changed substantially, although the structure of the argument remains, as Michael Sprinker has shown, profoundly dialectical; and the "wish" (Althusser's as well as Rousseau's) for the appearance of a "miraculous Minerva" of *material* effects persists, though remarkably transformed. The movement toward a *décalage* and the regression from it, *fuite et regression,* remain posed as operating within a discontinuity between the theoretical and the real.[28] It is when the last discontinuity shows itself to resist a theoretical solution that Althusser opens the possibility of discussing the "fictional" Rousseau as an allegory of the failure of the "political" or theoretical one:

---

28. "'Fuite en avant dans l'idéologie, ou regression dans l'économie'" is the title of the essay's last section.

If no possible discontinuity remains—since it would be useless in the region of theory, which has lived off of these discontinuities, chasing before it its problems in their solutions until it finds a real, insoluble problem; if no possible discontinuity remains, there is still one avenue of recourse, but of a different sort. It consists this time in a *transference*, the transference of the impossible theoretical solution into the other of theory: into literature. The admirable "fictitious triumph" of a writing without precedents: *La Nouvelle Héloïse, Emile,* and the *Confessions*. Its being unprecedented may not be unrelated to the admirable "failure" of a theory without precedents: The Social Contract.[29]

The movement from Rousseau's "theory" to his "fiction," the therapeutic completing of the project, this "determining" of each by the other, stands here as a "transference" in the shape of a narrative: the narrative of a victory, a determining narrative of determination as the appearance of a recognizable "fiction." In this sense Althusser proposes a role for fiction or literature that, if it seems to be *sui generis*, in fact can be understood as a general program for aesthetics (as a close reading of Althusser's essay on Cremonini and "A Letter on Art" would confirm): the aesthetic is the region of a double, paradoxical embodiment. It is able to express as "fiction" the persistent troubling of cause and effect—the *production*—which cannot operate "in theory"; and it arrives at this "fiction" by means not of a conceptual, but of a "literary" movement. For this reason fiction or literature— aesthetics—is the labor of the concept, the form and direction of its "transference" from theoretical "failure" to fictional "success." But the specific *means* by which the "décalages" take place in this essay

---

29. "S'il n'est plus de Décalage possible—puisqu'il ne servirait plus à rien dans l'ordre théorique, qui n'a fait que vivre de ces Décalages, en chassant devant lui ses problèmes en leur solution jusqu'à la rencontre du problème réel, insoluble, il reste pourtant un recours, mais d'une autre nature: un *transfert*, cette fois, le transfert de l'impossible solution théorique dans l'autre de la théorie, la littérature. Le 'triomphe fictif', admirable, d'une écriture sans précédent: *La Nouvelle Héloïse,* l'*Emile,* les *Confessions*. Qu'elle soit sans précédent n'est peut-être pas sans rapport avec 'l'échec', admirable, d'une théorie sans précédent: le Contrat Social." Althusser, "Sur le 'Contrat Social' (Les Décalages)," *Cahiers Pour l'Analyse* 8 (1966): 42. My translation. Compare the much more optimistic conclusion of Alain Grosrichard's essay in the same volume, "Gravité de Rousseau": "Rousseau's 'literature' is nothing but the displacement, into the interior of his writing, of a problem posed by theory. His literature is the mise en scène, the dramatization of theory . . . . Literature verifies theory and makes theory true; theory justifies literature and makes it necessary. This is why Rousseau's work is inseparably both literature and theory of literature, theory and literature of theory," (64). My translation.

argues for another engagement as well. The terms "flight," "regression," "wordplay," and finally the "transference" to the "other" of theory suggest that Althusser was seeking to articulate this "flight" in the language of psychoanalysis, the displacement from the theoretical region of the *décalages* to the region of fiction having the structure of a recognizable analytic movement: the externalization-projection by means of which a therapeutic fantasy can be represented, the "real embodiment" of what remains unconscious, or the dynamic of the transference.

If this marked turn toward the language of psychoanalysis is not in itself surprising—"Sur le 'Contrat Social' (les Décalages)" was, after all, published in *Cahiers pour l'analyse*, and at a time when Althusser's engagement with Lacan was almost constant—some of what it suggests about Althusser's "theoretical" as well as his "biographical" or literary trajectory is immediately problematic.[30] In the first place, the pedagogical model of historical influence at issue in "Contradiction and Overdetermination" is recast here, by virtue of the seemingly open sequence of *transferts*, as a question of identity: the problematic identity or supplementarity, in the first instance, of the "admirable 'fictitious triumph' of a writing without precedents" with the "admirable 'failure' of a theory without precedents"; the equally problematic identity or supplementarity of the Rousseau of the *Social Contract* with respect to the Rousseau of *La Nouvelle Héloïse, Emile,* and especially of the *Confessions*; and finally the complex identification, at issue already in "Contradiction and Overdetermination," between Althusser and the figure or figures of Rousseau.

30. I am at odds here, clearly, with David Macey, who has recently argued that the "Décalages" piece seems "out of place, if not archaic" in the project announced by *Cahiers pour l'analyse*: a proposed genealogy of the social sciences. Althusser's article on "Freud and Lacan" dates from 1964–65, but see also "Trois notes sur la théorie des discours" of 1966, collected in Louis Althusser, *Ecrits sur la psychanalyse*, ed. Olivier Corpet and François Matheron (Paris: STOCK/IMEC, 1993), 111–70, especially 143–44: "We can suggest that the ideological formations in which the formations of an unconscious being considered are said to 'take'—that these formations are the 'matter,' although the unformed matter, in which certain of the typical formations of this unconscious 'take.' It would be by means of these ideological formations, among others, that the unconscious could communicate according to the phenomenon that Freud describes, and by means of them, too, the situation of transference would occur. This point deserves careful attention, especially as concerns definition and conceptual refinement; for one cannot simply accept the category of 'matter.' It has the grave disadvantage of masking the very important fact that the discourse of the unconscious is produced in and by means of ideological discourse, the fragment of ideological discourse where the unconscious discourse 'takes,' while being absent from that discourse." My translation.

For we cannot be blind to the pathos of the essay's concluding lines. The topos of the flight from reason—*theoria*—to "an avenue of recourse, but of a different sort" is not only the narrative of the birth and the therapeutic necessity of fiction or of literature, or the narrative of the failure of all merely theoreticist positions whose effectivity must be completed or supplemented by a passage or transference into the material region of theoretical practice (Marx: "Philosophers have interpreted the world; the point, however, is to change it"). It is also, as its roots in Romanticism serve to remind us, the narrative of a flight into madness. The flight or regression into fiction described for Rousseau—the flight from theoretical impasses—will be read also as the fundamental moment of this identification between Althusser and Rousseau: the recourse of madness that derives "theoretically" from the effort to overcome *décalages* internal to the genealogy of the concept, and "biographically" from the conditions described in the autobiographies, and condensed there, with the rigor of denegation, in the opening pages: "Alas," Althusser writes in *The Future Lasts Forever*, "I am no Rousseau. But in planning to write about myself and the dramatic events I lived through and live with still, I often thought about his unprecedented boldness. Not that I would ever claim as he did at the beginning of the *Confessions:* 'I am embarking on something which has never been done before.' Certainly not. But I can in all honesty subscribe to the following declaration of his: 'I shall say openly what I did, what I thought, what I was.'"[31]

But in the second place, and to a great extent in contrast, the dynamic of transference, for all its descriptive power and suggestiveness for the question of identity, poses fundamental problems as well. *Transfert* in "Sur le 'Contrat Social' (les Décalages)" conveniently straddles the field of intentional acts as well as nonintentional events, for important theoretical reasons: the movement toward resolving the last, most stubborn *décalage* in Rousseau is not Rousseau's own, "proper" act or decision, nor does it obey a structural necessity that might immediately have "produced" the literary "recourse" from the

31. Althusser, *The Future Lasts Forever and the Facts*, ed. Olivier Corpet and Yann Moulier Boutang, trans. Richard Veasey (London: Chatto and Windus, 1993). Laclau and Mouffe's description of the argumentation on the problem of determination in Althusser bears repeating, as a description of a pathology: "From the very beginning, an attempt was made to render it compatible with another central moment in Althusserian discourse that is, strictly speaking, incompatible with the first." This transference of the language of "theory" to that of "biography" is most explicit in Peter Sloterdijk's comments on Althusser in *Critique of Cynical Reason*.

failure of the theoretical. Instead, and as the strikingly depersonalized grammar of the last sentences conveys as well, the *transfert* from "failure" to "victory," the therapeutic supplementation of theory by fiction obeys the impersonal difficulty of distinguishing, on any grounds, between an intentional act and an event. It should be remarked that the same is generally true for descriptions of analytic transference: it *occurs*, it happens that the analyst or another figure acquires for the patient the characteristics of a figure from the pantheon of the analysand's recollections—and the intentional form of that transference is what remains to be produced in and by means of the analysis.[32] The consequences of this depersonalization for the phenomenology of embodiment are again mixed. If we seek in the engagement with Rousseau the transference (back) to the realm of "theory" (miraculous Minerva, philosophical, literary, and political) of concepts from psychoanalysis and from literature, then we need to account also for the contingent movement that the language of psychoanalysis consistently associates with every such narrative. Thus although Rousseau's strategy in moving from *décalage* to theoretical solution is one of condensation—two or more concepts or senses of a word condensed in one signifier—there is no reason to suppose that the closing "transference" from failure to victory, from the arena of theory to that of fiction, follows the same pattern. The "recourse" to the other in this instance is made to seem necessary, to take the form of a narrative reaching a foreseeable and determined closure—but the association of Althusser with Rousseau here is indeed as contingent as the object of transference in the analytic situation can be. To put it differently: the *transfert* from theory to literature or to madness can be described as therapeutic, as producing identification or personification when not identity, only from the per-

---

32. See Mladen Dolar's quite different treatment of Althusser and transference as the more restricted *transference-love* in "Beyond Interpellation," *Qui Parle* 6/2 (1993), 84–5: "This love of the patient for the analyst . . . springs up with an astonishing, almost mechanical regularity in the analytical situation, regardless of the person of the analyst and that of the patient. . . . The minimal mechanism of transference is embedded in the very basic function of speech as addressed to the Other, the Other as an instance beyond all empirical interlocutors." Dolar is careful to note that the "dialectics of transference" requires another moment or aspect: "the emergence of transference-love as . . . a halt of repetition, when the free flow is cut short, when words fail; it emerges as a resistance, or, as Lacan puts it, as the closing of the unconscious." From this "dialectic," Dolar suggestively concludes, the remainder—love—emerges to provide a way of understanding the possibility of subjectivity "beyond interpellation," though the more extensive sense of transference I am suggesting here considerably changes the nature and ethical dimension of that "emergence."

spective that it has abandoned: the perspective of theory. From the perspective of literature or of psychoanalysis, and a fortiori from the perspective (if one can still call it that) of madness, the dynamic of *transfert* is always an "avenue . . . of a different sort" from the terms that theory can use to describe it, or transfer onto it. Again, from the perspective of literature or of psychoanalysis, indeed from the perspective (for instance) of the *Confessions*, the "transference" (of guilt or of responsibility, say) does not occur (necessarily) from theory to its other or from one person to another, but to what is at hand, a metonymic "flight" to an other whose connection to theory this flight then *produces*.³³ "Transference" no longer straddles—that is, participates in and joins—two distinct arenas; it is not a trope for the free movement [*phorein*] of the word from one to another, from theory to fiction or from Rousseau to Althusser; it is not a *jeu de mots* condensing two concepts under a single term so as to retain and limn for and in us the synthetic consciousness of the concept of identity to a concept.

Let us call it instead a *rule*, though of a paradoxical sort: the *form* of a gerund, transference as *transfering* cannot, to return to Kant's initial formulation, *"serve* as a rule" [*zur Regel dient*] that would predict the direction (*from* theory *to* fiction, or to practice, or to matter) of any concrete content or instance, including particular rules. As a rule, "transference" happens, it is an event; but because of the rule of its occurring, "transference" has in itself no regulative content. The issue immediately becomes considerably broader than the local question of the status granted "literature" in the failure of the *Social Contract*. It is by now understood that it is not possible to settle on either of the two models of causation that Althusser deploys in "Sur le 'Contrat Social' (les Décalages)" and in *Reading "Capital,"* a "metonymic causality" on the one hand, and on the other the hypothesis of a structuring, "disconcerting but inevitable absence, the absence of the concept" in the mode of a *deus absconditus* in Pascal's tradition. Doubtless, this undecidability constitutes the closest point of contact between the project

---

33. This is of course the point best made by Paul de Man about the *Confessions*, in "Excuses (*Confessions*)," his chapter on the Marion episode in *Allegories of Reading* (New Haven: Yale University Press, 1979), 278–301, esp. 288–9: "Because Rousseau desires Marion, she haunts his mind and her name is pronounced almost unconsciously, as if it were a slip, a segment of the discourse of the other. . . . But Marion just happened to be the first thing that came to mind; any other name, any other word, any other sound or noise could have done just as well and Marion's entry into the discourse is a mere effect of chance. She is a free signifier, metonymically related to the part she is made to play in the subsequent system of exchanges and substitutions."

of *Reading "Capital"* and the unsutured field of the social envisioned by proponents of "radical democracy," from Laclau to Judith Butler. One can, indeed, express this undecidability as the interference of two models, one transcendental and the other materialist, the first accounting for intentional acts and the second for nonintentional events, whose complex history includes the encounters and failed synthesis, within and between the foundational texts of Marxism, of a theology and a materialism, of an apocalyptic rhetoric and an empirical one, the rhetoric of the *Communist Manifesto* and of Lenin's *Materialism and Empirio-criticism*. But most importantly: the rule of "transference" records this undecidability as a fundamental break that cannot be sutured, forgotten, or sublated by a transference into the arena of fiction or of practice. For it is not just that the "concept of identity to a concept" operates in the "system" as a concept precisely *not* identical to itself, but that, to the extent that it is a *product*, in a formal sense, such a concept does not *exist*, although it does *occur*. What *happens*, what is an event, as the irreducible difference between what is *de tous* and what is *general*, as the form of justice, happens "upon a play of words," and is inescapably literary.

To approach Althusser's understanding of this therapeutic literary model requires passing from what I have been posing as a *formal* discussion of the incompleting or unfinishing of reflection in the occurring of a certain *transfert*, to the *concrete content* furnished by this reflection. I have, in fact, been making this transition throughout—or rather, it has been occurring throughout, for reasons that are inextricably both historical and theoretical. Marx's own engagement with Hegel, for instance, is determined by the necessity of passing from the formal to the material, and from the form to the content of propositions—a necessity that Marx is careful to address both theoretically and allegorically. In the *Critique of Hegel's "Philosophy of Right,"* to take the best-known example, Marx expresses his understanding of Hegel's description of the passage from the "logical forms of the concept" to "the vital spirit [*lebendige Geist*] of the actual world" as a symmetrical confusion: although Hegel believes that in the *Philosophy of Right* he is able to derive and develop the determinate—the concrete—reality of the organism of the state from its idea, Hegel in fact derives the concrete from the presupposed concept: "He does not develop his thought out of what is objective [*aus dem Gegenstand*], but what is objective in accordance with a ready-made thought which has its origin in the abstract sphere of logic." Hegel, it seems, makes the necessity of the movement toward the concrete universal derive from this "abstract sphere," and as such the necessity is not itself "critically demonstrated" as internal to the various powers proper to the organic state. This process of deriving the necessity of an internal movement from an "alien" principle Marx then describes in these terms:

> Just as their necessity is not derived from their own nature, still less is it critically demonstrated. On the contrary, their realization is predestined by the nature of the concept, sealed in the holy register of the Santa Casa (the *Logic*). The soul of objects, in this case that of the state, is complete and predestined before its body, which is, properly speaking, mere appearance. The concept is the "Son" within the "Idea," within God the Father, the *agens*, the determining, differentiating principle.[34]

The unsystematic theology of the passage works in a number of different ways around the same knot, rendering allegorically the circularity that the *Critique* points out analytically: if the concept is not to be like the soul or the idea, subsisting and eternal, transcendent if not Platonic, but is instead a derived or produced representation, then its origin, its appearing, must be external to it: a matter of labor. And if *necessity* is not to be equally transcendent ("predestined by the nature of the concept") then the realization of the objective and of the form of logic also require deriving, if only in the form of a narrative or myth of origin. Here Marx makes use of the traditional problem in Platonic Christianity: when the preexisting or the ontological priority of the soul *vis à vis* the body is translated into the structure of the Trinity, God-the-Father becomes the *agens* of whom the Son is either the soul or the mere appearance. What is a resolute ontological as well as temporal hierarchy in the case of the soul and the body clashes with the theological need for mutual immanence in the case of the theology of the Trinity.

To be sure, the niceties of dogma are not Marx's main object, just as they are not in Althusser's well-known uses of theology in "Ideology and Ideological State Apparatuses": the *Critique of Hegel's "Philoso-*

---

34. Marx, *Critique of Hegel's "Philosophy of Right,"* trans. Joseph O'Malley (Cambridge: Cambridge University Press, 1970), 15. Marx is here poking fun especially at the *Zusatz* to the *Logic*, paragraph 161: "The movement of the notion is as it were to be looked upon merely as play: the other which it sets up is in reality not an other. Or, as it is expressed in the teaching of Christianity: not merely has God created a world which confronts him as an other; he has also from all eternity begotten a Son in whom he, a Spirit, is at home with himself" (225).

106 *Yale French Studies*

phy of Right" is concerned instead with the possible solutions to the circular phenomenology of "derivation" gingerly advanced in the *Philosophy of Right*, the transcendental model of annunciation and predestination (the concrete universal would appear according to a "necessity . . . derived from the nature" of what is objective) and a dialectical one (the concrete universal would be produced from the difference between the objective and its first formalization in the *Logic* as a concept). The sealing of the concept in the *Logic* or Santa Casa is an effort by Marx to show, at the level of the image, how Hegel is condensing these incompatibilities, and it is worth dwelling for a moment on this parodic materialization of the argument of the *Logic*. Transported miraculously to Loreto in the thirteenth century, the Santa Casa, the setting of the Annunciation to Mary, is already by the time of the Renaissance a thick cultural icon that condenses a number of tropes both literary and theological: the transference of the house corresponds to a *translatio imperii* from Nazareth to Italy and hence to the Holy Roman Empire; site of miraculous cures, by the sixteenth century it had acquired around it a second "casa," the Sanctuary in which it was sealed and shielded, and in which it became by the early seventeenth century an emblem of a "holy register" defined architecturally also by the traces of those cures, a scaffold of crutches, canes, and objects cast off by pilgrims whom a vision of the Santa Casa had made whole.[35] An armature of discarded tokens, phantoms of bodies that have been cured in turn concealing, clothing, or embodying a house sealed within a sanctuary—the abyssal presentation of the absent cause by its successive, hollow embodiments could hardly be more compactly rendered, the parentheses in Marx's text ("their realization is predestined by the nature of the concept, sealed in the holy register of the Santa Casa [the *Logic*]") materializing at the level of the sentence the logic of metonymous substitution of inside for out, container for contained, form for content or for matter, on which the *Philosophy of*

---

35. Cervantes's characteristically ironic description of the Santa Casa is perhaps the best known: Tomás Rodaja, who will become the mad Master Glass, visits "Our Lady of Loreto, in whose holy temple he saw neither walls nor battlements, for they were covered entirely with crutches, shrouds, chains, cuffs, metal bands, hair pieces, half-weights of wax, paintings and tableaux, which made manifest the innumerable gifts that many had received from the hand of God through the intercession of his divine Mother, who enriched and legitimated that holy image with a flock of miracles, as a reward for the veneration in which it is held by those who decorate the walls of her house with such gifts." From *"El licenciado Vidriera,"* in Miguel de Cervantes, *Novelas ejemplares* (Madrid; Castalia, 1986), vol. 2, 112–3. Translation mine.

Right seems to rest. The Santa Casa, standing for the body of Mary in whom the concept and the word (the Son) are materialized, "seals" for Marx the form of the Logic, body, outer shell, or architecture to the concept which it produces and which it *serves*, as Mary serves to contain and bear the concept, *ancilla Dei*.

Whatever humor attends the form of this encounter between Marx and Hegel concerning the origin of the concept should not conceal what is at stake "sealed within" its register: the determining fantasy of philosophical language—the production of "new" concepts—is the narrative of a miraculous birth, to which Marx will seek to restore the elementary resistance of the object and the suffering of its production, which is to say the element of material labor. Miraculous, because it is both spontaneous (that is: unannounced) and determined, both the labor of the objective that bears the concept and the labor of reflection upon the object. Miraculous, finally, because the doctrine of the concept expresses as early as Kant both the fantasy of immaterial conception, the mother merely *bearing* [*trägt*] what is immediate to the *agens*, the father; and, indissociably and consequently, the fantasy of the maternal father, bearing like Jupiter the body of philosophy and armed wisdom, miraculous Minerva midwifed by Vulcan. To speak in slightly less allegorical terms: the story of the production of the object of knowledge from the object or vice-versa is always embodied as a fantasy of the spontaneous reproduction of the identity to itself of the concept from which the new concept is produced—even though the "new" concept is the mark of the nonidentity to itself of the concept in general, and even though if the concept is going to be *common*, like the law, its parentage and birth need to be established or derived *according to the law*. "Thought" does not "derive from the objective" [*aus dem Gegenstand*], even when the objective is itself already symbolic, as its therapeutic cure or completing, "fiction" to its "theory" or "theory" to its "fiction," but as its vestige, its discarded crutch, so to speak: assembled about the hidden "register" of a translated or transferred container [*Träger*], phantom of the wounded or broken body *as well as* of the whole one reborn miraculously, spontaneously. This improper condensation of the complete and the incomplete, identity to self and nonidentity to self, is a formative aspect of the doctrine of the concept. Concepts "come from" a labor that effaces/produces its property over what it conceives, a labor that labors to efface itself as such, as the production of the concept as the nonidentical to itself. Miraculous Minerva, indeed: just as Marx both overturns Hegel (requiring that he

108 *Yale French Studies*

"develop his thought out of what is objective") and changes his terms, Althusser reads Rousseau as expressing the leaving out of a determinant—the labor of the coming-together of the general will, that is to say, the labor of the production of consciousness, the material conditions of the construction of consciousness.

If we now must understand that the riven "production of the concept" of effectivity is *for us* the site of a strong interference between two concepts, the "life" and the "work," then we must expect to find that in "Althusser" any reflection upon the production of the concept has to occur as both theory and biography.[36] We have seen in outline the stakes of this occurring in the notion of a "metonymic causality" in *Reading "Capital."* It should be no surprise that in the "life"—that is, in the autobiographies—we discover a reflection upon the production of the concept, embedded within a reflection upon the possibility of passing from exceptional experience to a rule about that experience. It is a story told as a joke or a jibe, which, having to do with the origin of what was to become *Reading "Capital,"* allows me to return to the ideological project with which I opened. Like so many jokes, which for reasons that must remain enigmatic concern the propriety of the act of naming, Althusser's strange tale has to do with theft and with desire—though nominally it concerns the seminar on *Capital:*

> [Jacques-Alain] Miller was the [member of the seminar] with the most fixed ideas on the subject, but he dropped out completely in the course of the year. He was living in a hunting-lodge at Rambouillet with a girl who "produced," so he said, "at least one theoretical concept a week." ... After [Rancière's] intervention everything was easy because he opened up the debate effectively and in areas to which we were already giving some thought; this was after a talk of mine on Lacan during which [Jacques-Alain] Miller intervened to announce a "conceptual discovery": "metonymic causality" (otherwise known as the absent cause), which caused quite a stir.... When Miller returned ... and read the duplicated pages of the papers people had given, he discovered Rancière had "stolen" his own concept of "metonymic causality" [*son concept personnel*]. Rancière suffered terribly when charged with this. And is it not the case that concepts belong to everyone? ... My reason

36. The biographical sense of this is not unimportant: *Reading "Capital,"* like *For Marx,* breaks from the "humanist" reading of Marx that privileges the early, more Hegelian work. Vigorous defenses of a more "humanistic" reading of both Marx and Hegel abounded, of course. Lucien Goldmann is perhaps the best known, but see also Jacques d'Hondt, *De Hegel à Marx* (Paris: PUF, 1972), especially 219–28.

for relating this ridiculous incident is not to put Miller down. After all, youth must have its fling. Furthermore, it seems he began his magisterial course on Lacan this year by solemnly declaring, *"We are not studying Lacan but being studied by him."* This proves he too was capable of acknowledging someone else had invented and owned a concept. . . . None the less, this absurd idea of the "theft of concepts" touched on a point of principle which concerned me deeply and caused me great anxiety: the question of *anonymity*. [The Future Lasts Forever, 208–10]

The moment is recounted differently in two earlier passages in *The Facts*: "Some students at the Ecole [Normale Supérieure] had been quite impressed by [Lacan], among them Jacques-Alain Miller, whose famous concept had been plagiarised and who was wooing Judith Lacan" (*a qui on avait volé le fameux concept de sa vie*, a suggestive phrasing that joins the "concept of a life"—its correlative on the level of concepts—to the "concept of a lifetime," the best or most important one). And:

> We [Balibar, Macherey, Establet, and Rancière] organized a seminar on *Das Kapital* during the academic year 1964–5. Rancière set it going and got us over our initial difficulties, for which he deserves our thanks, as no one else was prepared to start the ball rolling. . . . It was a masterly exposition . . . slightly formalist and Lacanian (the "absent cause" kept coming up) but it showed real ability. . . . Jacques-Alain Miller, who was already going out with Judith Lacan, displayed great initiative in October 1964, which brought him to prominence, and then disappeared completely (he had gone off with a girl to the forest of Fontainebleau and was teaching her how to produce theoretical concepts). He reappeared again without warning in June 1965 to reveal, much to everyone's astonishment, that someone had "stolen one of his concepts." . . . In actual fact, [the incident] was quite exceptional. Concepts circulate freely as they are being developed without any controls placed on them. [The Facts, 333]

Why would this anecdote matter enough to Althusser to be repeated? If one sets aside momentarily the rather sophomoric tone in which the scene is told and retold, a different configuration emerges, signaled by Althusser's repeated effort to move from the arena of the biographical to the theoretical, the incident becoming "exceptional" when considered against the analytic description of the concept in general: "And is it not the case that concepts belong to everyone?" and: "Concepts circulate freely as they are being developed without any controls placed on them." The "property" of the concept of metonymic causality that Miller had proposed is the immediate precursor, it needs to be recalled, to the development or production of the concepts of "structural causality" and of "suture" upon which Laclau and Mouffe rest their project. One quick answer to the question of the scene's recurrence is indeed that it touches upon what Althusser perceives to be most *his own*, "a point of principle which concerned me deeply and caused me great anxiety," what most clearly affects the representation of himself and his relation to his work and to the concepts he "produced." It touches upon this "point of principle" both as a problem of *names* and *anonymity*, and in the form of a question: what about concepts—and not just any concept: *metonymic causality* is the notion that will make it possible to discuss the "effectivity of a structure upon its elements," or to apply the notion of overdetermination in the first place—can be said to be *personnel*, and what can be said to be *de tous*? What about concepts can be "discovered," moveable, nonproper, what about them cannot be stolen? What, in a word, is *immaterial* about the concept? The answer, covertly offered, is that what is immaterial about the concept (that is: ideally and indivisibly an aspect of it regardless of the concrete content of its occurring) is its freedom to circulate, or, more precisely, its spontaneous circulating, its occurring *as* spontaneous circulating.

Is it enough to observe, then, that the project of *Reading "Capital,"* the production of the concept of the *"effectivity of a structure on its elements,"* and the complex passage from reflection to the rule of its incompleteness need to be reread in the light of this strange "theft" to which the concept seems susceptible? For surely the notion of the prepositional immateriality of the concept is at odds with the notion of the *production* of the concept, of the notion of the spontaneous labor to which works like *Reading "Capital"* and "Sur le 'Contrat Social' (les Décalages)," I have been arguing, are devoted. The proposition that an ideal "freedom" of circulation underlies the concept's various material embodiments (as *raepresentationes*) need only be recast in the language of "rights" to square with formulations we might expect in the doctrines of classical humanism (the doctrines of "inalienable rights," for instance). On reflection, however, it cannot be simply coincidental that Althusser's idealization of the concept occurs at the very moment in which a sense "not identical to this one" is being proposed for and within the story that his autobiography tells: the "proper" conceptual content of "this ridiculous incident" is a didactic allegory posing that the ideality of the concept as such precludes its becoming the property of any one. Neither can it be coincidental that Althusser fancifully engages here the two familiar tropes for the spontaneous production of the concept—the "miraculous Minerva" or birth of the concept from a man, and the *ancilla Dei*, Mary as the handservant [*Dienerin*] of the Holy Spirit, the carrier of the concept. The tone and nature of Althusser's remarks in the autobiographies should give us an indication that something else is sealed in this register with the problem of the self-identity of the concept, something or some process constantly exceeding the ideal borders of a subjective sense of freedom. Remark, first, that the enviously infantilizing quality of these passages remains constant: the "wooing of Judith Lacan" is imagined contiguously with a libidino-political "teaching" in the forests of Fontainebleau, the "production of theoretical concepts" encoded here as an eroticized act, a form of intercourse or pedagogy in which Miller, the "owner" of the "concept of his life," becomes a disappearing and reappearing principle; even the scene's locations acquire, in this context, a pseudorustical genealogy linking them to literary *topoi* of pastoral retreat and contemplation on one hand (Fontainebleau), and to sexual strategy, chase, and violence on the other ("a hunting-lodge at Rambouillet"). Other micronarratives concerning identity and anonymity soon emerge from behind questions, sometimes with the crass insistence one expects of soap-opera plots, sometimes with the open subtlety of the *roman policier*: Who "produced" the concept whose "discovery" was announced—Miller or the "girl" who "produced at least one theoretical concept a week"? Are Judith Lacan and "a girl" or "the girl" the same? If "teaching" how to produce theoretical concepts is a libidinal or erotic act (but whose?), what would it then mean to "study" or be "studied" by another? What role does the name "Lacan" play in Althusser's description? What other names are screened here?

The point of this explication and of these questions is neither to catch Althusser in contradictions that may express nothing more than the license of rhetorical ornament or the momentum of a joke, nor to provide these contradictions with a psychobiographical intent or motivation. The passages I have cited from the autobiographies give rise to three separate observations that bear upon the *occurring* of "rhetorical ornament," undecidable and overdetermined "micronarratives," and "jokes"—that bear, that is, on the dynamic of *transfert* or of what Laclau and Mouffe call "deconstructive effects" at work where "life" and "concept" seem to meet. In the first place, and concerning what I can still call the form of the argument: where the "production of concepts" is being established *as a concept* and as a concrete, even humorous *raepresentatio,* and where the formal ideality of concepts in general is being located in the *freedom* of their circulation, Althusser's "life" produces *literary* effects that are not concepts, that are not identical to themselves, and which circulate "freely" by putting into question the possibility of distinguishing between what "everyone" owns and is responsible for and what "someone else" has invented and owned. Freely circulating though these literary effects may be, what is not free about them—that is, what cannot be separated from these effects—is their *occurring* as events: reading-events, to be sure, but also, in the form of their insistent return in the autobiographies, writing-events. The practical consequences to be derived from the questioning they make necessary and from the rule of their occurrence are nowhere more poignantly, and threateningly, felt than where what "everyone owns" and what "someone else" has invented is the set of *raepresentationes communes* that we call our *life,* Althusser's life or autobiographies, or another's, "le concept de sa vie." These scenes from the autobiographies tell allegorically the story of the "production" of Althusser's "life" and of the concept of *life* as what cannot properly belong either to an "owner" or to a community. One understands why the story never stops being told.

If these literary effects occur spontaneously, however, then they cannot have the status of a *rule*—or, rather, one can again argue, as with Althusser's reading of the *Social Contract,* that as a rule they occur, but that no rule formalizing the occurring of literary effects or their production can be produced. If this is so, then the occurring of this allegory of desire and of excessive *transfert* at the moment when the concept of metonymic causality is discussed and thematized in the "life" could not, in principle or as a rule, have been foreseen or repeated. The coincidence of the thematics of "birth," "concept," "theft," and "desire" with the spontaneous overdetermination of literary effect would itself, in this case, become an instance of metonymic causality, a true event which would always only *have been,* its present as an occurrence always an absence "to be measured" or reconstituted after the fact. That it is, quite to the contrary, a foreseeable and indeed repeatable occurrence—for Althusser, the story is told three times, with differences that make no difference—suggests to what extent this *formal* rule has to be understood as also parasitized, contaminated by or embodied already in the discursive and material rules of "life" or of "biography." It is for this reason that "the totality of . . . deconstructive effects" of the notion of determination may never be accessible: there is no "totality" of deconstructive effects, because the effort to establish the rule for the occurring of transference or of literary effect is itself a practical, not a transcendental one. (It is not accidental that one can express this impasse *upon a play of words* about the word "as": "As a rule, it occurs; it does not occur as a rule"). Efforts in Laclau and Mouffe, in Žižek, in Sloterdijk, and in others (including Althusser himself) to measure Althusser by means of the concept of development toward determination in the last instance repeat therapeutically the narrative transference from "theory" to "fiction" or to madness that characterizes the form of the concept's production. And to put it differently: to the extent that they are readings of Althusser as well as repetitions of his work, narratives that determine the effect of his work or life are indeed "deconstructive effects" showing that the heterogeneity of their own text concerns its necessary reliance (for example) on the structure of the confessional narrative, the narrative of excuses. The effects of this unfinishing are themselves always unfinished because the story or the allegory of the becoming-concept of life, and the becoming-life of the concept, that is, the story of "theory" and the story of "fiction," are never identical to each other or to themselves.

Matters are not finished yet, however. For in the second place, and as to the concrete content or embodiment of this story: the transference from theory to fiction, its status as an *event* and as a rule of occurring, serve to account for the political movement from *volonté de tous* to *volonté générale,* and to account for the comparable epistemological movement from the law to the concept (in order to understand the *volonté générale,* one needs to eliminate and elevate the particular laws which are its manifestation) in terms of a procedure that can no longer be conceptualized. At this point the difficulties of the *transfert* are no longer matters of singular identity. For the narratives distinguishing one from the other, "theory" from "fiction" or *volonté de tous* from *volonté générale* accord a temporal priority to the epistemological effort that becomes "embodied" after the fact, an annunciation that fixes the word in flesh—and these narratives are themselves the product and the record of that "embodiment," as their organic concept. The embodying of the concept that must follow its philosophical production does so only to the extent that an organic figure for temporal relation—for "following"—is presupposed. In Althusser as in Marx, this circular figure or figure for circularity is again classically double: the *concept* of the law, sealed within the *representation* of the (hidden or appropriated) body of the *woman* that gives birth (that "produces theoretical concepts") to what in turn conceives and bears her as *agens*.

Two programs of thought concerning this organic concept follow. One, which can be associated with the early work of Luce Irigaray, contrasts the specularity of the (history of the) concept to the nonidentity to itself of the woman or of women, a sex always not-one. This process of association serves as a representation for what is unpresentable: the philosphemes of "transcendental" and "empirical," or "conceptual" and "material," embody their nonidentity to themselves in a body—a *raepresentatio communis*—culturally available to them as both single and double, single to itself and double as it is maternal or labile, self-identical and always not-one. The woman "serves" the concept that she bears as mother or as labile body, serves it by becoming useful, as representing the not-one of its "birth," *pedagogically:* she teaches the concept "how to produce theoretical concepts" and how to forget (as one forgets the "mere" representation) the labor of that production. And two: to the contrary, the woman ideally absent from the Santa Casa as from the history of the doctrine of the concept is herself a concept "produced" from the forehead of the *agens* as a hypostasis of the material, another concept or another goddess—*Materia*, as miraculous in her way as Minerva. Her body is not already available to represent for philosophy the circularity of its origin as a concept or system of concepts, but is produced and fashioned so as to take that pedagogical function (of carrier, of servant, etc.). In this formulation, sealed as alternative directions within the languages of philosophical feminism, both projects are unmistakably idealizing. It would be a glaring error, for instance, to claim that their philosophical and cultural role as the therapeutic *Materia* is the guiding reason for the fashioning of women's bodies as not-one. It would also be a mistake to assert that this therapeutic role preexists in any simple way the philosophical need or impasse—*décalage*—that it unmistakably serves to resolve. The conditions of fashioning and production as well as the measurement of their motives are both over- and underdetermined: their economy, the patient and violent labor of the discourses and pressures of culture, the spontaneous resistance of matter are themselves as objects of thought the product they seem to fashion.

This does not mean that we abandon the concrete content of the body, that because the always divided body of *Materia* does not necessarily seal within it, does not necessarily *bear* (the form of) the material body of a woman, we abandon the rigor of this circularity. For in the third place, and finally, if the nature of the occurring of the concept unfinishes the possibility of reflecting upon Marxism as a system of concepts, it also becomes the condition for a *practice* whose task—whose necessity—it is to account for the coincidence of the thematic ("birth," in this case, "desire," "concept," "suffering," and so on) with the theoretical in "literature" about "life," or to account in "theory" as in "fiction" for the force with which the concept's embodiment seals culturally the mother's body within *Materia*'s form and vice-versa. I do not—it must be clear—mean by this that Althusser, Balibar, Macherey, and their closest readers make this necessity a general *law*, but rather that they pose it as a rule of reflection and of action, a practical, rather than a transcendental, rule; as a reflection that does not exist *formally*, but that does occur. We can, for instance, reflect that "fiction" constantly incompletes or undetermines the theory from which it is born, and that "theory" does the same to the fiction that bears it. But when we seek to know what form this reflection could have, and why and how it imposes itself, we find ourselves, whether we like it or not, in the unstable region of *Witz*, of practical gaming, of linguistic materiality. This "region" should not be unrecognizable: for this necessity of the occurring of reflection also takes historically the form of a movement toward and within psychoanalytic language (and practice), which poses as a literary matter that its object of inquiry is not (only) a concept, but the becoming-concept of its incompleteness as a field riven by the occurring of transference.[37] It is here, precisely at the opposite point from where Laclau and Mouffe introduce the notion of suture in their argument, that the seduction of psychoanalysis in the form of a meditation on *transfert* arises in Althusser. The language of psychoanalysis, and in particular its notoriously *divided* relation to the figure of the woman, then provides a way to return to the question of the "effectivity" of a structure upon its elements; to argue that any reflection upon agency has to be understood outside of the horizon of the ultimate arrival of the concept, that is, outside of the apocalyptic

---

37. On the relation between Althusser's Marxism and psychoanalysis, see especially Warren Montag's "Marxism and Psychoanalysis: The Impossible Encounter," *Minnesota review* N.S. 23 (Fall 1984): 70–85. I understand Montag's stress on the complex, analogous materiality of ideology and of the unconscious as complementing my suggestion about the role of transference in incompleting both sides of the "encounter."

horizon of a dialectic; to pose that the concept, like a symptom, is always born, always arrives, both too late and too soon.

The witticisms, hesitations, and imponderables at issue in the autobiographies as in the work on Rousseau may then reflect an anxiety about the concept in its *psychoanalytic* usage, and about the seductiveness and violence of psychoanalytic language more broadly (both as it might draw Miller, the student "with the most fixed ideas on the subject," away from Althusser and towards Lacan or Lacan's daughter, and as it might serve to seduce or chase, hunt, do violence to Althusser himself). Jacques-Alain Miller's work was indeed construed, as Elizabeth Roudinesco shows, as designating the juncture *between* Althusser and Lacan, a place institutionalized and polemically named by and in the very *Cahiers pour l'analyse* in which the "Suture" essay would appear.[38] The line associating these moments to the *transfert* in the essay on Rousseau, and to the overdetermined appearance of psychoanalytic vocabulary there, is clear: what Miller "has," desires, or has produced should "belong to everyone"—the concept of metonymic causality, the "girl" who produces theoretical concepts weekly, and finally Judith Lacan and *through her and in her name* the language and the concepts of her father. The process of "embodying" concepts serves here to make them figuratively "proper" to a body (Judith Lacan and Miller, or Althusser, whose "talk on Lacan" was the occasion for Miller to announce his "discovery") just where this sense of property is most aggressively in question. The argumentative impasse is posed baldly: "And is it not the case that concepts belong to everyone?" the passage from *The Future Lasts Forever* rhetorically asks—answering both that "[Miller] too was capable of acknowledging someone else had invented and owned a concept," and that such a notion of property is "absurd."

The condition this impasse sketches is to a great extent our own as well, since it is now hard to tell in principle whether the language of psychoanalysis historically arises, like the miraculous figures of Minerva and of Materia, to complete a philosophical language that it also unfinishes, an effect of the doctrine of the concept and inseparable from it; or if it is culturally available to that end, independently and contingently. Like the system of concepts that we call Marxism, the

---

38. Serge Leclaire indeed shows that Miller's work is associated with a notion of an "unconscious concept" deriving from Freud, and concerning the nonidentical to itself. See Serge Leclaire, "L'Analyste à sa place?" *Cahiers pour l'analyse* 1 (1966): 51.

life, the concept or the desire we call "Althusser" and the practices of reading Marx outlined in the project of *Reading "Capital"* "belong to everyone" today precisely to the extent that "someone else" or "something else" has always "invented and owned" them. Here we must again depersonalize these reflections: for no "concept personnel" or "concept de sa vie" attaches to "someone" or "something else," as no allegorical form can hope to embody or represent it, him, or her. And yet Marxism today and in its futures remains the study of the legitimacy and conditions of possibility (material, conceptual) of such property *in general,* as well as the condition of possibility of its constant redistribution across the competing discursive fields of the social. As such, Marxism survives where the substituting of allegory for concept fails, where (on a different level) the circulation between concept and object is blocked: between "concept" and "personne" and between bodies and their concepts, as it were, where the nonidentity to itself of each fails to complete itself in the other, miraculous *Materia.* It survives as the reiteration of a *transfert* whose therapeutic "effects" can never become concepts, that is, as literature, as the language of psychoanalysis, or, more precisely, as the endless, disruptive birth or occurring of "deconstructive effects" where the concept of life and the concept of person seek to take meaning. The occurring of reflection is the name we give to Marxism's spontaneous labors: for if literature and psychoanalysis are born from the incompleting of its philosophy, it is no less true that the concept of a philosophy for Marxism is born at the same moment from the incompleting—the *deconstruction*—of literature and of psychoanalysis.

ANDRZEJ WARMINSKI

Hegel/Marx: Consciousness and Life

> *For the philosophers relationship = idea.* They only know the relation of 'Man' to himself and hence for them, all real relations become ideas.
>
> *Verhältnis für die Philosophen = Idee.* Sie kennen bloß das Verhältnis 'des Menschen' zu sich selbst, und darum werden alle wirklichen Verhältnisse ihnen zu Ideen.[1]

To begin reading the Hegel/Marx relationship, we may as well start with their differing versions of the relation between consciousness and life: "It's not consciousness that determines life," writes Marx in a well-known sentence of *The German Ideology*, "but rather life determines consciousness" (37). If the sentence is well known, it is no doubt because both in its content and in its form, it expresses what we all know about Marx's relation to Hegel and the Hegelian philosophy: that is, an apparently straightforward substitution of "life," "real life," for "consciousness," for the primacy of consciousness in the understanding of the human being, by means of an apparently equally straightforward (chiasmic) inversion or reversal of the terms ("life" and "consciousness") in a hierarchical opposition or relation. Of course, in context the immediate targets of this operation are the *Young* Hegelians, but it is clear enough that they can *be* its targets because, despite their claims and pretensions, they do *not* challenge the primacy of consciousness (over life) and hence do *not* differ from the Old Hegelians (or, presumably, the Old Hegel). For despite their attempt to *criticize* everything—in particular the concepts of idealist philosophy—by taking it as the product of man's self-alienation in religious or theological projections, the Young Hegelians nevertheless agree with the Old Hegelians in their belief in the rule of religion, of concepts, of the universal in the existent world. In other words, because all they do is substitute one conscious-

---

1. Marginal note by Marx in Karl Marx and Frederick Engels, *The German Ideology*, vol. 5, *Collected Works*, trans. Richard Dixon et al. (New York: International Publishers, 1976), 91.

ness for another—for instance, a human, man-centered consciousness for a religious, God-centered consciousness—the Young Hegelians never challenge the primacy of consciousness itself. Rather than changing the world, they manage only to interpret it differently, that is, only to *know* it by means of another interpretation.

All this is indeed very well known. If I rehearse it here one more time, it is only in order to remind us that from the outset of *The German Ideology*, the main thrust of Marx's critique is directed against those who would *criticize* Hegel or the Hegelian philosophy by performing a species of inversion, of mere overturning, of setting the Hegelian philosophy back on its feet by substituting a purported materialism for a purported idealism. As *The German Ideology* never tires of telling us, a mere inversion does nothing to change either the terms inverted or the relation between them. A self-proclaimed "materialism" that defines itself as the symmetrical inversion and negation of idealism winds up being defined and determined by that idealism as its own determinate negation. This is pithily illustrated by Feuerbach's predicament: in short, because his stress on human sensuous existence, his conceiving man as an "object of the senses," is an abstraction from human "sensuous activity" in given social relations, Feuerbach winds up with an abstract materialism that cannot account for *men* as products of a history of production and hence cannot provide a "criticism of the present conditions of life." Whereas as soon as he does try to account for the historical conditions, Feuerbach has to have recourse to idealist conceptions:

> [Feuerbach] gives no criticism of the present conditions of life. Thus he never manages to conceive the sensuous world as the total living sensuous *activity* of the individuals composing it; therefore when, for example, he sees instead of healthy men a crowd of scrofulous, overworked and consumptive starvelings, he is compelled to take refuge in the "higher perception" and in the ideal "compensation of the species" (*ideelen Ausgleichung in der Gattung*), and thus to relapse into idealism at the very point where the communist materialist sees the necessity, and at the same time the condition, of a transformation both of industry and of the social structure. As far as Feuerbach is a materialist he does not deal with history, and as far as he considers history he is not a materialist. [*The German Ideology*, 41]

The dialectical edge of Marx's critique could not be clearer: an abstract "materialism"—the ahistorical reification of "man" and his sensuous existence—all too easily turns over into an equally abstract idealism.

Rather than being a critique of Hegelian absolute idealism, such a materialism only comes up with a more naive, because undialectical, precritical idealism.

The upshot would be that whatever Marx may mean by all the formulations that suggest a reversal or an inversion of the terms of a hierarchical opposition—like "consciousness" and "life," for instance—the one thing he *cannot* mean is a *mere* inversion, a *mere* reversal, for that is precisely the (non-)critique of Hegel performed by the German Ideologists who thereby fall back into a *pre*-Hegelian position. And, indeed, in the case of the life/consciousness relation, it is easy enough to see that for a dialectical thought, it makes no difference which determines which, as long as their relation remains one of determination. For Hegel—as for Spinoza—*omnis determinatio est negatio*, and therefore it does not matter whether consciousness is said to determine (*bestimmen*) life or life consciousness—as long as one determines the other, it is mediatable with it thanks to the work of the determinate negative. For life to determine consciousness means for it still to be the negation *of* consciousness, consciousness's *own negation* that needs to be negated in turn so that consciousness can verify and become itself, consciousness (and so that life can be relegated to an essential, necessary moment [of truth, of verification] of consciousness: consciousness = life sublated, *das aufgehobene Leben*, one could say). So: if Marx's statement that life determines consciousness (rather than vice versa) is going to make a difference, is going to mean anything different from the eminently sublatable differences of determinate negation, then both the nature of the terms ("life" and "consciousness") and the nature of the relation (of "determination" [*bestimmen*]) between them before and after the inversion need to be rewritten, reinscribed: Marx's operation cannot be one of mere inversion, mere overturning—that is what the Young Hegelians do and what he criticizes them for. Rather, it has to be an operation of inversion and reinscription—in short, a full-scale "deconstruction" of both consciousness *and* life and the "relation" between them. However symmetrical the chiasmic reversal may seem—and however parallel the determining (*bestimmen*) before the inversion and after the inversion—what Marx is actually saying (and *has* to be saying if he is to be Marx and not just another Young Hegelian or German Ideologist) is that life, real life, determines consciousness in a way that consciousness cannot master, cannot come up against as a merely, determinately negative object *of* consciousness, of itself *as* consciousness. In short, life *over*determines consciousness—it is made up of contradictions and a negativity, call it, that cannot be reduced to (i.e., mediated, sublated, into) one, simple, determined negation.²

We do not have to look far in *The German Ideology* to begin to determine what the nature of this overdetermination is. Life, the real life of human beings, is not biological, appetitive existence, but rather the product of a history of production: men distinguish themselves from animals not by consciousness, not by knowing, but by producing their means of subsistence. In other words, life is not a given, positive fact but rather produced by the labor of human beings who constitute themselves *as* human in this history of material production. Consciousness, on the other hand, is the (historical, material) *relation* of these human beings first to nature and then to other human beings—a relation that is historical and material because it is not one "mediated" by knowing (and all the determinations that come with it: subject and object, truth and certainty, in itself and for itself, etc.), but by the historical materiality of relations of production (and *its* determinations: like the division of labor, class divisions, etc.). It is no surprise, then, that according to *The German Ideology*, consciousness and its products, when they come into existence, do so as the "conscious expression" (*der bewußte Ausdruck*) or the "direct efflux" (*der direkte Ausfluß*) *of* these relations of production, what the text calls "the language of real life" (*die Sprache des wirklichen Lebens*) (*The German Ideology*, 36). Indeed, consciousness, when it comes on the scene, appears not as "pure spirit" but rather as "burdened" with *matter* "which here steps on the scene in the form of moving layers of air, sounds, in short, language" (43–44). Only if this language of real life is alienated from itself—only if in addition to the spirit (*Geist*) of real, material individuals a spirit apart (*einen aparten Geist*) is invented, only if a consciousness other than the consciousness of existent praxis is imagined—can consciousness free itself from the world and go over (*überzugehen*) by means of a species of metaphorical transport to the formation (*Bildung*) of "pure theory," theology, philosophy, morality—i.e., ideologies (45). Much is implied about language—about the language of a material spirit or a material consciousness as distinguished from the language of a ghostly redoubled *Geist* or consciousness apart,

---

2. For the distinction between simple and overdetermined contradiction, our reference is, of course, Louis Althusser, "Contradiction and Overdetermination," in *For Marx*, trans. Ben Brewster (New York: Vintage, 1970), 87–128.

the language of ideology—and not least of all a certain hint as to *why* a mere demystification of an ideological formation by an inversion always remains insufficient: that is, if the language of ideology is the projected figure for a second, spectral *Geist* or consciousness apart, then an interpretation *of* those figures that confines itself to unmasking them *as* figures, *as* projections, will only manage to uncover and return to the literality of the *Geist* or consciousness apart—a still abstract, reified consciousness like the sensuous consciousness of Feuerbach. This amounts to saying, in other words, that the language of ideology is what one could call an "allegorical" language: one that represents, figures, one thing but that actually *means*, signifies, points to, refers to, something else. Hence it can never be enough to unmask or demystify its phenomenal appearance, its figural, representational function—this would be to fall into the trap that ideologies set for critics. Rather, its allegorical, pointing, re-ferential (carrying back) function also needs to be *read* in its overdetermined historical materiality.[3] (Althusser's famous statement that "Ideology represents the imaginary relationship of individuals to their real conditions of existence" could be read as very much consistent with our account of it as an "allegorical" language. That is, ideology "represents" all right, but what it represents [in distorted form or otherwise] is *not* the real conditions, but rather the *imaginary relation to* those real conditions. This is why an operation of demystification can uncover only the *imaginary* relations and *not* the real conditions. A second operation is necessary to read not what ideology *represents*, but what it actually *means*.)

But that's easily said. That is, it may be easy enough to wield terms like "overdetermination" or "overdetermined contradiction" and to insist that what is necessary for Marx to become Marx is not only an inversion but also a "reinscription" of the life/consciousness relation; more difficult is to take the full measure of what lurks behind these more or less convenient ciphers or place-holders—ciphers or place-holders for what actually *happens*, what is historical and material in the reading (or the writing) of a text. In the case of the text Hegel/Marx, to say that what Marx performs is a "deconstruction" of the relation of consciousness and life in Hegel does not mean that there is a "deconstructible" Hegelian relation there "before" the operation (of inversion and reinscription) and a "deconstructed" Marxian relation there

---

3. Cf. Althusser, "Ideology and Ideological State Apparatuses," in *Lenin and Philosophy*, trans. Ben Brewster (New York and London: New Left Books, 1971).

"after" the operation (of inversion and reinscription). In fact, to think that about Hegel/Marx (or, for that matter, about deconstruction) is precisely German Ideology—the operation that "critiques" not Hegel but a caricature of Hegel, not Hegel as the text that *happens* (historically, materially) but Hegel as a cliché of intellectual history. For indeed if "Hegel" *were* just some kind of subjective idealist who reduces "life" to "consciousness"—all sensuous otherness to sublatable moments in the progress of self-consciousness to absolute knowing, to an utterly transparent self-consciousness of self-consciousness—then it would be hard to understand not only how such a Hegel could be Hegel (rather than, say, a relatively simple-minded Fichte) but also how Marx could ever have become Marx by critiquing (however "deconstructively") *such* a Hegel: that is, how Marx could ever have found the resources he needed in Hegel to become Marx, i.e. to *happen* (historically, materially) *as* Marx and not as a Young Hegelian.[4] In short, I am asking about that which would be the historical, the material, in, *of*, "Hegel," of Hegel's text. What is it that could be said to be *alive*, living, in Hegel's text? This "life" of Hegel's text—if it is understood in a Marxian (historical, material) sense—would be a life that exceeds consciousness by *over*determining it and hence a life that threatens to interrupt irrevocably the entire project of a "science of the experience of consciousness" or a *Phenomenology of Spirit*.[5] So: how do we read the life of Hegel's text, a life that would also be the death of the *Phenomenology of Spirit*?

The moment of what Hegel calls "life" in the *Phenomenology of Spirit* is very precisely determined, and, as it turns out, even thinking its *determinately* negative relation to consciousness is no simple matter. That is, "life" appears in one of the most difficult passages in the entire *Phenomenology:* i.e., the short introductory section to the chap-

---

4. That is, one of the "ingredients" that went into producing "Marx" (again, *as* Marx) would be missing. Cf. Althusser, "Marx's Relation to Hegel," in *Montesquieu, Rousseau, Marx, Politics and History*, trans. Ben Brewster (London: Verso, 1982): "Which means very schematically that Marx (*Capital*) is the product of the work of Hegel (German Philosophy) on English Political Economy + French Socialism, in other words, the *Hegelian dialectic* on: *Labour theory of value* (R) + *the class struggle* (FS)" (170).

5. "Science of the Experience of Consciousness" is, of course, one of the titles of the book that came to be called *The Phenomenology of Spirit*. On the question of the titles, see: Otto Pöggeler, "Zur Deutung der Phänomenologie des Geistes," in *Hegels Idee einer Phänomenologie des Geistes* (Freiburg/Munich: Karl Alber, 1973), and my "Parentheses: Hegel by Heidegger," in *Readings in Interpretation* (Minneapolis: University of Minnesota Press, 1987).

ter on "Self-consciousness" entitled "The Truth of Self-certainty." This eight-page passage is *so* difficult, in fact, that many otherwise diligent commentators simply give up on it—sometimes very explicitly—and prefer immediately to go over to the master/slave dialectic which is its result.[6] Those who do *not* just skip it and do manage to say something about it nevertheless do not really read it and instead content themselves with telling what *should* happen, what *must* happen, what *must have* happened, in order for us to understand why and how it is that we are reading about a fight for recognition between self-consciousness and self-consciousness that issues in one's becoming master and the other slave. But even a perfunctory account of what should happen or should *have* happened in the dialectics of life and desire cannot occult the fact of this section's absolutely crucial importance for the project of the *Phenomenology of Spirit*. The passage is crucial most obviously because it marks a moment of transition between the end of the section on "Consciousness" and the beginning of the section on "Self-consciousness." Marking *this* transition has particular importance because its burden amounts to being able to explain why and how self-consciousness *as* self-consciousness is possible. This explanation is absolutely necessary because it turned out that consciousness in order to be what it is—i.e., knowing as knowing something—has to be, has to have *already* been, in truth, in essence, *self*-consciousness, i.e., self-knowing. In other words, consciousness can be what it is only because it is essentially self-consciousness—self-consciousness in its truth—and hence self-consciousness is the new object of knowing that comes on the scene, appears, in this presentation of apparent knowing—the new object (which, clearly, is also a *subject*) of knowing whose claim to truth has to be examined and verified in turn. In short: self-consciousness *is*; what would it have to be in order to *be* (in truth, in essence, in itself, *an sich*) self-consciousness? Formally speaking, the answer is very easy: to go by the

---

6. One example would be Richard Norman in his otherwise very helpful and extremely clear *Hegel's Phenomenology: A Philosophical Introduction* (London: Chatto and Windus for Sussex University Press, 1976): "The section on 'Self-certainty' is extremely unrewarding, and since I find large parts of it unintelligible I shall say little about it. The one important point to be gleaned from it is the claim that in order to be conscious of one's own existence one must experience *desire*. . . . The experience of desire, however, does not constitute self-consciousness in the full sense. Why is this? In 'Self-certainty' Hegel offers a preliminary explanation, but the whole question is dealt with much more satisfactorily in the 'Master and Slave' section, to which we may now gratefully turn" (46).

model of the dialectical movement of consciousness, if the truth of consciousness is *self*-consciousness, the truth of knowing *self*-knowing, then the truth of *self*-consciousness, of *self*-knowing, would have to be self-consciousness *of* self-consciousness, self-knowing *of* self-knowing—in other words, a necessary redoubling of self-consciousness would be the necessary and the only *sufficient* condition of the existence of self-consciousness *as* self-consciousness. We all know this—this is indeed what *has* to happen in order to issue in the dialectic of master and slave—but, of course, what *we* know is in fact only the formal side, the formal aspect of the arising of the new figure (*Gestalt*) and the new object of apparent knowing (as the "Introduction" to the *Phenomenology* had put it).[7] The *content* of this new figure of apparent knowing has to be gone through, and this can only be done by the consciousness going through the experience of *knowing*, of thinking that first *this* and then *that* is the true object of a certain knowing—the experience of itself, consciousness, on the way to absolute consciousness, absolute knowing. We can't *tell* it what it has to be in order to be what it is but rather can only observe how on its own it comes to know what it is in and for itself. How does it?

It does it by becoming desire (*Begierde*). That is, when self-consciousness arises as the new object, the new truth, the new in-itself, of consciousness, it appears as *desire:* self-consciousness is first of all desire. Why so? To paraphrase the second paragraph of "The Truth of Self-certainty": When the truth of consciousness turns out to be self-consciousness, knowing as the knowing of an other (*Wissen von einem Andern*) turns out to be knowing of itself (*Wissen von sich selbst*). In this dialectical movement of the experience of consciousness, the *other* that consciousness claimed to know in truth would seem to have disappeared—knowing of an other has become knowing of itself. But the moments of this other (of knowing) have at the same time been preserved, they are in fact present as they are in themselves, in their essence—which essence consists of their being essentially (in truth, in themselves) disappear*ing* essences (*verschwindende Wesen*), essences

---

7. See the end of the "Introduction" to *Phenomenology of Spirit*, trans. A. V. Miller (Oxford: Oxford University Press, 1977): "Thus in the movement of consciousness there occurs a moment of *being-in-itself* or *being-for-us* which is not present to the consciousness comprehended in the experience itself. The *content*, however, of what presents itself to us does exist *for it;* we comprehend only the formal aspect of that content, or its pure origination. *For it*, what has thus arisen exists only as an object; *for us*, it appears at the same time as movement and a process of becoming" (56).

whose essence is to disappear, or, better, to *be* disappearing. As such, these essences are preserved as *moments* of self-consciousness—a self-consciousness that (as the result of the dialectic of consciousness) has turned out to be a reflection out of the being of the sensuous and perceived world and essentially a return out of other-being ("Aber in der Tat ist das Selbstbewußtsein die Reflexion aus dem Sein der sinnlichen und wahrgenommenen Welt und wesentlich Rückkehr aus dem Anderssein"). "It [self-consciousness] is as self-consciousness movement (Es ist als Selbstbewußtsein Bewegung)." But—and this "but" articulates the negative moment in the dialectic of what will shortly be given the name "desire"—but since these essences of other-being are essentially disappearing essences, the movement of self-consciousness out of the sensuous and perceived world and of return out of other-being remains a tautologous movement in which it goes out from and comes back to only itself because it differentiates *only* itself *as* itself *from* itself. The differentiation between itself and its other-being *is* not, has no being, and hence it falls back into the movement-less tautology of the "I am I." And *as* bereft of *movement*, it *is* not self-consciousness, since *as* self-consciousness it is movement.

This dialectic is in fact already the dialectic of self-consciousness as desire. That is, self-consciousness is here desire because it appears under the sign of a double lack, a negativity proper to itself as desire. In brief: because self-consciousness at this (preliminary) stage has only itself, the unity of the tautologous "I am I," as its truth, it does not have an other-being that, simply put, is *other* enough for it to be able to verify itself (the unity of the "I am I") in it, to make itself *true* in an essence (an in-itself, a truth) that would have enough *being*, enough existence, to verify self-consciousness, that is, an essence whose own being, truth, in-itself, essence, did *not* consist in being a disappear*ing* essence. Hence it is desire: desire first of all for self-verification in an other that would be other enough as its own other—the other *of* itself (i.e., the unity of the "I am I"), of self-consciousness. The other-being of the other of itself, self-consciousness, as desire always turns out to be not *other enough:* it is in fact all too easily annihilated, sublated, like the object of an appetitive desire for nourishment. Take the potato. The two moments of self-consciousness as desire can be demonstrated on it—before and after eating. First, there is the moment of other-being (*Anderssein*). I recognize myself in the otherness of the potato: this is my potato in which I can recognize myself, verify myself, it is my other, etc. In this case—before eating—I depend on an other external to me, to the "I," for my identity, and therefore I cannot recognize myself in it *as* a self, *as* an "I." I can recognize myself in it only *as* a potato. The "I" becomes a potato—i.e., *not* a self-consciousness. Then, there is the second moment: the unity of self-consciousness with itself, the "I am I." That is, I eat the potato, thereby annihilating its otherness, negating the negativity of its other-being; but, in doing so, I also negate that in which I recognized myself, the other on which I depended to verify myself (albeit as a potato), and hence I am thrown back on my sheer self, the empty, movementless tautology of the "I am I." In short, I negate myself not *as* a self but as a potato—i.e., *not* a self-consciousness. In the first moment—before eating—the other-being of the other is *too* essential, that is, it negates me too immediately to be, to allow me to be, the negation *of* self-consciousness. In the second moment—after eating—the other-being of the other is not essential enough, and my negation of its otherness is too immediate. So: in the first case, the potato negates self-consciousness too immediately; in the second case, I negate the potato (*my* negation) too immediately. In the first case, I revert to the position of mere *consciousness*—i.e., that for which the truth of knowing is the otherness of the sensory outside—in the second case, I remain a merely one-sided, abstract, tautologous *self-consciousness*. What's the point? The point is that the potato is not yet essential enough for self-consciousness. That is, it is essential enough for self-consciousness *as desire,* but not for self-consciousness *as self-consciousness.* And the point becomes clearer perhaps once we recall that the objects of desire, of self-consciousness as desire, are *living,* are *life.* The potato I desire to eat is the object of self-consciousness as living and desiring—in fact, as desiring to live—and not of self-consciousness as self-consciousness, as self-knowing. This means that in the potato, for example, life is not yet essential enough for self-consciousness. And this sentence has to be read in two registers, as it were, according to two emphases, two stresses: either on the word "self-consciousness" or on the word "life." On the one hand, we need to emphasize the word "self-consciousness"—life is not yet essential enough for *self-consciousness*—that is, life may be essential enough for self-consciousness as living and desiring, but since the essence (truth, *an sich*) of self-consciousness is not the otherness of life but rather the unity of itself with itself (the "I am I"), life *cannot* be essential enough for *self-consciousness.* But, on the other hand, we need just as much to emphasize the word "life"—*life* is not yet essential enough for self-consciousness—that is, until self-consciousness can make *life* essential for itself *as* self-consciousness, it cannot become truly self-consciousness but rather remains at the stage of the tautologous "I am I," the merely immediate unity of itself with itself. Now the first hand—the stress on the word "self-consciousness" (Life is not yet essential enough for *self-consciousness*)—would certainly be obvious enough in the case of an idealism that would want to dissolve all non-conscious otherness, all merely living existence, into knowing, consciousness, mind, spirit, etc. It is no wonder that life would not be essential enough for *self-consciousness!* But the second, other hand—the stress on the word "life" (*Life* is not yet essential enough for self-consciousness)—should make us pause a bit and elaborate its considerable implications. Namely, first of all, there is the inescapable fact that whatever is going on here in the dialectics of desire and life does not conform to the received idea of idealism. The burden of the passage is not at all a matter of self-consciousness' attempt to rid itself of any otherness that it cannot reduce to itself, but rather, if anything, precisely the opposite. That is, self-consciousness does indeed have to rid itself of all *merely immediate* otherness (because such other-being does not have enough existence, enough essence—it is a merely apparent, i.e., merely *disappearing,* essence), but in order that it may make otherness essential for itself. In short, it is not trying to annihilate, negate, the potato—it can do that easily enough, immediately enough, by eating it—but rather to make the potato essential, other enough, for self-consciousness. *Life* itself has to become (essential for, the essential other of) self-consciousness.

Another, more general, way to put this is to say that Hegel here does not take the "easy" idealist way out. He does not begin with some kind of absolutely self-positing "I" that can then take all "non-I" as its own negation, but rather arrives at idealism's formula "I am I" as the result of a dialectical movement of the experience of consciousness. And, to boot, *this* self-consciousness, whose truth (essence) is the unity of the "I am I," is not one that can be satisfied by, or verified in, an immediate negation of its other-being. No, it has to make its other-being—the object of self-consciousness as desire that is life—essential for itself, it has to show how it is that self-consciousness can emerge out of life itself, how self-consciousness *as* self-consciousness can emerge out of self-consciousness as desire (whose object is life). This is indeed quite a task that the *Phenomenology* has imposed on itself (by a dialectical necessity) at this point, and the enormity of the stakes has not gone unnoticed in the commentaries, especially in the "anthropologizing" or "existentialist" interpretations of readers like Kojève and Hyppolite, who see the *enjeu* as the question of how man, the human being (which they identify [too quickly] with self-consciousness), can emerge out of merely biological, appetitive, desiring, animal being.[8] How indeed? How will "life" itself become the essential other of self-consciousness—again, the essential other of self-consciousness *as* self-consciousness and *not* of self-consciousness *as* desire? How can life by itself produce, as it were, *its* other *as* self-consciousness? And lest we think that the answer is easy—as "easy" as the answer to the question of how self-consciousness is possible—and answer that the only way self-consciousness can emerge out of life *as* self-consciousness and *not* as desire is precisely by a negation of itself *as* desire, i.e., by means of a "desire of desire," let me say straightaway that this is *not* what happens in the Hegel. It may indeed be what *should* happen, what *must* happen, what *must have happened*, in order for us to arrive by the end of "The Truth of Self-certainty" at the stage of a self-consciousness for a self-consciousness, but . . . it is in fact not what happens in Hegel's text. What in fact happens is weirder, odder, more *over*determined, hence something that produces a "Hegel" other than the successfully Hegelian Hegel of Kojève and Hyppolite. Let me begin to spell it out.

What happens is this: in order to demonstrate how it is that life—the object of self-consciousness as desire—can in fact become an other essential enough for self-consciousness to emerge *as* self-consciousness out of it, Hegel's argument goes over to the one side of the dialectic of desire—namely, its object, life—and presents its dialectic. The burden on this presentation is clear: it has to be able to show that life itself, the object of self-consciousness as desire, undergoes the same movement, the same process of reflection, into itself, as consciousness did in becoming self-conscious by a reflection out of the sensuous and perceived world and a return from other-being. In other words, self-consciousness is going to have to make the experience of the independence of its object—life—and learn that life is in fact independent enough—other enough, say—as independent as self-consciousness at this stage. And *for* it to be independent enough for self-consciousness, life is going to have to be shown to be self-negating enough for self-

---

8. See Alexandre Kojève, *Introduction à la lecture de Hegel* (Paris: Gallimard, 1947) and Jean Hyppolite, "The Concept of Existence in the Hegelian Phenomenology," in *Studies on Marx and Hegel*, ed. and trans. John O'Neill (New York: Harper and Row, 1973).

consciousness: it will have to negate itself just as self-consciousness does at the stage of desire. This is indeed what takes place, and it is certainly no surprise that it does so, for it is based on the most important element of Hegel's phenomenological presentation of apparent knowing: namely, the fact that for this presentation, knowing is always essentially knowing of something, of an object and a truth that are always determinately *the* object and *the* truth of *that* particular form of knowing. In short, when the knowing changes, so does the object known, for a new object (of knowing) arises along with a new subject of knowing. So here if consciousness undergoes a movement of reflection into itself—i.e., it becomes self-consciousness as desire—so does its object—the apparently disappear*ing* essences of the figures of consciousness—undergo a dialectical movement of reflection into itself. And *how* it does so is for us of less interest here—in part because the dialectic of life amounts to something of a mirror repetition of what took place on the side of the dialectic of desire—than its result. To be brief, suffice it to say that in the end the determinations of life— like the subsistence and finitude of the individual and the fluidity and infinity of the genus—wind up going through a dialectic of self and other at least like that of self-consciousness as desire: a self- constitution and a self-annihilation of life like that of the desiring self- consciousness and its potato. And whereas eating was an apt analogy for this process in the one case, so procreation is an appropriate analogy in the other: that is, in procreating, the individual living being annihilates itself as individual by rejoining the infinite fluidity of the genus (*Gattung*) *and*, at the same time, also reproduces itself *as* individual living being in the progeny that is the result of this procreative act. (In summary form: "Thus the simple substance of Life is the splitting-up of itself into shapes and at the same time the dissolution of these existent differences; and the dissolution of the splitting-up is just as much a splitting-up and a forming of members" [*Phenomenology of Spirit*, 168].) Life, in the result of its dialectic—i.e., genus (*Gattung*), the universal reflected (and hence no longer immediate) unity of itself with itself—seems to be independent enough for self-consciousness insofar as it seems to be self-negating enough for self-consciousness.

But, sooner or later, one has also to ask: is it knowing, conscious— self-knowing and self-conscious—enough for self-consciousness? Or, another way to put it, does life when it negates itself, *know* that it negates itself in such a way (i.e., determinately) that its other will have to be knowing, consciousness, self-consciousness? Or, again, is there a necessity in life's self-negation (i.e., death!) that necessarily results in the production of knowing, consciousness, self-consciousness? Perhaps the awkwardness of the question can be lessened if we put it in the somewhat jocular terms of the analogy of procreation. In short, does the cat, for example, when it desires to eat and procreate know that what it desires is (essentially, actually) to dissolve itself into the genus (the cat-*Gattung*?) and yet dialectically be reborn as individual? I don't know about you—or the cat—but I prefer to leave the question open. And, as it turns out, so does Hegel—or, at least the "Hegel" that is the writing of the text. For, in fact, when the dialectic of life is finished up (in *Gattung*), when the argument is ready to take us back to the *other* side of the relation, namely back to self-consciousness, the text does not make the transition by means of a determinate negation that could mediate life and self-consciousness. Instead, what the text actually says is that life—in the result of its dialectic, i.e., genus (*Gattung*)—points to or indicates or beckons toward an other than it (life) is, namely consciousness, for which it (life) can be as this unity, or the genus ("... in diesem *Resultate* verweist das Leben auf ein Anderes, als es ist, nämlich auf das Bewußtsein, für welches es als diese Einheit, oder als Gattung ist") (*Phänomenologie des Geistes*, 138). The implications of this pointing of life toward, at, an other than itself are far-reaching, and I can only begin to outline them here. First of all, it means that whatever happens at this moment of transition, of return, from life back to consciousness and self-consciousness, the transition itself does not take place, is *not* said to take place, by means of a determinate negation. Consciousness here is not the *other* of life as its determinate negation but rather an other pointed to, indicated, beckoned to, referred to, by life. The argument that would demonstrate the possibility of the existence of self-consciousness (*as* self-consciousness) certainly *needs* this pointing operation to be that of a determined negation—and it needs to have this *other* of life be life's own other—but the *text* just as surely does not work this way, does not perform *this* operation. Rather what the text does is introduce something of a "linguistic moment" into the relation of life and consciousness and, in doing so, threatens to render impossible not only the emergence of self-consciousness (*as* self-consciousness) out of life but also the project of the *Phenomenology of Spirit* as such. Life's pointing introduces this threat because it opens the possibility of an unmediatable break or gap between life and consciousness: that is, if the "relation" between life and consciousness is "mediated," not by a determinate negation but, rather, by an act of pointing that can, perhaps, point to many living things (just as it can point to their "other," many dead things) but that, by itself, can never make the other of life—consciousness as consciousness, knowing as knowing—*appear*, then this "relation" would in fact be a disjunction, the falling apart of life and consciousness. And when life and consciousness are un-mediated or "de-mediated" in this way, then the possibility of spirit's appearing—the possibility of a phenomeno-logic of spirit's appearing in the phenomena of its own self-negations—would also be very much in question. It is in question because a linguistic act or function of pointing or reference cannot make anything *appear* unless it is itself phenomenalized, only if it is given a figure, a face, as it were, only if the *logos*, speech, is made to, *said* to, appear—only if speaking is said to appear, only if the speaking (*logos*) of the apparent (*phenomena*) is said to be the appearance of speaking.

But if the speaking of the apparent can turn into the appearance of speaking only thanks to the figural, rhetorical function or dimension of language, then the authority for this tropological substitution or transfer—this trope or figure—is most unreliable. It is unreliable because the only authoritative ground for this figure—a figure that would turn life (in its result, *Gattung*) into a determinate figure for consciousness—would be the system of consciousness itself, i.e., the system of (apparent) knowing, here taken as a *closed* tropological system (i.e., a system of substitutions and exchanges based on a *knowledge* of entities and their exchangeable properties). The only way to stabilize the figure that would turn life's pointing, referential function into a phenomenal appearance (and hence into an object that would be the determinate negation *of* consciousness) would be to ground it in the "proper sense" of consciousness itself: in short, to know "language" here, the "linguisticality" of life's pointing, on the model of consciousness ("proper") and its determinations. The trouble is, however, that the integrity and self-identity of the system of consciousness as a closed tropological system cannot be taken for granted here, for it is precisely the linguistic function of pointing or reference that is said to make *consciousness* possible and not vice versa. That is, according to the text, it is only by virtue of life's pointing that anything like "consciousness proper"—i.e., a system of consciousness that would include life *within itself* (as its own determinately negative other) and thereby constitute itself as a *closed* tropological system—can come into existence in the first place. Consciousness is the only thing that could authorize the trope that turns life into a reliable phenomenal figure for consciousness, but consciousness can emerge, be itself, i.e, *become* itself (self-consciousness), *appear*, only thanks to this trope. Since it is the very burden of this passage to demonstrate how consciousness, and thereby *self*-consciousness (i.e., consciousness in its truth), is possible in the first place as a system of knowing that emerges, as it were, out of life itself and thereby includes life within itself as its own other, consciousness cannot be called upon to validate and verify (as in "make true") this demonstration as though it were already existent in its truth, as though we already *knew* what consciousness was in its truth—*as though we had already verified it as self-consciousness!*⁹ How should we understand, how should we know, "language" on the basis of the model of consciousness, when "language" is that which is supposed to make consciousness possible in the first place? And if

---

9. The commentators who do not just skip over life's pointing in our passage and valiantly try to re-mediate the relation between life and consciousness (into a determinately negative relation) can do so only by having recourse, in one way or another, to self-consciousness, when the burden of this passage is precisely to demonstrate how it is that self-consciousness (*as* self-consciousness) is possible! One intelligent example would be that of Johannes Heinrichs in *Die Logik der 'Phänomenologie des Geistes'* (Bonn: Bouvier, 1974): "Wieso verweist das Leben auf die fürsichseiende, sich wissende Einheit? Der Übergang ist nicht ein solcher der Bewußtseinserfahrung, sondern ein solcher für uns. Selbst der Phänomenologe scheint hier aufgefordert, die Sache logisch zu nehmen, d.h. von der bloß ansichseienden substantiellen Einheit als Möglichkeit (Leben) zur fürsichseienden Einheit überzugehen, die das Selbstbewußtsein ist: als die sich selbst wissende und somit wissend-wirkliche Gattung seiner selbst" (176). Although to say that the transition takes place not for consciousness but rather for us is an ingenious solution, its questionable character becomes apparent when we remember *who* the "we" of the *Phenomenology* is. If we follow the rigor of Hegel's logic (in the "Introduction") to its end, it turns out that the "we" of the phenomenological presentation—who observe the progression of consciousness through the various figures of apparent knowing and who put themselves in by leaving themselves out—are not some vague "philosophical observer" or "phenomenologist" but none other than self-consciousness! This is so because the single indispensable determination of the "we" is "our" being those who give up the position of consciousness in relation to the consciousness "we" are observing when we realize that "our" relation to it is a relation *internal* to consciousness. In other words, "we" are the negation *of* consciousness, consciousness' *self*-negation, i.e., *self*-consciousness. But the positing of this "formal" self-consciousness has to be verified in turn when consciousness' essence and truth turns out to be self-consciousness, and this is precisely the burden of the dialectic of life and desire. In any event, a painstaking reading of the "Introduction" is necessary to demonstrate this, and we will do so in another essay. It should be noted, however, that many interpretations of the *Phenomenology* fall short of Hegel's rigor and precision because their understanding of the "we" is far too vague. For a helpful survey of various (insufficient) interpretations of the "we," see Kenley Royce Dove, "Hegel's Phenomenological Method," *The Review of Metaphysics* 23 (1970), 615–41.

"language" turns out to be a disjunction between reference (life's pointing) and phenomenalism (the appearance of consciousness as the determinately negative other of life), mediatable only by a trope that is necessarily aberrant because it is not grounded in any proper sense (but rather is an arbitrary imposition of sense), then "language" is here also that which makes consciousness *im*possible.[10] That the very "linguisticality" of this "linguistic moment" would prohibit the emergence of consciousness as the determinate negation of life is finally not all that surprising, for what Hegel's claim amounts to here is that the limit of life (i.e., in its result, *Gattung*), namely death, is the determinate negation of life and therefore can become the object of consciousness: death is, death becomes, consciousness, insofar as it is the limit of life that pushes consciousness beyond its own immediate existence to its (self-)mediated essence, self-consciousness. But, as Bataille and others well knew, death can become (self-)consciousness—that is, can *appear* as the limit (and therefore the determinate negation) of life rather than *occur* as the random violence of sheer exteriority—only thanks to a subterfuge, a spectacle, a comedy of sacrifice which will allow me both to die and, at the same time, to watch myself die.[11] The

10. Putting this disjunction in terms of "reference" and "phenomenalism" is intentional, for I want to mark explicitly the close relation between my reading here and Paul de Man's "definition" of ideology in "The Resistance to Theory" as the confusion "of reference with phenomenalism." See *The Resistance to Theory* (Minneapolis: University of Minnesota Press, 1986), 11. Indeed, the reading can be taken as just a commentary on or an elaboration of de Man's hints in this essay and in the short but very difficult reading of sense-certainty in "Hypogram and Inscription," also in *The Resistance to Theory:* "Consciousness ('here' and 'now') is not 'false and misleading' because of language; consciousness *is* language, and nothing else, because it is false and misleading. And it is false and misleading because it determines by showing (*montrer* or *démontrer, deiknumi*) or pointing (*Zeigen* or *Aufzeigen*), that is to say in a manner that implies the generality of the phenomenon as cognition (which makes the pointing possible) in the loss of the immediacy and the particularity of sensory perception (which makes the pointing necessary): consciousness is linguistic because it is deictic. Language appears explicitly for the first time in Hegel's chapter in the figure of a *speaking* consciousness. . . . The figure of a speaking consciousness is made plausible by the deictic function that it names" (41–42). For an extended reading of de Man on ideology, see my Introduction, "Ideology, Rhetoric, Aesthetics: An Essay for Paul de Man," to de Man's *Aesthetics, Rhetoric, Ideology* (Minneapolis: University of Minnesota Press, forthcoming, 1996).

11. See Georges Bataille, "Hegel, la mort et le sacrifice," *Deucalion* 5 (October 1955), 32–33: "Pour que l'homme à la fin se révèle à lui-même il devrait mourir, mais il lui faudrait le faire en vivant—en se regardant cesser d'être. En d'autres termes, la mort elle-même devrait devenir conscience (de soi), au moment même où elle anéantit l'être conscient. C'est en un sens ce qui a lieu (qui est du moins sur le point d'avoir lieu, ou qui a lieu d'une manière fugitive, insaisissable), au moyen d'un subterfuge. Dans le sacrifice,

subterfuge or comedy of sacrifice here consists in Hegel's wanting to turn an act of sheer linguistic imposition—indeed, the giving of a name (to death!): "In its result, at its limit, life points to an other than it is, call it consciousness"—into an apparent, knowable, reliable, phenomenal figure of consciousness. To put it as bluntly as possible: at the moment that Hegel's text says that life (in this result: *Gattung*) points to an other than it is, consciousness, "Hegel," or at least the Hegel who would want this to be a self-determination and self-negation of life— *this Hegel* hallucinates, he is seeing things, instead of death or *the* dead he sees ghosts (*Geister*). This Hegel is a *Geisterseher*, and the *Phänomenologie des Geistes* would be the confessions of a seer of ghosts, the speaking of the appearances of ghosts.

The idealizing nature of Hegel's impossible trope is nicely legible here in the word *verweisen*, to point. Even though Hegel presumably would never be caught trying "to grow grapes by the luminosity of the word 'day,'"[12] we can read him here, at least *this* Hegel, trying to make consciousness appear by the light of the verb *verweisen* which, conveniently enough, comes from the same roots as *wissen*, to know, and hence as *Bewußtsein*, and which ultimately comes from the same root (*weid*) as Greek *eidos*—"visible appearance," say—and *Idea*—visible appearance *as* visible, visibility as such. The proto-idealist operation is clear: the *Idea*, the spiritually (and truly) existent, is constituted (linguistically) by a (pseudo-)metaphorical transport from that which is visible for the sensuous eye of the body to that which is *in*visible, nonvisible, except for the nonsensuous eye of the soul—call it *Idea*. Like all such idealizing operations, this is an arbitrary act of linguistic imposition of meaning. And as an imposition, it works not by the determinate negation *of* the sensuous and physical but rather by a blind marking, naming, which is then taken as the mark or the name *of* the blindness, of the blindness as a negation of seeing and visibility, etc. In short, it is a catachrestic act, not a substantial metaphor at all but a "blind metonymy," as Paul de Man would put it,[13] a mutilated and mutilating metaphor that brings monsters into the world, precisely the monsters necessarily created by the language that does nothing so much as to figure our own self-mutilation by figures, our own

---

le sacrifiant s'identifie à l'animal frappé de mort. Ainsi meurt-il en se voyant mourir, et même en quelque sorte, par sa propre volonté, de coeur avec l'arme du sacrifice. Mais c'est une comédie!"

12. De Man, *The Resistance to Theory*, 11.
13. De Man, "Genesis and Genealogy (Nietzsche)," in *Allegories of Reading*, 102.

self-blinding as we go about our business giving legs, arms, feet, faces, mouths, and eyes to things that are legless, armless, footless, faceless, mouthless, and eyeless.[14] But the catachrestic nature of the aberrant trope that would "mediate" reference (as a function *of language*) and phenomenalism (reference taken not as a function of language but as an intuition) in this idealizing operation is not the point here. The point is rather that this idealizing operation—the phenomenalization of a linguistic function—would be quite clearly an ideological operation, and *ideo-logical* in the most basic sense: making speech appear, and appear as an *ideal* entity, which is ideological through and through (the representation of an imaginary relation to the real conditions of existence) because speaking, if and when it appears, does not "appear" as ghost or *Geist* but, say, as moving layers of air (in Marx's phrase) or as inscribed letters—that is, as historically, materially overdetermined, i.e., made up of contradictions that will not be returned to a master negation, a master dialectic, *dia-logos*, of determinate negation. In other words, although "Hegel" here might indeed want to be the German super-Ideologist who would transform life into consciousness, the text does not, cannot, make the mediation by self-negation of life and consciousness—of self-consciousness as desire and self-consciousness as self-consciousness. Instead, the text writes a "properly" linguistic moment into the workings of the dialectic of desire—"linguistic" because it amounts to the introduction of a moment of reference that can be phenomenalized, that can *appear*, only thanks to an aberrant trope (i.e., catachresis)—and thereby threatens not only to make the emergence of self-consciousness (*as* self-consciousness and *not* as desire) impossible but also to turn Hegel's history of the experience of consciousness into an allegory of the mutual interference and inevitable ideologization of linguistic functions.

But in *not* making the mediation, in being unable to make the transition between life and (self-)consciousness—except by way of a "linguistic moment"—the text introduces what could be called a material "moment" into "itself," indeed, the moment of text *as* text. "Material"—because it is a moment when "Hegel," the text, is simply too much of a materialist, too intent upon having (self-)consciousness emerge *out of life, from within life*, to "fake" the transition here (by saying something like: life determines or negates itself here in such a

---

14. On catachresis and its (self-)mutilations, see my "Prefatory Postscript: Interpretation and Reading," in *Readings in Interpretation: Hölderlin, Hegel, Heidegger* (Minneapolis: University of Minnesota Press, 1987), liii–lxi.

way that consciousness itself, the other or negation of life itself, appears). Instead, the moment is "material" because what "appears" is neither "life" nor "consciousness" nor the mediation by negation of the two but rather . . . what? . . . the text appears, or, more precisely, *text happens* here as a linguistic artifact, a bit of material produced by the workings neither of life and appetitive desire nor of consciousness and its negations but rather the *work* (in a fully Marxian sense) of language in its materiality—i.e., the irreducible referential function, its overdetermined potential for meaning, and its inevitable phenomenalization and ideologization in an aberrant trope. And *as* material, this moment is also truly "historical" in the sense that it is what *happens*— and it happens precisely because it will not allow itself to be inscribed *as* a moment into Hegel's history of the experience of consciousness, of the presentation of apparent knowing. (If it did allow it, it would by definition be a non-happening, a non-event, something whose role is to be *only* a moment in a process whose meaning is the [self-]negation of *all* moments *as* moments—i.e., whose meaning is the phenomenologic of the process itself.) If we are right about this historical/material moment—better: event, happening—of the *Phenomenology,* then *this* Hegel, the text, would be a Hegel much closer to Marx than most Marxists, and especially closer to Marx than those Marxists who go one better than Hegel, out-Hegel Hegel as it were, and do in fact accomplish the mediation of life and consciousness, of self-consciousness as desire and self-consciousness as self-consciousness.[15]

15. The most famous successfully "Hegelian" re-mediation of self-consciousness as desire and self-consciousness as self-consciousness—by means of a "desire of desire," i.e., by means of a rigorously "Hegelian" negation of negation—would, of course, be that of Kojève. The ironies attendant upon this interpretation are many: in being more Hegelian than Hegel and "succeeding" where Hegel "failed," Kojève winds up being closer to "Hegel" than "Hegel" is to "Marx." Ironically (but consistently and predictably) enough, Kojève's anthropologization of phenomenology—i.e., his identification of man and self-consciousness—ends up with neither man nor self-consciousness. That is, he ends up with the thesis of the end of man in either animal (or the automaton) or god, an utter falling apart of life and consciousness. See not only his *Introduction to the Reading of Hegel,* but also his correspondence with Leo Strauss published in Leo Strauss, *On Tyranny,* ed. Victor Gourevitch and Michael S. Roth (New York: The Free Press, 1991): "Besides, 'not human' can mean 'animal' (or, better—automaton) as well as 'God.'* In the final state there naturally are no more 'human beings' in our sense of an *historical* human being. The 'healthy' automata are 'satisfied' (sports, art, eroticism, etc.), and the 'sick' ones get locked up. As for those who are not satisfied with their 'purposeless activity' (art, etc.), they are the philosophers (who can attain wisdom if they 'contemplate' enough). By doing so they become 'gods.' The tyrant becomes an administrator, a cog in the 'machine' fashioned by automata for automata" (255).

But lest this "other Hegel"—a "Hegel" closer to Marx than to Hegel—get lost in my claims about "language," let me recapitulate why and how life's pointing makes such a difference—for Hegel, for Marx, and for us. Going back to the crucial sentence may be the most economical way to do this: ". . . in this result [namely, the *genus*, the simple *genus*] life points to an other than it is, namely toward consciousness, for which it [life] is as this unity, or as genus (*in diesem Resultate verweist das Leben auf ein Anderes, als es ist, nämlich auf das Bewußtsein, für welches es als diese Einheit, oder als Gattung ist*)." If we bracket the phrase "life points to an other than it is, namely" for a moment, the essential appropriateness and adequation to one another of life as *Gattung* and consciousness is clear: this result can be only *for* consciousness because it is indeed only consciousness that can have this result—i.e., life as genus, as *Gattung*—for it, for an object that is consciousness' own object. It is only *for consciousness* that life can *be* the "unity" (*Einheit*) that is genus (*Gattung*). This is certainly clear and understandable enough: life, that which is living, can be the identity of identity and difference that is genus only for a consciousness that *knows* this, that *knows life as* genus. But, however clear this relation of genus and consciousness may be, it is equally clear that the being of life for consciousness (i.e., genus) is not life's own for itself, it is not something that life can ever have as its own object, that could ever be a unity *for* life. No matter how much life may negate itself and no matter how much consciousness may want to recognize itself in this self-negation of life (as its own, consciousness' negation), the fact nevertheless remains that life *cannot* have itself as the unity that is genus for an object. In short, life cannot have itself as an object of consciousness—because, quite simply, life is *not* (yet) consciousness, and it is precisely the burden of this passage to demonstrate how it is that it (life) *can be* consciousness. Again: this result, the unity that is genus, can be only for consciousness. This is why life *points* and can *only* point to consciousness. That is, life can be only a sign for consciousness—it can only signify it, refer to it—because by itself it will never be able to go beyond the limits of its immediate existence, as Hegel had put it in the "Introduction" to the *Phenomenology*, except when it is forced to do so by an other: death.[16] And even though con-

---

16. Cf. Hegel's distinction here between that which would be death for "natural life" and that which would be the "death" of consciousness: "Whatever is confined within the limits of a natural life cannot by its own efforts go beyond its immediate existence; but it is driven beyond it by something else, and this uprooting entails its

sciousness may be able to make this other—death—its own other, a negation in which consciousness can recognize itself, *for life* this death remains always other, a sheer exteriority in which life will never be able to recognize itself. Again: this is why life *points* and has to point to an *other* than it is. And that this other will be, will *have* to be, consciousness—that which can have life as genus, and therefore death, for an object, for its own object, a negativity proper to it, consciousness— is most uncertain once we take the full measure of this pointing into account. Life may indeed point to an other than it is, but this other will necessarily be consciousness—the determinate negation of life—only for life in its result, the unity that is genus, that is, only for a life, the life, that consciousness can make its own object, only the life that can be (only) *for* consciousness. In other words, the last thing that Hegel's argument wants life to do is to point at an other than it is, for such a pointed-at other need not be a consciousness that would be the result of life's own self-negation (the essential, true, determinately negative other *of* life) but rather could be "simply" (that is, *over*determinately) other—an other other, as it were, that could as well be called "consciousness" but that would not be a consciousness mediatable with life (as its determinate negation, as its essential other). *This* consciousness would indeed be a ghost, and all the more ghostly because *when* it appears, it can appear not in symbolic incarnations or phenomenal figures for the spiritual but rather can only signify itself, point to itself, by a sheer act of signification when it converts sensory appearance into signs, allegorical signs, for itself.

If one could pinpoint this moment of arbitrary allegorical signification in the text's sentence—the moment when spirit, rather than appearing in phenomenal form, signifies itself in an allegorical sign—it would have to be when *"an* other" (*ein Anderes*) that life is said to point to gets identified, determined, as the other that is and has to be

---

death. Consciousness, however, is explicitly the *Notion* of itself. Hence it is something that goes beyond limits, and since these limits are its own, it is something that goes beyond itself. . . . Thus consciousness suffers this violence at its own hands: it spoils its own limited satisfaction" (*Phenomenology,* 51). In a sense, at this moment of decision (i.e., cutting apart), Hegel here sets himself the task of transforming the sheer exteriority of death into a "death" proper to consciousness: in short, he has to transform death into consciousness. This is the "decision" that catches up to him in "the truth of self-certainty" and needs to be verified. It is no wonder that it "fails," for the sheer exteriority, otherness, of death can be transformed into the *self*-limiting of life only thanks to an impossible, aberrant trope.

consciousness: "Life points to an other than it is, namely to consciousness." It is in this "namely" (*nämlich*) perhaps that the mediation of life and consciousness is most legible as *not* a mediation by determinate (self-)negation at all but as a disarticulation of life and consciousness in the act of an arbitrary imposition of a name: life points to an other than it is—writes the text (and in doing so *over*determines this other as the [historical material] *product* of "the language of real life")—"namely consciousness"—says the dialectic of self-consciousness (and in doing so wants to determine this other as the determined other of a life that can be only *for* consciousness). So: instead of being able to mediate life and consciousness (and thereby bring us back to self-consciousness) by demonstrating how it is that life could not be life except *as* consciousness, the text converts life into an allegorical sign for consciousness—which points to an other than it is, call it consciousness. In doing so, it brings into "existence" a ghostly consciousness or *Geist* apart, as Marx might (did) put it (the Marx that, in a sense, read this passage in Hegel very well), *not* consciousness as the product of the historical materiality of the *work* of Hegel's text, but the shadow consciousness that would phenomenalize itself and appear *as* the essential (determinately negative) other of life, life's own negation, death itself. This ideological consciousness—or, better, consciousness as ideology[17]—nevertheless always bears the marks of its material production—and these marks, like life's allegorical pointing, can always be read in turn on the body of the language of ideology—*not* in what that language represents but in what it points to, signifies, refers to: an allegory that itself has to be read allegorically in turn. This is especially the case here in the *Phenomenology of Spirit* at the moment when life catches up with consciousness, as it were, and demands that the arbitrary decision between man as a living creature (the object of anthropology) and man as knowing, as consciousness (the object of phenomenology)—a decision that one might as well locate in the very first sentence of the Introduction to the *Phenomenology* ("Es ist eine natürliche Vorstellung, daß . . . " or, to paraphrase loosely, "There is

17. See Louis Althusser, "On Marx and Freud," *Rethinking Marxism* 4/1 (Spring 1991): "In the category of the self-conscious subject, bourgeois ideology *represents* to individuals what they *must be* in order for them to accept their own submission to bourgeois ideology . . . *consciousness* is *necessary* for the individual who is endowed with it to realize within 'himself' the unity required by bourgeois ideology, so that every subject will conform to its own ideological and political requirement, that of unity, in brief, so that *the conflictual violence of the class struggle will be lived by its agents as a superior and 'spiritual' form of unity*" (24–25).

knowing, consciousness; what does it have to be to be what it is, for it *is?"*)[18]—that this decision (or cutting, *Unterscheidung*) be accounted for. The account offered by the text is to be read allegorically, for it is itself an account of allegory—the allegory of allegory, one could say— the story of how consciousness at the stage of self-consciousness as desire needs to verify itself (as itself) in the disappearing essences that are the (sublated) objects of consciousness and how its attempt to do so fails and has to fail. It fails because the attempt to verify self-consciousness in disappear*ing* essences can only make self-consciousness itself disappear, or, better, itself *be* disappearing. In fact, it would not be going too far to say that this constant, persistent, disappear*ing* is the very "truth"—the very *allegorical* truth—of self-consciousness. Its disappearing essence is the truth of this infinitely (or rather [irreducibly] finitely) unhappy self-consciousness[19] because the only way it *has* to appear, to verify itself as itself in an other that appears, is to mark, signify, point to, itself by converting this phenomenal other into an allegorical sign for itself. But as an always disappear*ing* essence, this sign can ultimately be the sign only for self-consciousness' own disappear*ing* essence, its constant wearing away and wearing down, the ceaseless erosion of material history.

---

18. On the first sentence of the "Einleitung" to the *Phenomenology*, see my "Parentheses: Hegel by Heidegger," in *Readings in Interpretation: Hölderlin, Hegel, Heidegger*.

19. That our reading should, in a sense, collapse the *first* figure of self-consciousness (i.e., desire) and the *last* figure of self-consciousness (i.e., the unhappy consciousness) is no accident, for the disarticulation of the dialectic of life and consciousness would indeed mean that self-consciousness gets stuck here, as though in a stutter or a "syncope" that can only repeat allegories of its self-erosion, the impossibility of constituting itself as self-consciousness.

ETIENNE BALIBAR

The Infinite Contradiction[1]

In the short time allowed for this presentation, I will provide you neither with a summary of what you have read, nor with a framework for whatever questions you may eventually want to pose. I will try instead to review the general issues whose insistence I now recognize, after the fact, in many of the texts that make up this file. What I am suggesting is not that these issues derive from some simple initial idea, but that a number of their hypotheses and formulations can now, I believe, be inserted in an on-going project. For the most part, this series of works has been driven by events and summations (or by events that I perceived to be summations), which means that it is governed by disparity and abounds in palinodes. I could try to confer a fictitious unity on these works, but that would not deceive anyone. Still, I would like to suggest that the necessity of presenting them together, and thus of linking them, comes at a moment when (maybe for the first time) I believe—and the feeling may turn out to be an illusion—that I am able to understand, in light of today's questions, what was and may remain of interest about, and some of the presuppositions of, the issues formulated twenty or thirty years ago in circles to which I belonged, and which have not all vanished, at least not as far as *I* am concerned.

Therefore, I would like this review to revolve around three themes: *philosophical practice*, the *construction of the subject*, and the theme

---

1. Except for the initial acknowledgments, which have been cut, this is the same paper I read to present the body of my work during my Research Director *habilitation* on 16 January 1993 at the Université de Paris I. Members of the jury included Olivier Bloch (Research Director), Paulette Carrive (President), Georges Labica, Gérard Lebrun, and Alexandre Matheron.

YFS 88, *Depositions,* ed. Lezra, © 1995 by Yale University.

of *structural causality* and historical materialism. I will try to conclude with a few remarks or questions regarding the maxims of an ethics that seems indispensable to me when one proposes, with Marxism, but also against it, that there are truth effects in politics.

I. WRITING AND CONJUNCTURE

Philosophy *is* indeed a practice, even if it is not *practice* itself. To add that this practice is essentially "theoretical" is a useful but insufficient precision. It arms us in advance against the risks of empiricism or subjectivism that are bound to arise out of the inevitable use of such words as activity, operation, intervention, experience, and work. It also prevents us from getting lost in a pointless discussion on the means of overcoming (or, conversely, of preserving) the gap that is often thought to divide theoretical activities (especially philosophy) from practical activities—even in the form that consists in claiming that thought should be action and, therefore, nonphilosophical or postphilosophical, as with the Heidegger of the *Letter on Humanism*. Finally, it warns us that, if all practice requires matter exterior to it, this matter must nonetheless be transformed in a way that shows precisely its materiality as such, in the field of theory. Now, with regard to the undoubtedly diverse ways and means of such a truly philosophical transformation (a paradoxical one, to be sure, since in a sense it must be a nontransformation or, to parody Wittgenstein, a transformation that *leaves things as they stand*, which is to say, a transformation that *returns them to where they stood*) and notwithstanding any idealization, the expression "theoretical practice," in its generality, does not yet tell us anything specific.

In the essays you have before you, I have tried to practice philosophy in a way that is surely not the only possible one, but that unquestionably assembled and addressed matter—a great deal of it—much of which came and still comes from outside what is officially defined as philosophy. And yet as I was reading, rereading, or translating philosophers among whom I was hoping to find my material or whose secrets I was hoping to whatever degree to penetrate (Kant, Marx, Spinoza, Descartes, Wittgenstein, and Fichte, among others), I formed a notion of the way they themselves practiced philosophy: frankly, no philosopher has held any interest for me as long as I was aware only of his ideas, and not of his practice. From the confrontation between what I was trying to achieve and what I perceived of our models, I drew a hypothesis about the specific modality of theoretical practice in philosophy. I would put it this way: philosophy constantly endeavors to untie and retie from the inside the knot between conjuncture and writing, or if you will, it works from within the element of writing to untie the elements of conjuncture, but it also works under the constraint of conjuncture to retie the conditions of writing. This is the double materiality, both indissociable and heterogeneous, that I will briefly try to characterize by going back to some of the themes and examples that are scattered here and there in these texts.

I hold, then, that philosophy is never independent of specific conjunctures. It should be clear that I use this word in a qualitative rather than a quantitative sense, stressing by it the very brief or prolonged event of a crisis, a transition, a suspense, a bifurcation, which manifests itself by irreversibility, i.e., in the impossibility of acting and thinking as before. Without necessarily using this terminology, but always trying precisely to tie from within the register of the event and that of the theoretical intervention (however indirect, and however much performed primarily in the field of theory itself), I have analyzed a number of exemplary, even privileged conjunctures—for instance, the reversal of the relations between the State and the labor movement, which Marx and Engels "answered" by means of the "rectification of the *Communist Manifesto*,"[2] of the tendential change from the conception of "the party as conscience" to that of "the party as organization,"[3] and of the distinction between *classes* and *masses*;[4] or the Orangist Revolution of 1672, which can be interpreted, after the fact, as the Dutch aristocracy's abandoning their efforts to organize the world economy into a free-trade network, which Spinoza "answered" by substituting a "science of the State" for a "democratic manifesto," i.e., by moving from an ethic of freedom of expression to an ontology of absolute power.[5] Finally, I have analyzed both the annihilation of German freedom under Napoleon, and the resistance it occasioned, including Fichte's *Addresses to the German Nation*, both a stab at resistance and

2. Etienne Balibar, *Cinq études du matérialisme historique* (Paris: François Maspéro, 1974). [All other notes below refer to works by Balibar, unless otherwise indicated—Editor's note.]
3. *Marx et sa critique de la politique* (in collaboration with Cesare Luporini and André Tosel) (Paris: François Maspéro, 1979).
4. See "The Vacillation of Ideology" and "Politics and Truth," in *Masses, Classes, Ideas: Studies on Politics and Philosophy Before and After Marx*, trans. James Swenson (New York and London: Routledge, 1994), 87–123; 151–74.
5. *Spinoza et la politique* (Paris: Presses Universitaires de France, 1985).

a way to escape the repetitions of the *Wissenschaftslehre* and to offer with the expression "interior border" a concrete solution to the aporia of the self and the "non-self."[6] But individual examples are not the only ones: *collective* examples, i.e., examples that show how philosophers see their discourses internally connected to one another (and connected to nonphilosophical, e.g., theological, legal, scientific discourses) in the same conjuncture, are in a sense more significant. For instance—and bearing in mind that these are in part the same examples as those given above—"the invention of consciousness" in the conjuncture of "1690" (the mechanistic or spiritualist Cartesians, Malebranche, Leibniz, and Locke);[7] the invention of the "subject of history" (or of "historicity") in the conjuncture of "1807–1809" (*Addresses to the German Nation, Phenomenology of Spirit,* and Schelling's "*Freiheitsschrift*").

Such a notion poses the immanence of philosophical work to history, but it is resolutely opposed to all the variants of the notion of *Zeitgeist,* or of the "culture" or "spirit" of a time, including the form that Marx's concept of "dominant ideology" gives it and the form Foucault gives it by means of the concept of *épistémè*. On the other hand, this notion seeks to link itself, freeing up the concept's critical and analytical potential, with Foucault's *points d'hérésie*—heretical points "shared by" a number of philosophies, insofar as these points designate in their very language what is at stake in their confrontation. Marx's "contradictions," Spinoza's "aporias," Descartes's "ambivalence," and so on, around which I have organized the study of their argumentations and concepts, should help to clarify one another as terms of a contradictory conjuncture and as reflection of these collective *points d'hérésie at the heart of* each philosophical discourse. This is why I proposed, in reference to Fichte, that "the philosophical text carries to an extreme contradictions that go beyond it, but that nowhere else find so constricting a formulation."

This leads us to the second point: not only do philosophers always write *within a conjuncture,* but conversely, within the conjuncture, *they write.* They "think," no doubt (how could they not?), but only through writing and in constant confrontation with the problems writ-

---

6. "La Frontière intérieure. Réflexion sur les *Discours à la Nation allemande* de Fichte," *Cahiers de Fontenay* 58/59 (June 1990). An English translation appears in *Masses, Classes, Ideas,* 61–84.
7. "L'invention de la conscience: Descartes, Locke, Coste et les autres," in *Traduire les philosophes,* ed. Olivier Bloch (forthcoming).

ing poses for them, while also benefiting from the terms and conveniences it offers. All philosophy is essentially written, and philosophers have a particular relation to writing that necessarily includes the issue of its forms, "technical" modes or genres (which Valéry rightly emphasized), or styles (which Granger rightly emphasizes). More: the philosopher's original relation to writing is determined especially by the fact that a singular experience of thought is always an experience of writing, and that "philosophical practice" is one that, consciously or not, seeks in and by means of writing to go back to the very constraints the latter imposes on thought.

I do not want to treat here the crucial question of knowing what happens to philosophers in their texts. Let me instead allude only to three increasingly constraining modalities under which I have come across it in my work:

First modality: *aporia*, in that it determines the need for a constant rewriting of the philosophical text. Allow me at this point to elaborate on the type of *incompleteness* [*inachèvement*] proper to philosophical texts—an incompleteness that my readings constantly illustrate, and that has led me to use the verb *to incomplete* [*inachever*] in the active form: Marx *incompleted* Capital (and toiled all his life to incomplete it); Heidegger *incompleted* Being and Time. At the risk of superstition, I have even proposed that there would be a certain logical benefit in reading the interruption of Spinoza's *Political Treatise* as if it were an active incompletion, comparable to that of the *Regulae* or *De intellectus emendatione*.[8] One might go even further and assert that the nature of a great philosophy is not only to incomplete itself, but to *incomplete others*, by introducing itself or by being introduced in their writing: thus, from the "Manuscripts of 1843" up to *Capital*, Marx prodigiously incompleted Hegel's *Philosophy of Right*. And if it is true that the regulating idea of "system" is fundamentally a modern version of the old *imago mundi*, the meaning of all these aporetic undertakings is, if not to "transform," probably *to incomplete the world*, or the representation of the world as "a world."

Second modality: *dispersion* or *dissemination*, understood as the fact that no philosopher can write "the same book twice," not only because every book is undertaken in order to try to overcome the apo-

---

8. "Spinoza, l'anti-Orwell—la crainte des masses," *Les Temps Modernes* 470 (September 1985): 353–98. An English translation appears in *Masses, Classes, Ideas*, 3–37.

rias of the previous one, whether by reversing its point of view or by introducing a difference—even, perhaps, an imperceptible difference—in its project, but because each writing experience is an unpredictable adventure. Derrida would say: writing is opening up a trace (for oneself), in which the concept is exposed to after-effects, to the backlash of words, and especially of its own *names*. I have tried in particular to demonstrate that each of Spinoza's three great books, each of his great theoretical practices, is a singular experience of writing that leads to *other propositions*. I am ready to attempt the same demonstration in regard to Descartes, Marx, Hegel, or Kant. This does not mean that a philosopher has no doctrine, but that this doctrine lies nowhere but in the intersecting [*recoupement*] of his or her different writing paths.

Hence, finally, a third modality underlying the first two: the *intersecting of the signifying chain itself*. This point, which seems to me particularly important, was the last of these modalities to become explicit, in the course of efforts to reread Descartes's statement: *Ego sum, ego existo*.[9] I had already used the same expression, however, in addressing the function of the word "dictatorship" in the history of the problem of the "dictatorship of the proletariat" in Marx and surrounding Marx.[10] And in many respects, the portmanteau word I fashioned in "La Proposition de l'égaliberté"[11] is my own attempt both to intersect a signifying chain and simultaneously to make its existence manifest. Again, I am not proposing here a general theory that is nowhere to be found in my essays, but rather drawing attention to a fact of theoretical experience: in the practice of philosophical writing, the words and propositions around which aporias crystallize and inventions take place always belong to long signifying chains; most often they constitute its element of *Unruhe*, of uneasiness or uncertainty—the one that constantly returns to the "origins," i.e., to the necessity for new uses and interpretations.

The odds are good, then, that an intrinsic relation exists between

---

9. "*Ego sum, ego existo:* Descartes au point d'hérésie," a paper presented to the Société française de philosophie on 22 February 1992, and published in the *Bulletin de la Société française de philosophie* 86/3 (July-September 1992): 81–123.

10. "Marx le joker—ou le tiers inclus," in *Rejouer le politique* (Paris: Editions Galilée, 1981); "Dictature du prolétariat," entry in *Dictionnaire critique du marxisme*, ed. Georges Labica and Gérard Bensussan (Paris: Presses Universitaires de France, 1982).

11. "La Proposition de l'égaliberté," *Les Conférences du Perroquet* 22 (November 1989); *Les Frontières de la démocratie* (Paris: La Découverte, 1992). A partial English translation of *Les Frontières* appears in *Masses, Classes, Ideas*, 205–25.

the intersecting or overt reversal of a signifying chain that *lets itself be seen* more or less cryptically in the fabric of philosophical writing, and, on the one hand, the radical alternatives or *points d'hérésie* that divide philosophers; and, on the other hand, the lines of demarcation or forms of collusion between philosophical and nonphilosophical discourses (or between the philosophical and the nonphilosophical aspects of discourses—for instance, scientific, legal, or theological discourse).

We must therefore think through together both determinations of philosophical practice: its necessary relation to conjunctures (which leads philosophical texts to organize themselves into sets that are themselves dependent on a conjuncture) and its relation to writing as a permanent short-circuit or short-cut between the immediacy of thinking and its longer history. These two determinations entail two distinct but equally constraining materialities.

I see this conjuncture first of all in the way philosophy formulates historical or experienced divergences that require choices to be made in the creation of words and in the stating of propositions. Philosophy poses these divergences in terms of antinomies and introduces universal antinomies into each particular writing. Next, I see it in the fact that the great philosophical moments are those in which theoreticians (concurrently and against one another) bring back into play, in the heat of the conjuncture, the very forms or categories of the theoretical, as Althusser might say. Finally, I see it in the indirect but unique capacity of philosophical writing to show why, although not unintelligible, a historical conjuncture (in the strong sense of the word) is nonetheless fundamentally unmasterable: it always contains even *more divergent positions* than any strategic representation can apprehend (this is why philosophers, at least seemingly, constantly "shoot at their own camp," be it revolutionary or conservative).

These observations lead me both to adopt the point of view of those who believe that a "hermeneutic of philosophy" is structurally impossible (which is not the case of a "pragmatics" of philosophy—a point on which I would agree with Pierre Macherey), and to assert that, if there can be no separation between philosophy and ideologies (and indeed, the "matter" we treat in philosophy is always, in a sense, ideological), there nonetheless remains between them a difference of practice. Unceasingly recreated, this difference of practice forbids any confusion between philosophy and ideologies. Let me then come to my second point.

II. THE CONSTRUCTION OF THE SUBJECT

With your permission, I will not justify at great length the fact that this part of my recent work, concerned with the comparative history of philosophy, turns upon the issue of the "subject" (more precisely, the confrontation between the notions of "subject" and "citizen"). Hints of this organizing question crop up in my earlier work, to be taken up again sooner or later. Foremost among these would be my attempt to reread Spinoza's *Theologico-Political Treatise* from the point of view of the "construction of the subject,"[12] which I undertook between 1982 and 1985. I could even go back as far as the notion of "forms of historical individuality," which in my contribution to *Reading "Capital,"* I argued to be a sort of touchstone for the relevance of structural Marxism—a notion that was, we can now agree, more a way of denying the need to address in specific terms the problem of the subject and the meaning of the concept, than a first sketch of or priming for such an engagement.[13] I should also mention, however briefly, the relation of complementarity between this and other investigations (which you have in hand and which fall within the province of political philosophy, if you will) concerning past and present forms of nationalism and racism, and more generally what Wallerstein and I have called *the intrinsic ambiguity of individual and collective identities*.[14] The meeting point of these issues of politics and the history of philosophy is finally the complementary light they try to shed on the moment of extreme uncertainty in which the intellectual and institutional figure of the "citizen" finds itself again today.

But all this will probably come up during our discussion. Let me instead give you some reference points about the origin of my work. What is the source of this incomplete investigation of the history of the concept of "subject" and, as a consequence, of the problems, forms, and meaning of anthropological questions in philosophy? It started with three successive moments of surprise, which I came to understand more clearly once they had reconfigured themselves around certain questions bearing upon conjuncture.

---

12. "*Jus, Pactum, Lex*: sur la constitution du sujet dans le *Traité théologico-politique*," *Studia Spinozana* 1 (1985): 105–42.
13. "The Basic Concepts of Historical Materialism," in *Reading "Capital"* (in collaboration with Louis Althusser, Pierre Macherey, Jacques Rancière, Roger Establet), trans. Ben Brewster (London: Verso, 1979), 201–308.
14. *Race, Nation, Class* (in collaboration with Immanuel Wallerstein), trans. Chris Turner (London: Verso, 1992).

First surprise: there exists in Spinoza a causal theory of the construction of the subject (what one might call an etiology of the subject), presented essentially as the theory of the "first kind of knowledge" in that it is also a way of life, a structure of behaviors and images that give meaning to individual and collective existence. It does not characterize *first person* discourse as a mere way of taking (a) place in the imaginary, but demonstrates that it is itself conditioned by the existence of symbolic narratives, institutions, and representations: "*Jus, Pactum, Lex.*"

However, not only is this etiology not merely a reduction of the subjective moment (from the point of view of philosophy itself), but it coexists with two (and maybe three) resurgences of the "subject" that can be identified with similar philosophical movements (at least by analogy), even though their unity is far from obvious. Here, I am thinking of the *Theologico-Political Treatise* and the insistent, irreducible reference to the *dictamen rationis,* or voice of reason, which is the basis for the establishment of the "regime of tolerance" that is both the goal of the State and the condition of its continued existence. I am thinking of the emergence of a transindividual subjectivity in the *Ethics,* understood as a practice of communication. The scientific use of "common notions" is no more than the base of such a practice, which also requires the sharing of certain active affects: the shared knowledge and love of bodies.[15] Finally, I have in mind the way the *Political Treatise* directs the analysis of the institutional mediations of the monarchic and aristocratic regimes or the double process of democratization of equality and liberty, not only toward a theory of collective power, but toward a theory of decision. Thus, it is Spinoza himself, master of all the great critiques of philosophical subjectivism (whether it be the epistemology of the "I think" or the ontotheology of creation), who discovers for us in each of his works a horizon of subjectivization: an unremovable remnant, but also the priming, the first moment of a movement to pass beyond such subjectivization. But he discovers it almost at the margins of his writing and according to three apparently incompatible modalities. First surprise, first puzzle.

Second, and to a certain extent, contrary surprise: there can be no doubt that Marx is, among other things (as Althusser helped us under-

---

15. "Spinoza: From Individuality to Transindividuality," a lecture delivered in Rijnsburg on 15 May 1993, forthcoming in *Medelelingen vanwege het Spinozahuis* 71.

stand), a philosopher of the subject in the most classical sense. More precisely, Marx is a philosopher of the self-construction of the subject and its liberty in and by means of revolutionary practice. From this point of view, Marx belongs to the great tradition of historical idealism, where he follows and intervenes at the same speculative level as Kant, Fichte, Hegel, even Schelling, clarifying finally (if it were indeed necessary to do so) the intrinsic relation between modern, Idealist philosophy of history and the trace of the revolutionary event as well as the anticipation of its accomplishment. All this is expressed quite clearly in the *Theses on Feuerbach:* and the schema thus constituted will never be refuted [*récusé*].[16]

Now, the category in which *we* spontaneously conceive this self-construction of the subject is obviously that of the "subject of history" —theme of the impassioned discussions of our youth. In Marx, the Proletariat is the subject of history—like Humanity in Kant, the People in the Fichte of the *Addresses to the German Nation,* or the World-Spirit in the Hegel of *Lessons on the Philosophy of History.* And yet, however much you may search for the "subject of history" in the young or old Marx, I challenge you to find it expressed *in so many words,* i.e., in its explicit theoretical wording. The term's absence "in the flesh" [*en personne*] (as Althusser would have put it) is not the only surprise encountered when Marx's texts are read *to the letter:* for you will be equally unable to find other expressions that, rightly or wrongly, have been attributed to Marx—for instance, "proletarian ideology" or "class consciousness." It is unquestionably in Marx's intellectual wake that we philosophize and write the history of philosophy in terms of *Subjekt der Geschichte.* This category, however, is nonetheless not to be found and may in fact be impossible in his writing, however clearly we think we discern it between the lines of many published or unpublished pages. Neither is it to be found in Kant, or in Fichte, or especially in Hegel— although again we cannot help but discern it between the lines. According to my preliminary investigations, the *inventor* of the "Subject of history" is none other than Lukács—quite specifically in *History and Class Consciousness.* And the round of debates on this issue, or of theoretical innovations related to this problematic, ends with Althusser's "process without subject."[17]

16. *La Philosophie de Marx* (Paris: La Découverte, 1993).
17. "Le Non-contemporain," in *Ecrits pour Althusser* (Paris: La Découverte, 1991), 91–118.

It is therefore a history quite internal to Marxist circles (although it is decentered and delayed vis à vis the development of Marxism), and yet of an order of necessity and universality such that all of the modern philosophy of history can no longer be perceived without at least an implicit reference to it. Second surprise, second puzzle.

The third and last moment of surprise comes when, distancing ourselves from the traditions of spiritualism, neo-Kantianism, Hegelianism, and phenomenology (which are convergent on this point), we ask ourselves when and for what reasons we *began to read in Descartes a philosophy of the subject and, a fortiori, of the "sovereignty of the subject,"* when, once again, such a term is radically not to be found in his writing—is, indeed, I think I have shown, impossible in his thought. I began to study the problem myself some years ago when Jean-Luc Nancy formulated, in deliberately paradoxical terms, a question that forced me to make old inquiries crystallize with new preoccupations and to take up, as much the enlightened amateur as I could be, areas of history or philology that philosophy has always in fact *presupposed.*[18] The question was "Who comes after the subject?" And the answer—to my mind, the inescapable answer, inescapable not in speculative or moral terms, but from the point of view of historical facts themselves— was this: *after the subject comes the citizen.* For the "subject," which has haunted the whole problematic of liberty and of the individual [*personne*] for fifteen centuries, is not an ontological figure, that of an *objectum* or *hypokeimenon,* but a legal, political, theological, and moral figure, that of a *subjectus* or *subditus,* i.e., a dependent, believing, and obedient individual.

What—or rather *who*—comes after the subject (first around 1789–93), is the universal, national, and cosmopolitical citizen who is indissociably both a political and a philosophical figure. And here my surprise, or, if you prefer, my third puzzle comes into focus: there is no doubt that with the revolutionary event the *subjectus* irreversibly cedes his place to the *citizen;* that the humility of the one who listens to the Voice of an external or internal "master" gives way in principle to the autonomy of a collective legislator: this break is recorded in the insurrectional *negativity* of the Proposition of Equaliberty as "*de jure* fact" and "truth effect," from then on ineffaceable even as they are

---

18. "Citoyen Sujet—Réponse à la question de Jean-Luc Nancy: Qui vient après le sujet?," *Cahiers Confrontation* 20 (1989). An English translation appears in *Who Comes After the Subject?*, ed. Eduardo Cadava, Peter Connor, Jean-Luc Nancy (New York and London: Routledge, 1991), 33–57.

denounced. Still, *nothing changes* (or very little), except for a slight displacement, inscribed in a play on words—although this play on words fits into a very old and long signifying chain almost indissociable from the history of universal languages and law in the West. I mean by this displacement the transition from the *subjectus* to the *subjectum*, or *Subjekt*. Nothing changes unless everything does, and *this* is the puzzling nature of what is called "modernity," for the individual can be a citizen effectively only if he or she *becomes a subject again*. It is to this end that institutions and discourses, including philosophical discourse, then seek a "psychological," a "moral," or a "legal" subject dissociated or united in the figure of the "transcendental subject," according to the schema that Michel Foucault characterized so aptly as the "empirico-transcendental doublet." Thus, for two centuries the history shared by institutions and anthropological discourse has been that of the *becoming-subject of the citizen* and of the denominations and conflicts of its "*subjectivity*"—an endless task, but always already under way, engaged, in truth, from the very moment of the break.[19]

I said that nothing (or hardly anything) changes, for, in this production of the citizen as subject or of the "subject Citizen," the *subjectus* is still and always present, submitting to the inner voice of "consciousness" that informs him or her of his or her responsibility. But I also said that everything (or almost everything) changes, for we know that the permanence and insistence of the *subjectus* in the *subjectum* in the last two centuries have only been possible in conjunction with and maybe under the domination of quite different modalities of subjectification and subjection. I am thinking here not of schemata of transcendence, but of immanent ones, like the inscription of the individual within the framework of norms, normalities, capacities, and disciplines—whose other face, as we know, is the individual or transindividual outcome of anomies, deviances, inferiorities, minorities, and incapacities.[20] I have in mind also mainly *communal* schemata that combine immanence and transcendence—in particular, the two great rival schemata of "nation" and "class," both secretly haunted by a third schema (the schema of "race") producing what we call identities through the play and investment of anthropological differences.[21]

19. "Ce qui fait qu'un peuple est un peuple: Rousseau et Kant," *Revue de Synthèse* serie 4, 3/4 (July-December 1989): 391–417.
20. "Crime privé, folie publique," in *Le Citoyen fou*, ed. Nathalie Robatel (Paris: Presses Universitaires de France, 1991), 81–104.
21. "Cultura e identità" (an Italian translation of the keynote speech for a confer-

154 *Yale French Studies*

Enough philology, however. What conclusions have I drawn from this investigation, some of whose themes I have just evoked? Let me offer two, and run the risk of being too cavalier after having been too fragmentary.

First of all, I have convinced myself, not that the question of the subject is or should be the specific object of philosophy—far from it; but nevertheless that *on the issue of the subject* (inextinguishable as such, and anything but circumscribed in an "age of subjectivity," precisely because it is not univocal) only *philosophical* work can be critical work. The history of the figures of the subject, of subjection, subjugation, subjectivity, and subjectification (we now know that all this is not "the same thing," but that it is the same problem) is to a certain extent nothing but philosophy ruminating on the great "historical play on words," *subjectus/subjectum,* and a few others that are closely linked to it, like *conscience/consciousness/self-consciousness* or *Gewissen/Bewusstsein,* or the double meaning of *Beruf* ("election" and "profession"). Philosophy has no metatheoretical position or external vantage point in relation to the signifying composites that constitute it. It is, however, quite illusory to rely on disciplines other than philosophy in order to display the margin of freedom or *capacity of variation* that these problematic notions conceal, and thus to point toward what I called earlier the contradictions or *points d'hérésie* of a conjuncture. Perfectly illusory, *unless,* under the name of this or that discipline, what is really taking place is philosophical work—as is the case, to offer some notable examples, in Max Weber, Kelsen, Mauss, Freud, Benveniste, and Lacan. Fundamentally, this criticism is always already philosophical, since, being immanent to writing, it can neither resort to an analytical metalanguage nor bring about a reduction to external processes. To put it concretely, this means that we will always learn more on this point from philosophers themselves (whatever they call themselves) than with the nonphilosophical users of philosophy for whom the philosophical text is merely an element of an archive or the reflection of another structure.

And this means that by rereading philosophers with "the greater force of the present," i.e., with the uncertainties and questions of *our* conjuncture, in which *we too* want to philosophize or, in Alain Bad-

---

ence organized by the Division de philosophie et des Sciences Humaines de l'UNESCO, Paris, on 14–15 December 1989), in *Problemi del Socialismo* 3 (1989): 13–34.

iou's wonderful expression, to "take another step" [*faire un pas de plus*] in philosophy, we are bound not only to rectify preconceptions but always to discover something new, perhaps even something unknown. Thus, after I thought I had made sure that the reading of Descartes as a "philosopher of the subject" and a "philosopher of consciousness" could only be a Kantian and Cousinian philosopheme, I had to ask myself what, in Descartes, occupied the space that had thus been as it were cleared out. I came to understand that it was the far more radical thesis of a *nonsubjective freedom*. This led me to surmise (contrary to what I—along with many others—had believed for twenty-five years on the strength of an almost unanimous French and German academic tradition) that Descartes and Spinoza were not that incompatible (as prototypes of the "philosopher of the subject" and the "philosopher of substance"), or, more precisely, that they *were* irreconcilable, to be sure, but also indissociable, so that it is most unlikely that we will ever be able to choose between them—for instance, on such issues as the personality and impersonality of thought.

My second conclusion is that the major task of the philosophical or philosophico-philologico-historical work in which we are involved is to establish a program of investigation of *modes of subjection*.

I use this term (perhaps provisionally) for several reasons. First, because the two aspects of the issue before us need to be subsumed under a single two-sided word: subjugation in its different forms (*servitus*, as Spinoza used to say) and subjectification—or becoming a subject on one's own—in its different forms (*esse sui juris*, as Spinoza also used to say). The terminology that we need should include both activity and passivity, and consequently raise, in itself, the problem of their difference and the movement of this difference. All philosophies of liberation have been reflections, each in its own way, on the conditions and forms of this *conatus*, or transition, that differentiates activity from passivity as such.

But I also use the expression *modes of subjection* because there are, or used to be, *modes of production*. At this point, however, we should back up: in most of the texts I have submitted to you under the common label "essays in philosophical anthropology," we are dealing with a determined *mode* of subjection, whose transformations have at times been announced and at times reflected after the fact by modern philosophy. Because of the closeness of its conflicted relation with theology (even when the point has been to denounce it), classical philosophy has naturally privileged the schema that Althusser called "the interpellation of the individual as a subject," and that I call the schema of the "inner voice," i.e., the schema of transcendence, of the Law that always remains withheld behind the mouth that utters it. This is only *one* mode of subjection, or rather, it is the trait shared by a series of modes of subjection. By isolating and privileging it, modern philosophers have built the fiction that the evolution of thought followed a single path—which easily grants it the allure of a goal or a destination. No doubt I risk contributing to this fiction by focusing my research on the revolutionary relieving and replacing of the subject by the citizen, and on the becoming-citizen of the subject. And yet, even in the rough sketch of a phenomenology of this becoming-subject, there appear already, as we have just seen, irreducible forms of subjection, whose history should also be recounted. Clearly, there are *modes of subjection other* than the "inner voice" that, similarly, may combine relations of power, an economy of language, and imagination of the body and soul.

This would have become apparent, I think, if instead of comparing Descartes, Locke, Kant, and Fichte with one another, we had confronted them with, say, Aristotle—the first of the great structuralists in whom the egalitarian figure of the *politès* is studied and defined against a quite different relation of subjection (characterized by what I call *unilateral discourse*), distributed according to the triple inequality of man to woman, master to slave, and father to son, i.e., to disciple.

It would have become apparent, too, if, rereading Marx's texts (especially his analysis of "fetishism") from this angle, we had looked not only for a critique of alienation, but for a similarly structural theory of the articulation of commercial and legal forms of exchange, which establishes individuals as carriers or holders of value and thus creates *within* the very fabric of their activities an empire of objectified signs, working indeed like a "spiritual automaton," like an *a priori* material form of generalized equivalence or a language of things, a "language-object."

But since I have just evoked Marx and time is running out, I will now take a new short-cut or short-circuit and discuss briefly the way I studied him and how I use him today, deferring any further elaboration to my answers to whatever questions you may wish to pose on this point.

III. MARXISM AND STRUCTURAL CAUSALITY

I worked continuously and almost exclusively with Marx's texts, and often with his very words, for nearly twenty years. Needless to say, I would not write any of the studies I devoted to him in precisely the same way today, either because they seem abstruse and dubious to me, or because the positions they uphold now seem quite untenable. And yet, there is not one of my previous studies (at least those I kept as part of the thesis I submitted five years ago and which, under other circumstances, you have before you again) from which I would not retain some element. So I would not write that historical materialism is a *science* (as I did in the late 1960s),[22] or that class struggle is in itself the instance of the irreconcilable in the materiality of history and, consequently, the "engine" of its irreversible transformations (as I did in the 1970s),[23] although I am certain that any explanation of historical process, sequences, or conjunctures should be principally causal and that the effectivity of class divisions and struggles (even overdetermined by other structures) is harder than ever to overlook or ignore today.

Similarly, I would not write (as in my 1976 book, *Sur la Dictature du prolétariat*)[24] that the general form of development for democracy beyond its class frontiers lies in the dismantling of the State apparatus and generally in the decline of the State. For the political experience of the 1970s and 1980s has taught me (or so I believe) that the existence of a social movement "outside the State" is a contradiction in terms. Indeed, it is on this very issue that I began to part company with Althusser in 1978.[25] And the course of thought I have tried to follow for the past ten years or so, either alone or in collaboration with Immanuel Wallerstein and others, which focuses on present and past forms of racism and nationalism, and their ambiguous combinations with class struggle, has suggested to me that class struggle experienced, thought, and organized *under its own name* is the exception, not the rule. Today I believe that what can be called the theoretical anarchism shared by Marxism and the entire libertarian tradition (whether socialist or not)

---

22. "La Science du Capital," in *Le Centenaire du Capital*, Décades de Cerisy-la-Salle: Exposés et Entretiens sur le marxisme (Paris and The Hague: Mouton, 1967).

23. "A Nouveau sur la contradiction," in *Sur la Dialectique*, ed. Guy Besse (Paris: C.E.R.M.—Editions Sociales, 1977).

24. *Sur la Dictature du prolétariat* (Paris: François Maspéro, 1976).

25. "Interrogativi sul partito fuori dello Stato," in Louis Althusser et al., *Discutere lo Stato: posizioni a confronto su una tesi di Louis Althusser* (Bari: De Donato, 1978).

is mainly responsible, at least from the standpoint of its theoretical component, for its inability to size up the crisis it has faced since at least the years of its confrontation with Nazism, and from which it has never emerged.[26] And I believe, *a fortiori*, that it is not on these grounds that we are likely to contribute intellectually to solving the crisis of democratic politics that today threatens in different ways to open a new door to various neo-Fascisms.

However, this in no sense leads me to abandon the idea that a new practice of politics is a mass practice. On the contrary, knowing that such a notion is necessarily ambivalent, I believe that it is all the more indispensable to include the "insurrectional" dimension (or, if you will, that aspect of movements of collective liberation that exceeds the functioning of institutions and apparatuses) in any reflection on democratic citizenship. Neither does this lead me to consider as meaningless one or another of the issues that Marxist tradition has subsumed under the notion of "communism" and to which from the start I had attached particular importance: for instance, what classical theoreticians called the "end of the division of manual and intellectual labor," and which did not fall within the domain of a description of the forms of nineteenth-century industrialization so much as it referred to one of the underlying anthropological forces of the transhistorical division between governors and governed.[27]

If I wanted to give a brief, schematic recapitulation of the successive stages of my work on Marx, I would say that the first task, undertaken with Althusser, was to *reconstruct* or remodel Marxism: in a sense, to complete it or to find at last the shape of its coherence and systematicity. This program was widespread at the time, although oriented in directions contrary to one another.

I then undertook a long and, in a sense, opposed process of *deconstruction* of the Marxist text. The most significant thresholds of this second task were crossed when I too came to realize that the contradictions of Marxism—as a political theory and as a historical movement—cannot be accounted for outside of Marx's own contradictions, for they are nothing other than these contradictions rendered effective. It then

---

26. "Fascism, Psychoanalysis, Freudo-Marxism," in *Masses, Classes, Ideas*, 177–89.

27. "Sur le concept de la division du travail manuel et intellectuel," in *L'intellectuel, l'intelligentsia et les manuels*, ed. Jean Belkhin (Paris: Anthropos, 1983). See also my article "Division du travail manuel et intellectuel," in *Dictionnaire critique du marxisme*, second edition, 1985.

became clear that, in its strongest realizations, the history of Marxist theory itself is nothing but a displacement or evasion of certain fundamental *aporias* whose trace and terms must be sought in the very texture of Marx's writing—the most fundamental of all these aporias, the one which in fact governs the whole fate of Marxism (as Althusser had perfectly understood and shown), being the aporia of the concept of ideology.

Aporia does not mean error, of course, but the *double bind*[28] of a discovery or simply of a revolutionary theoretical question, posed in the very terms of its denial or in the impossibility of its solution. I believe that in commenting upon and analyzing Marx's tests, and beginning as early as my 1974 essays included in *Cinq etudes du matérialisme historique,* but especially in those published in 1979 (*Marx et sa critique de la politique*) and most clearly in those of the early 1980s (my articles from the *Dictionnaire critique du marxisme* directed by Georges Labica and my study on *La Vacillation de l'idéologie dans le marxisme*),[29] I established the close correspondence in Marx between the aporia of ideology (that is, the complete impossibility of conceptualizing the ideology of the "proletarian masses" that, Marx tells us, make history) and the successive, conjunctural versions of his critique of political economy and theory of the State apparatus, dictatorship of the proletariat, and revolutionary party. From my point of view, this first negative result is attained, and it helps us understand how the historical cycle of dogmatic and critical Marxisms circled back upon itself.

This work of deconstruction, however, which is never by definition finished and which has much to gain in not limiting itself to a confrontation with Marx alone, was never an end in itself. It only makes sense to the extent that it allows us to think otherwise, i.e., to tease out positively, affirmatively, *another problematic,* or, to rely upon our old terminology, another topic or another schema of historical causality. For the concept of ideology in Marx has more than a merely descriptive or even critical function: as the very concept of the *discrepancy* between tendencies [*tendances*] and events, it represents the key moment of the interworking—*Wechselwirkung* or *Rückwirkung*—of

28. In English in the original text—Translator's note.
29. See the following entries in the *Dictionnaire critique du marxisme:* "Appareil," "Bakouninisme," "Classes," "Critique de l'économie politique," "Contre-révolution," "Dictature du prolétariat," "Droit de tendances," "Lutte de classes," "Pouvoir." See also "L'idée d'une politique de classe chez Marx," in *Marx en perspective,* ed. Bernard Chavance (Paris: E.H.E.S.S., 1985), 497–526. An English translation appears in *Masses, Classes, Ideas,* 125–49.

causes and effects upon each other; it is therefore the touchstone of everything that has taken the name of "historical materialism."

Can we then "take another step"? I believe so; indeed, I even think that we can describe what such a schema would ideally consist of. It would not be the sum of a "base" and a "superstructure," working like a complement or supplement of historicity, but rather the combination of two "bases" of explanation or two determinations both incompatible and indissociable: the *mode of subjection* and the *mode of production* (or, more generally, the ideological mode and the generalized economic mode). Both are material, although in opposite senses. To name these different senses of the materiality of subjection and production, the traditional terms *imaginary* and *reality* suggest themselves. One can adopt them, provided that one keep in mind that in any historical conjuncture, the effects of the imaginary can only appear through and by means of the real, and the effects of the real through and by means of the imaginary: in other words, the structural law of causality in history is the *detour through and by means of the other scene*. Let us say, parodying Marx, that economy has no more a "history of its own" than does ideology, since each has a history only through the other that is the efficient cause of *its own effects*. Not so much the "absent cause" as the cause *that absents itself*, or the cause whose effectivity works through its contrary.

This, then, is the theoretical point of view, if not properly the *object*, of *Race, Nation, Class* and *Les Frontières de la démocratie:* not the object, for these two collections of essays do not seek only to illustrate methodological postulates, but to question events and describe tendencies [*tendances*] so that a democratic practice can arise in them. It is a theoretical point of view, then, whose validity can only be tested in its practice. Indeed, in these texts I illustrate again and again the idea that only imaginary communities (including political communities) are "real." I suggest also, however, that collective formations of the imaginary and their symbolic frame (therefore all *traces* of the ideological past fraught with the most ambivalent effects: nationalism, patriotism, institutional or cultural racism, but also religion and socialism) do not prescribe any future outside present-day constraints of accumulation, the State, and class struggle.

The problematic that is thus undoubtedly outlined is not conceivable without the totality of intellectual experiences and issues raised by Marxism, but it deliberately plays *Marxism against itself* as much as against its adversaries. In this sense it is irreversibly post-Marxist, though the more pedantic "meta-Marxist" might make clearer that the issue is not to declare "out of date" or surpassed—in a historicist way—the concepts and issues of Marxism, but to confront them with their antithesis.[30] Precisely because it is radically *causal*, such a problematic has no part in any *deterministic* representation of the course of history. No one who has tried to school himself or herself in the work of Spinoza can confuse the two notions. Besides, we know that determinism is indeed a teleology. In contrast, to the extent that it opens the way to a philosophy of history, or better, a philosophy *in* history, the conception of causality I am advancing can only allow a *conjectural* philosophy: not an attempt to compute probabilities of events, but an attempt to diagnose the configurations of forces that will face the political and the symbolic issues that will divide it within itself.

Must such a problematic be *given a name?* Instead of the terms "sur-rationalism" (used by Gaston Bachelard) or "sur-materialism" (coined on the same model by Dominique Lecourt), and especially "surrealism" (the first and best term of the series, but which might have us confused with poets or lunatics), it may be worth reviving the word *structuralism* (and I must say I am increasingly tempted to do so). The term is certainly not that old, though nobody (or almost nobody) today seems to want to have anything to do with it—so much so, indeed, that someone recently thought it possible to chronicle its history in a few hundred pages as, and I quote, the story of a "collective shipwreck." Structuralism, then—provided, however, that we understand it not as a combinative or hierarchical schema for constructing sets or totalities, but, on the contrary, as a problematic of differential identities; an analysis of the double inscription of causes and their excess of productivity within the representation of functionalities; finally, as an infinite topic of the noncontemporaneity of events to themselves.

* * *

If you grant me a few more minutes to conclude, I will propose not an argument, but a number of theses on the ethical attitude that is implied, it seems to me, by this way of philosophizing within what I have called the infinite contradiction of history.

One cannot propose that history is causally overdetermined with-

30. In the same spirit, see my "Foucault et Marx: l'enjeu du nominalisme," in *Michel Foucault philosophe: rencontre internationale, Paris, 9, 10, 11 janvier 1988* (Paris: Editions du Seuil, 1989). An English translation is available in *Michel Foucault, Philosopher*, trans. Timothy J. Armstrong (London and New York: Routledge, 1991).

out positing that there are truth effects in history.[31] All materialism (and I intend to propose ways of remaining within materialism) is incompatible with any relativism. It does not, though, seek the antithesis of relativism in some eternal truth or in what is no more than a lay version of such a truth, a law of evolution, i.e., some guarantee or *a priori* that anticipates a consensus. It seeks the truth effect only in the irreversibility of certain breaks, in the incoercible character of certain issues. Let me hazard in passing that I believe it to be a sort of intellectual point of honor, for someone who subscribed for years to a doctrine or ideology whose flag bore the inscription "Marx's theory is all powerful because it is true," not to abandon this position through any relativism, historicism, or pluralism, but instead by means of a renewed effort to understand the mode of existence of truth in history. That history is not the process of effectuation of truth does not mean that it is the process of its constant destitution.

Still, one can only posit that the structure of this historic causality is that of a double scene (real/imaginary) or that it is "surreal," if one presupposes that truth effects in history are first negative—in other words, that such effects make institutional constructions possible only by their capacity to interrupt or suspend the course of events. I believe I identified this formal characteristic in the proposition of equaliberty, as well as in its anticipations and reiterations. This means precisely, not that equaliberty is "empty," but that it is an *issue* or a question, and that this issue *is there,* whether one likes it or not. It fits, irrepressibly, into the history of subjection. It represents a point at which the history of economico-political systems of production reverses course. It transforms the whole of philosophical writing.

Finally, one cannot posit that because history is structural it is therefore conjectural, without—like Spinoza and, to a certain extent, like Hegel and Marx—reversing the terms of the classical issue of liberty and necessity (whose relation to theological narratives of subjection is well known): there will not be a leaving of the "reign of necessity" for the "reign of liberty," that land of milk and honey or wine and roses in which there will be neither social relations nor ideology, but, on the contrary, the *realization of liberty,* a *Verwirklichung* of the maximum of liberty *within* the field of necessity.

---

31. See *Theses,* defended on 11 December 1987 before the jury of the Université de Nimègue (Netherlands), for the degree of Doctor of Philosophy. Published in French in *Raison présente* 89 (1989): 15–17.

Better yet: the realization of the conditions for maximal liberty within the field of necessity. In other words, the proposition that because history is structural it is therefore conjectural supposes the *becoming-necessary of liberty* [*devenir nécessaire de la liberté*]. This means, and I admit it unreservedly, that politics is also ethics. Not in the sense of an *amor fati*, nor because the political would be subjected to moral means and ends, but in that politics acts so as to render liberty necessary, within the broadest possible limits and for the longest possible time.

Such a position is consistent—or I believe it to be—with the thesis I have maintained in the field of historical materialism: that formations of the imaginary or subjective formations are not the reflection or superstructure of economy and politics, but rather their psychic material—a material that cannot be manipulated at will. To act is therefore not to "master," it is not to *shape*, it is not even to *organize* history or humanity even by means of the law, science, and institution—as Hobbes and so many after him believed. Nor, however, is it to limit oneself to resisting heroically the immemorial attraction of the human species to "evil." Instead, to act is to play a game with many players, sometimes tricking or finessing, with and against the risks of ideology and economy.

Such a position is thus not incompatible with Gramsci's famous maxim (who claimed to have taken it from Romain Rolland): "pessimism of the intellect, optimism of the will"—an injunction that one should be careful not to interpret as a mere combination of activism and fatalism. Nor does it contradict Max Weber's seemingly opposite and no less famous maxim urging the joining of "the ethic of conviction" with "the ethic of responsibility," i.e., (if I understand it correctly) the *presumption of truth* with the *attention paid to effects*, or consequences. Such maxims, however, opposed both to the rationalist ideology of inevitable progress and to the mysticism of imminent catastrophe, should not be repeated too often. You have probably guessed that I would readily apply to them the last statement of the *Tractatus*, which, by definition, is also a rule concerning judgment in ethics: "Those things about which we cannot speak, we must pass over in silence." A contradictory injunction, of course, and therefore an ironic one, which could be glossed as: one should not make speeches [*faire des discours*], nor, even less, should one theorize about such an injunction; still, it should be set forth at least once (for it is neither a secret nor an initiatory rule), and even be made a thesis: silence should therefore be broken. Hence the compromise solution that I practice: we should talk about it as little as possible, or, if I may put it this way, we must speak about "those things" as little as possible, and make as much "silence" as possible.

—Translated by Jean-Marc Poisson with Jacques Lezra

GERALDINE FRIEDMAN

The Spectral Legacy of Althusser: The Symptom and Its Return

Althusser always wrote out of a conjuncture that was both philosophical and political, but even if we limit ourselves to the philosophical Althusser, we find that his legacy is already double. First, there is his tremendous theoretical effort to elaborate a rigorous dialectical materialism whose discourse would be adequate to its authentically materialist concepts. At its core, this effort to produce texts that say what they mean and mean what they say is a philosophical project, which, by purging the Marxian corpus and tradition of speculative and empiricist backsliding, hopes to arrive at a Marxist science that is truly scientific. What emerges as a surprise, however, is that the conceptual work that produces science takes place not at the well-established center of Marxian theory but at those marginal sites where Marx's theoretical rigor falters:

> A science only progresses, i.e., *lives*, by the extreme attention it pays to the points where it is theoretically fragile. By these standards, it depends less for its life on what it knows than on what it *does not know:* its absolute precondition is to focus on this unknown, and to pose it in the rigour of a problem.[1]

In these places, or "symptoms" as Althusser calls them, "Marx shows us in a thousand ways the presence of a concept essential to his

---

1. Louis Althusser and Étienne Balibar, *Reading "Capital,"* hereafter *RC*, trans. Ben Brewster (New York: Verso, 1979), 30; first published as *Lire le Capital*, hereafter *LC*, by Louis Althusser, Étienne Balibar, Jacques Rancière, Roger Establet, and Pierre Macherey, 4 vols. (Paris: François Maspero: 1971–75), vol. 1, 31. All subsequent references to this work are to these editions. English translations will be given in the text, except when the quotation is brief or I find it necessary to work with the original French in the main text.

YFS 88, *Depositions*, ed. Lezra, © 1995 by Yale University.

thought, but absent from his discourse" (RC, 30). The implied inadequation between meaning and language arises, in Althusserian terms, from Marx's "epistemological break" with the Feuerbachian and Hegelian traditions in which he was educated. In this view, the mature Marx works within a completely different theoretical structure or "problematic" from that of his precursors, a structure that determines what counts as a question as well as an answer (RC, 25).[2] The revolutionary character of this break is what produces the symptom. Precisely because the concepts Marx was inventing did not yet exist, he had no choice but to borrow the formulations of the problematic from which he had broken or to speak in metaphors. As an inadequate concept that demands the production of an adequate one, the symptom is the starting point for Althusser's philosophical work. The elaboration of a Marxist philosophy thus depends on first recognizing the "weak spots" in Marx's texts, and this can occur only by what Althusser calls a "symptomatic reading" or "lecture symptomnale" that attends painstakingly to Marx's figures and theoretical borrowings. For this reason, Althusser's philosophical legacy cannot be simply a search for the truth contained in Marxian concepts; it must also be a legacy of reading that takes Marx's language seriously. Yet work on or inspired by Althusser generally ignores this intimate connection, treating the text as the transparent embodiment of an ideal meaning. With very few exceptions, Althusserians have focused on Althusser's theory, especially his theory of ideology, at the expense of the *lecture symptomnale*. Now, this situation might be understandable in the social sciences, but it is puzzling in the study of literature, a field that could be defined as a reading practice. It is almost as if literary Althusserians had actively decided not to see Althusser's theory of reading.[3]

---

2. For Althusser's explicit elaboration of the "epistemological break," a concept at work everywhere in his writing, see the introduction "Today" to *For Marx*, trans. Ben Brewster (New York: Verso, 1990), 32–38; hereafter *FM*. In *Pour Marx*, ed. Louis Althusser (Paris: François Maspero, 1968), see 24–30; hereafter *PM*. As with *Reading "Capital"* and *Lire le Capital*, subsequent passages from and references to the English translation will generally be given in the text.

3. The most notable exception is Ellen Rooney's *Seductive Reasoning: Pluralism as the Problematic of Contemporary Literary Theory* (Ithaca: Cornell University Press, 1989), which develops a theory of reading from Althusser's *lecture symptomnale*. Terry Eagleton's *Criticism and Ideology* (London: New Left Books, 1976) and *Marxism and Literary Criticism* (Los Angeles: University of California Press, 1976) and Catherine Belsey's *Critical Practice* (London: Methuen, 1980) are works by students of literature that, despite their concern with language, bypass "symptomatic reading" to develop a Marxist theory of literature heavily inflected by Althusser's theory of ideology. Lan-

This persistent nonseeing partakes of the blindness that characterizes the symptom itself. For the symptom registers the necessary invisibility of Marx's revolutionary new objects within a pre-Marxian perspective that by definition excludes them. As Althusser writes, these objects

> are invisible because they are rejected in principle, repressed from the field of the visible: and that is why their fleeting presence in the field when it does occur (in very peculiar and symptomatic circumstances) *goes unperceived*, and becomes literally an undivulgeable absence—since the whole function of the field is not to see them, to forbid any sighting of them. [*RC*, 26]⁴

---

guage and Materialism, by Rosalind Coward and John Ellis, and "Reference and Dissemination: Althusser after Derrida," by Thomas E. Lewis (*Diacritics: A Review of Contemporary Criticism* 15/4 [Winter 1985]: 37–56), do not mention Althusser's theory of reading but nonetheless perform a symptomatic reading of him, in the first case of the "imaginary," "language," and the "subject" and in the second of "representation," "production," and "reproduction." Andrew Parker, in his excellent "Futures for Marxism: An Appreciation of Althusser," which appeared in the same number of *Diacritics* as Lewis's article, reads both Marx and Althusser in relation to the theory of reading he sees them to offer (57–72). Michael Sprinker's "Imaginary Relations: Althusser and Materialist Aesthetics," in *Imaginary Relations: Aesthetics and Ideology in the Theory of Historical Materialism* (New York: Verso, New Left Books, 1987) begins to do a symptomatic reading of Althusser's metaphor of the theater at the end of "Marx's Immense Theoretical Revolution," but the "empirico-aesthetic" turn that Sprinker's treatment of this figure takes mars an otherwise excellent discussion (289–95). As the title suggests, Steven B. Smith's *Reading Althusser: An Essay on Structural Marxism* (Ithaca: Cornell, 1984) addresses the problem of reading in Althusser but from a deeply empiricist perspective that cannot really engage the problem (75–82).

4. The symptom as blindness suggests an oedipal reading of *Reading "Capital,"* which we can only sketch here. According to Althusser, the vulgar Marxist interpretation sees in the materialist dialectic a "happy union" ("union heureuse," *LC*, 1:105) between Ricardo and Hegel that is theoretically unproblematic. The symptomatic reading, on the contrary, finds in Marx

> real theoretical lapses, in brief blank flashes, invisible in the light of the proof: words that hang in mid-air although they seem to be inserted into the necessity of the thought, judgements which close irreversibly with a false obviousness the very space which seemed to be opening before reason. [*RC*, 86]

Marx thus goes from being the potent, procreative father in a good marriage to an onanist or practitioner of *coitus interruptus* who disseminates his words in the air because he cannot insert his concepts into the maternal body of thought. In short, symptomatic reading, in revealing the "blinded eye" (*RC*, 26) of the pre-Marxian theoretical problematic, subjects Marx to symbolic castration, which is perhaps not unrelated to the concept of the social totality as an articulated body. I am indebted to Diane Rubenstein for suggesting this line of thought on Marx's position as father in Althusser.

The image of Marx as potent father in the first, immediate reading of the text also suggests a rather startling new understanding of the common Althusserian word "in-

But from the perspective of the new problematic, placing Althusser's theory of reading at the center of his project means reading not only Marx but also Althusser. In performing just such a reading, this paper will show the necessary dependence of Althusser's theoretical project on its figures, and, by implication, the inseparability of the two Althusserian legacies. This is, after all, only to assume the burden passed on to the reader in Part 1 of *Reading "Capital"*: ". . . the papers you are about to *read* . . . do not escape the law I have pronounced [the law of the symptom]—assuming that they have some claim to be treated, for the time being at least, as discourses with a theoretical meaning . . ." *RC*, 28). Since to read Althusser theoretically is to read his symptomatic figures, we shall see that we must apply to him the directive he formulates with regard to Marx: the necessity of approaching the text in the original (*RC*, 14). For if language matters, translation also becomes an issue.

As the production of adequate concepts, symptomatic reading is a philosophical work of correction that evokes a figure Althusser uses in *For Marx* for his nonphilosophical, politically engaged youth: "In our philosophical memory it remains the period of intellectuals in arms, hunting out error from all its hiding-places" (22). In *Reading "Capital,"* this political hunt is replaced by a philosophical one that tracks down the various misreadings of Marxism—the historicist, the humanist, the empiricist, the mechanist, the economist, and the Hegelian (mis)interpretations—in order to submit them to radical critique. Yet something strange occurs in the effort to purge these errors. The reading that works *on* the symptom works itself *as* a symptom, casting doubt on whether it is ever possible to read correctly. Thus, according to its authors, what makes *Reading "Capital"* a reading is its flaws:

> The following papers were delivered in the course of a seminar on *Capital* held at the École Normale Supérieure early in 1965. They bear

---

sert" ("insérer"), as, for instance, when Althusser speaks of "actions inserted into practices" in "Ideology and Ideological State Apparatuses (Notes Toward an Investigation)," in *Lenin and Philosophy and Other Essays,* trans. Ben Brewster (New York: Monthly Review Press, 1971), 168. Subsequent references to this collection will appear in the text as *LP*. All the above references and Althusser's formulation of the relation between Hegel and Marx as one of flirtation ("kokettieren"), which will be discussed below, suggest that desire is not simply absent from Althusser's texts, although he cannot see it from within his theoretical problematic. Perhaps it is most accurate to say that desire never receives theoretical elaboration in Althusser, but it is present in his texts as a symptom to be read.

the mark of these circumstances: not only in their construction, their rhythm, their didactic or oral style, but also and above all in their discrepancies, the repetitions, hesitations and uncertain steps in their investigations. We could, of course, have gone over them at our leisure, corrected them one against the other, reduced the margin of variation between them, unified their terminology, their hypotheses and their conclusions to the best of our ability, and set out their contents in the systematic framework of a single discourse—in other words, we could have tried to make a *finished* work out of them. But rather than pretending they are what they should have been, we prefer to present them for what they are: precisely, incomplete texts, the mere beginnings of a *reading*. [RC, 13; authors' emphasis]

In refusing the perfection of completeness, this passage tells us that reading is not the discovery of a preformed, already whole object but a work process, a production which leaves traces, because it is an activity with a history. Only when one reading has already taken place or another can still occur do certain moments emerge as discrepant, redundant, or uncertain.

If we look for the history of Althusser's reading, we find it most obviously in the lists of omissions and errors which he realizes retrospectively and then positions in the prefaces to his works. "To My English Readers," the prefatory text of *For Marx*, ends with what the author, in a self-consciously Stalinist idiom, calls a "'self-criticism,'" and its confessional pages make two related denunciations. First, Althusser judges his engagement of "the question of the union of theory and practice" to be one-sided, for he considers it only "within 'theoretical practice'" but not "within *political practice*." Second, he fails clearly to "distinguish[ ] philosophy from science" (*FM*, 15).[5] His first words in *Reading "Capital"* signal similar terminological ambiguities and the more substantive error of his "unilateral and therefore inaccurate . . . definition of philosophy as a *theory of theoretical practice*." (He later "corrects" this to the representation of "the class struggle in theory."[6]) Like that first inadequate definition of philosophy, all these slips point to a "'theoreticist' tendency" that Althusser finds and condemns in himself (*RC*, 8).

---

5. This liminary text, which precedes the preface "Today" ("Aujourd'hui"), does not appear in the French original, *Pour Marx*. In this quotation and the one below, the emphasis is Althusser's.

6. Althusser, "Philosophy as a Revolutionary Weapon," Interview Conducted by Maria Antonietta Macciocchi, in *Lenin and Philosophy and Other Essays*.

What is remarkable about these ritual *ex post facto* confessions is that they mime a rhythm of reading that Althusser discovers in Marx. Just as Marx writes that in the first volume of *Capital* he had "coquett[ed]" with Hegel's terminology (*FM*, 197n38), we could say that Althusser indulges in "raffish flirtation" (*RC*, 29) with the nonrigorous, which he then severely corrects. This pattern suggests that it is possible to read aright only after the fact, but this retroactivity gives the history of reading a paradoxically ahistoricist character, in the special sense that "Marxism Is Not a Historicism," as one of the chapter titles of *Reading "Capital"* announces. For the text, like the social formation, functions as an Althusserian "complex structured whole" with relatively autonomous levels.[7] (Thus we might conceive the theoretical problematic as the infrastructure and the ongoing work of corrective reading as the articulated superstructure.) As the *après-coup* prefaces and frequent appendices to Althusser's articles make especially clear, these levels each have their own temporal rhythm. There is no one textual moment that constitutes an "essential section," or a representative cross section of the whole, because in such a synecdochal relation, each part would be referable to the same homogeneous temporality. In contrast, Althusser's self-reading, constituted by a lag inherent in all reading, takes place in a nonpunctual, noncontemporaneous time, which precludes any full present in which Marx or Althusser could "get it right."[8] Thus, in correcting the empiricist or metaphysicist errors of other readers, Althusser produces new errors of his own, which he calls theoreticist. It seems that however many sins one preface discovers, another, later one will always find more.

These lapses might seem like accidents or subjective failings, which could have occurred or not. But in light of Althusser's theory of reading, they point to an inevitable error intrinsic to that theory, because for all its desired correctness, symptomatic reading is constituted by a certain guilt:

> Hence a philosophical reading of *Capital* is quite the opposite of an innocent reading. It is a guilty reading, but not one that absolves its

---

7. Althusser develops this concept in "On the Materialist Dialectic: On the Unevenness of Origins," in *FM*, 161–218, especially 193–200 and following.

8. Althusser's critique of historicism turns on his critique of the metaphysical conception of time at work in it. See the chapter "Marxism Is Not a Historicism" in *RC*, 119–44, especially 132–38, where the concepts of "contemporaneity" and the "essential section" are developed.

crime on confessing it. On the contrary, it takes the responsibility for its crime as a "justified crime" and defends it by proving its necessity. [RC, 15]

What is rendered as "crime" in this passage is "faute," a French word which also means "mistake." And this mistake is what the philosophical reading "defends," or in French "défend." But the original allows a sense which is elided in English, for "défendre," the infinitive of "défend," also means to prohibit. Yet this elision is necessary because English has no one word that combines the two senses of the French. Language thus forces the translator into an unavoidable error, precisely where the text speaks of its own "necessary" or "good" error, which it both defends and prohibits. Both necessary and disallowed and therefore neither quite one nor the other, this error has a curious status: by providing a starting place, it is the condition of possibility for rigorous Althusserian reading but also the unavoidable limit of that rigor.

The "faute" is the symptom in Marx's text, and, in principle, its faultiness is the inadequacy of its concept, signaled by its figuricity. But, in presenting the law of the symptom, Althusser himself seems able to write only in the most symptomatic of metaphors, of which "symptom" is in fact one.[9] Thus, in a footnote, he foregrounds the figuricity of the discourse in which he speaks of Marx's figures:

> The recourse made in this text to spatial metaphors (field, terrain, space, site, situation, position, etc.) poses a theoretical problem: the problem of the validity of its *claim* to existence in a discourse with scientific pretensions. The problem may be formulated as follows: *why does a certain form of scientific discourse necessarily need the use of metaphors borrowed from non-scientific disciplines?* [RC, 26n8; Althusser's emphasis]

As symptom, the figure, then, is not a mere decoration or convenient heuristic device but the necessary error, which requires that we study Marx's (and every theoretical author's) "typical metaphors." In cluster-

---

9. These remarks could be extended to include all Althusser's concepts, for he regularly registers a dissatisfaction with them that marks them as incomplete, borrowed, and not quite right. For example, he signals the "epistemological break" as Bachelard's formulation (FM, 32) and apologizes for using the psychoanalytic term "overdetermined" in preference to "the astonishing expression—complexly-structurally-unevenly determined" (FM, 209). Althusser's terminological anxieties indicate the symptomatic character of his concepts, which in turn indicates the novelty of his theoretical enterprise: he is hesitantly constructing a theory that does not yet exist in totality.

ing around the as yet unnameable concept, they are "part of a theory of the history of the production of knowledges" (*RC*, 121n13 and n14) and thus integral to Marx's and Althusser's theoretical work. Yet it is the very necessity of the symptom that has led even well-intentioned interpreters of Marx astray, producing conflicting interpretations. For, in being forced to think his radical break from Hegel in Hegelian concepts, Marx himself

> introduc[ed] an effect of dislocation between the semantic field of origin from which he borrowed his concepts, and the field of conceptual objects to which they were applied. . . .
> This, rather than any tendentiousness on their part, is the reason why so many of Marx's inheritors and supporters have produced inaccurate estimates of his thought, while claiming, text in hand, that they remain true *to the letter* of what he wrote." [*RC*, 121; emphasis Althusser's]

Ironically, it turns out that the very fidelity of the commentators to Marx's letter has kept them from reading his figures and from even posing the question of the relation of discourse to concept. Yet the dislocation between discourse and concept is "not peculiar to Marx but common to every scientific founding moment and to all scientific production generally" (*RC*, 121n14).

Althusser thus insists on the figure or error as not only necessary but also foundational, and this foundational error implies a radical Althusserian critique of metaphysics that for a certain distance travels step for step on the same path as Derrida's. Indeed, the place of metaphor in the discourse of philosophy is the problematic of "White Mythology," a problematic that in *Reading "Capital"* founds the practice of the symptomatic reading as "double reading."[10] It is in elaborating this textual theory that Althusser's metaphors focus most sharply on the concept, because its mode of appearance is what is at stake when we read. This becomes clearest in the passage on "innocent" reading, the degree zero from which the guilty "lecture symptomnale" deviates. An understanding of the world as a text to be taken at face value, innocent reading is what the still ideological "Young Marx" practiced before he invented Marxism and thereby switched to a scientific problematic:

---

10. From a very different perspective, Lewis's "Reference and Dissemination" makes metaphor a place from which to formulate the relation between Althusser and Derrida (45–53).

> For the Young Marx, to know the essence of things, the essence of the historical human world, of its economic, political, aesthetic and religious productions, was simply to *read* (*lesen, herauslesen*) in black and white the presence of the "abstract" essence in the transparency of its "concrete" existence. This immediate reading of essence in existence expresses the religious model of Hegel's Absolute Knowledge, that End of History in which the concept at last becomes fully visible, present among us in person, tangible in its sensory existence—in which *this* bread, *this* body, *this* face and *this* man are the Spirit himself. This sets us on the road to understanding that the yearning for a reading *at sight*, for Galileo's '*Great Book of the World*' itself, is older than all science, that it is still silently pondering the religious fantasies of epiphany and parousia, and the fascinating myth of the Scriptures, in which the body of truth, dressed in its words, is the Book: the Bible. This makes us suspect that to treat nature or reality as a Book, in which, according to Galileo, is spoken the silent discourse of a language whose "characters are triangles, circles and other geometrical figures," it was necessary to have a certain idea of *reading* which makes a written discourse the immediate transparency of the true, and the real discourse of a voice. [*RC*, 16; Althusser's emphasis]

This incarnational, consubstantial discourse, with all its Christian resonances, is a logocentric language if ever there was one, for it depends on a metaphysics in which truth inhabits the word as the soul of the body. In such a transparent language, the concept appears "in person," a phrase that has a noteworthy career in English translations of Althusser. In French, the phrase is "en personne," and, in either language, it is unusual, if not unheard of, in philosophical discourse outside Althusser. The translator, Ben Brewster, seems to have been disturbed by the oddness of the locution, because in his 1969 rendering of *For Marx*, he generally normalizes it as "as such." But when he Englishes *Reading "Capital"* the next year, he often translates it literally, as in the passage quoted above, as "in person." Brewster's two choices, it happens, are not unrelated to Althusser's theory of reading. On the one hand, the translator's decision to preserve the phrase suggests a realization that its very oddness signifies. The words "en personne" in fact point to themselves as an Althusserian symptom, which the translator reproduces when he translates literally. But the phrase also names the embodying personification of the concept that goes with innocent reading. Thus, when the translator elides "en personne," he again refuses the text as the transparent discourse of truth. This means that we have not a symptomatic original and a "normal" translation but two texts with two different kinds of symptoms.[11] In their own distinct ways, then, the strangeness of the French and the smoothness of the English both demand the symptomatic reading that is attentive to what Althusser calls the breaks in a seemingly full discourse (RC, 30),[12] to the places where the Hegelian formulae are neither the perfectly embodied concepts they claim to be nor mere play or raffish flirtation,

> but *the action of a real drama*, in which old concepts desperately play the part of something absent *which is nameless*, in order to call it onto the stage in person—whereas they only "produce" its presence in their failures, in the dislocation between the characters and their roles. [RC, 29; Althusser's emphasis][13]

According to this passage, the symptom is the radical impossibility of the concept to appear "in person," not just because it has no name but because it is still in the process of being produced. The symptom thus functions like an aberrant figure with no literal counterpart, a catachresis. When Althusser insists that "we must take these words [the words of his spatial figures] literally" (RC, 25), we should understand him to be referring precisely to their catachrestic status: they are

---

11. Compare the relation we are suggesting between the French original and the English translation with Althusser's account of the relation between Marx's symptomatic texts and a rigorous philosophical reading of them:

> I *heard* this silence as the possible weakness of a discourse under the pressure and repressive action of another discourse, which takes the place of the first discourse in favour of this repression, and speaks in its silence: the empiricist discourse. All I did was to *make this silence in the first discourse speak, dissipating the second.* [RC, 90; Althusser's emphasis]

12. It is not in order to blame the translator that we have pointed out his elisions, but rather to show that problems of translating *Reading "Capital"* are intimately caught up in Althusser's theory of reading. Thus we largely agree with Lawrence Venuti, who tries to develop a material model of translation from that theory. Arguing against the dominant practice of fluent, or transparent, translation, Venuti writes: "It is certainly a sign of the extremely unpropitious circumstances in which translation is practiced today that we must fasten on flaws in the translator's work in order to gain recognition for it" ("The Translator's Invisibility," *Criticism* 28/2 [Spring 1986]: 209). The notion of the necessary error is, however, outside Venuti's analysis.

13. The complete passage in French reads:

> Il n'est peut-être pas interdit alors de penser que si Marx "joue" si bien, en certains passages, des formules hégéliennes, ce jeu n'est pas seulement élégance ou dérision, mais, au sens fort, *le jeu d'un drame réel*, où d'anciens concepts jouent désespérément le rôle d'un absent, *qui n'a pas de nom*, pour l'appeler en personne sur la scène,—alors qu'ils n'en "produisent" la présence que dans leurs ratés, dans le décalage entre les personnages et les rôles. [LC, 1:31; Althusser's emphasis]

not, strictly speaking, figures, but a second proper sense where there is no first one. It would seem to be the goal of Althusser's theoretical work to produce the concept in person and thus renormalize the figure, as when he writes: "In the brief moment of [Marx's] temporary silence we are simply returning to him the speech that is his own" (*RC*, 144). But another metaphor for the symptom, the "blank" or gap in the seemingly full text,[14] suggests that this would be too quickly to recuperate Althusser's critique of metaphysics. In contrast to those modern critics who see Marx only as completing the classical economists "on the basis of their principles, and therefore of their problematic" (*RC*, 85), Althusser does not simply fill the gap at its site. Instead, he completely remaps knowledge from there, basing it on different principles. In this respect, we can again take his reading of Marx as a guide for reading him, because Althusser acts out in his own text the geographical metaphor of continents he applies to Marx. If the familiar sciences of mathematics and physics "have been installed in a number of great 'continents,' . . . Marx opened up a third continent to scientific knowledge: the continent of History."[15] What Althusser's theoretical work of reading does is to discover that opening and its radical newness. The consequential reorganization of knowledge, in which both Marx and Althusser participate, defers the "parousia" promised by the metaphysical conception of language, where, at the end of History, the concept would return to its proper name or body; for the opening of a new continent has created a completely different body.

It turns out that the original text has already spoken of this deferral, albeit symptomatically; for, in French, the "personne" in which the concept does or does not appear is also a negation. Thus, dislocating the incarnational logic of immediate reading, the phrase affirms and denies at the same time: the concept appears *in propria persona*, in the proper person, and in "no one"; there is no "one" in which the concept adequately personifies itself; or, most radically, "no one" *is* the proper person for the concept to embody itself in. Once more, the thematizing of this philosophical "error" produces a necessary error in translation, because English cannot capture the doubleness of the French phrase. Embodiment is thus the figure of an impossible personification, the

---

14. This figure appears, among other places, in *RC*, 22, 86, 143, 156. In the original, it is called the "blanc" (*LC*, 1:21, 105, 183, and 2:21).

15. Althusser uses the metaphor in "Interview on Philosophy," conducted by Maria Antonietta Macciocchi, included in *LP*, 15. The metaphor recurs frequently throughout the collection.

personification of an impossible figure, which is at once *the* problem for and of reading, since it poses the theoretical possibility of elaborating adequate concepts as the impossibility of that task. Now, according to Althusser, in producing such concepts, Marx breaks from the German ideologists and from his own ideological youth to establish a science, and the symptomatic reading of Marx repeats that break in more adequate form. Thus the burden of *Reading "Capital"* is to continue Marx's work of transforming an ideological problematic into a scientific one. Since the antithetical expression "en personne" names the incompleteness as well as completeness of that transformation, the couple ideology/science cannot be thought outside the couple figurative/literal. This is another way of saying what Althusser so often stresses: that ideology necessarily inhabits science from within, and scientific discourse cannot dispense with metaphor.[16]

Now, to insist, as I have done, on the Althusserian problematic as a problem in figuration might seem overwhelmingly to justify the charge that academics have flocked to Althusserian Marxism because of what one writer calls "its evident academic nature."[17] It happens, however, that personification, as the symptom of the symptom, arises where the philosophical project articulates with one of the strongest conjunctural pressures in Althusser's writing: "Stalinism" and the tasks it posed for later Marxists. This period in Soviet history presents in particularly urgent form the problem of the adequate concept, which is the theoretical necessity of "call[ing] things by their names" or *"their scientific names" (FM,* 240 and 247). For, in this case, the name, by virtue of having a function in a theoretical problematic, produces political effects and is therefore not a "mere" name. Thus, in "Marxism and Humanism" in *For Marx* and later in a "Note" appended to "Reply to John Lewis" in *Essays in Self-Criticism,* Althusser shows that the official labels, "the cult of personality" and "Stalinism," imply interpretations possible only within the pre-Marxian problematic of humanism, centered on the concept "Man."[18] From

16. For one statement of the necessary persistence of ideology in every social totality, including a Communist one, see *FM,* 232.
17. Ian Craib, "Criticism and Ideology: Theory and Experience," *Contemporary Literature,* 22/4 (Fall 1981): 489–90.
18. Althusser, "Note on 'The Critique of the Personality Cult,'" in "Reply to John Lewis," in *Essays in Self-Criticism,* trans. Grahame Lock (London: New Left Books, 1976); originally published as *Réponse à John Lewis,* Théorie, ed. Louis Althusser (Paris: Francois Maspero, 1973). Subsequent references to this essay will appear in the text under the shortened title "Note."

this point of view, all the difficulties of a historical period are reduced to questions of psychology and legality, the pathology that leads one man ruthlessly to violate the constitutional rights of others. And, since the question dictates the terms of the answer, the solution is to be a new humanism, the "Socialist 'Humanism'" that would recognize and respect Soviet legality.[19]

Nothing could sound more ethical than this switch from a terroristic rule to a benevolent one. Yet Althusser rejects the humanist interpretation because it is an instance of Marxists doing an innocent reading that takes the concept as appearing not only in person but in *a* person. If, in the "cult of personality," all was for Stalin, the man who on the level of immediate reading claimed to *be* the Spirit, now the slogan is "All for Man" (*FM*, 221). To avoid this substitution of one incarnational personification for another, Althusser contends that it is not enough for the Soviet Union to denounce the "crimes" and "deviations" of the Stalin years. The denunciation must also be made in terms of Marxist theory, because, otherwise, Marxists themselves advance the very arguments that their enemies have traditionally used against them. Insisting on a complete break with humanist concepts, Althusser, in "Marxism and Humanism," ascribes to Marx and himself espouses a "*theoretical antihumanism*" (*FM*, 229). Now, this term has been widely misunderstood by Althusser's Marxist and non-Marxist opponents alike as advocating brutality and apologizing for Stalin's crimes. But this is to confine Althusser to a position that remains within humanism as its internal negation. In fact, the "anti" of his neologism announces that Marxism establishes its theory on an entirely different basis: not a concept of "Man" (or even "real men") but "the ensemble of social relations" (*FM*, 243), which must be conceived in terms of such concepts as "mode of production, forces of production, relations of production, superstructure, ideology, etc." (*FM*, 244).[20]

19. As the official slogan of the de-Stalinization in the USSR, "Socialist 'Humanism'" also became, through Roger Garaudy, the doctrine of the French Communist Party in the sixties.

20. For lucid explanations of Althusser's antihumanism, see Kavanaugh (39) and Anderson (124–25). Kavanaugh's formulation of the humanist misunderstanding is worth quoting for its archness: Althusser is taken as "asserting that Marxists should not be nice to people, or take 'humanity' into account in political and ideological practice." The most notorious condemnation to date of Althusser's theoretical and political opposition to the "Socialist 'Humanist'" form of de-Stalinization has come from the pen of E. P. Thompson, who calls Althusser the consummate Stalinist. See the title essay in Thompson's *The Poverty of Theory and Other Essays* (Monthly Review Press, 1978).

From this perspective, Althusser reconceptualizes and thus also renames the years of Stalin's rule, proposing in his search for their scientific concept to call them, provisionally, the "Stalinian deviation." The advantage of this phrase, he tells us, is that it enjoys theoretical legitimacy and freedom from the guilty philosophical connections that taint the official labels. As a *bona fide* Marxist concept, "deviation" replaces the notion of a "personality cult," which is nowhere found in Marxist-Leninist theory. In its slight difference from "Stalinist," the adjective "Stalinian" is intended (whether or not it succeeds) to make a proper name refer first and foremost to a historical moment: "a certain *period* in the history of the International Labour Movement" ("Note," 81n3; Althusser's emphasis).[21] In this shift from persons to history, the phrase "Stalinian deviation" participates in the conceptual break from humanism, because the difference of Althusser's interpretation is that it locates causes precisely in historical necessity: the passage from "the dictatorship of the proletariat" to "the withering-away of the State apparatus" and "the creation of new forms of political, economic, and cultural organizations, corresponding to this transition" (*FM*, 238).

The recourse to "Socialist 'Humanism'" is, according to Althusser, a recourse to ideology, and we might guess that he denounces it so vociferously because its effect was to hinder the development of the new forms required for the full realization of Communism in the Soviet Union. Since, as the ISA's essay tells us, legal institutions belong to the State Apparatuses (*LP*, 143), the well-intentioned "Socialist 'Humanist'" emphasis on preserving legality also perpetuated the very state that was eventually supposed to disappear. These theoretical grounds combine with the political fact that "official blandishments of 'socialist humanism' were," as Perry Anderson puts it, "an ideological placebo—a substitute for genuine political measures to eliminate [terror, repression, and dogmatism] in the USSR" to make Althusser condemn the "cult of personality" interpretation as "*a right-wing critique*" [*une critique de droite*] ("Note," 82; Althusser's emphasis).[22]

Yet Althusser maintains that the wide currency enjoyed by the

---

21. It is not easy to see how "Stalinian" is less connected to an individual than "Stalinist" is, but Althusser seems to recognize the possible shortcomings of his coinage when he qualifies it as "provisional" and emphasizes the need "to look for" the name ("Note," 81 and 79).

22. The quoted lines before the phrase from "Note" come from Perry Anderson, "Stalinism," *Arguments within English Marxism* (London: NLB and Verso, 1980), 107.

ideological humanist explanation during de-Stalinization has a scientific, historical explanation: "[t]he present disproportion of the historical tasks to their conditions" (*FM*, 238),[23] in other words, the fact that the conditions in which the transition from class dictatorship to a classless society could be accomplished did not yet exist. What did exist were obstacles, among which Althusser emphasizes "the *theoretical conditions* currently inherited by Marxist theory from its past—not just the dogmatism of the Stalinist period, but also, from further back, the heritage of the disastrously opportunist interpretations of the Second International" (*FM*, 240; Althusser's emphasis). Later, in "Note," he identifies these interpretations as simultaneously economist and humanist, because their one-sided emphasis on productivity entails a silence on the class ownership of the means of production, a silence that gets filled with the ideological belief in the "liberty of the Person" ("Note," 86 and 88). His bold claim is that these linked problems set the stage for "the Stalinian deviation," which "can be considered as *a form* . . . of the *posthumous revenge of the Second International:* as a revival of its main tendency" ("Note," 89; Althusser's emphasis). Since this tendency comes from "profound causes in history and in the *conception* of the class struggle and of class *position*," Althusser bets on its surviving the death of Stalin and the Twentieth Congress, which denounced "Stalinism" ("Note," 92; Althusser's emphasis).

What can we say about this analysis? Purporting to proceed by Marxist concepts whose theoretical "necessity" is well "established" (*FM*, 239), Althusser explains the Stalinian deviation not simply on the basis of a person but in terms of the historical conditions that promoted one man's "'psychology' to . . . a historical fact" (*FM*, 241). Yet, theoretical sanction for its existence notwithstanding, the return hypothesized by Althusser makes Marxist history sound at least as Gothic as Marxist. For the survival acts as a ghastly and ghostly return from the dead: despite Lenin's lifelong struggle against economism, it has not "as yet been buried by History" (*FM*, 240; "la petite bourgeoisie, et son idéologie . . . n'ont pas encore été enterrées par l'Histoire," *PM*, 247) but continues to take its "posthumous revenge" ("Note," 89).

This uncanny narrative of a vampiric afterlife seems at first blush to stand in striking contrast to the total eradication of practical pseu-

---

23. In French, "cette inadéquation présente, entre les tâches historiques et leurs conditions" (*PM*, 245).

doconcepts that "Marxism and Humanism" describes as occurring in the elaboration of scientific Marxist concepts:

> The practical concept that pointed out for us the destination of the displacement has been consumed in the displacement itself, the concept that pointed out for us the site for investigation is from now on absent from the investigation itself. [FM, 244]

This displacement, which is perhaps the most punctual formulation of the epistemological break in Althusser, occurs when the practical concept that acts as a signpost "has been consumed," in French, "a été consommé" (PM, 255). But does the signpost disappear as definitively as the passage asserts? To be "consommé" also means to be completed, to be consummated, a state that connotes full presence, in direct opposition to the absence that results from being consumed. In the case of one practical concept, this ambiguity takes over the text with a vengeance. When Althusser rejects "real humanism" as an inadequate concept that merely points to a reality outside itself (FM, 243), he demands instead—what else?—a concept that "provide[s] the new content" of that reality "*en personne*" (FM, 242; emphasis added). Just where the person is refused as the foundation of one philosophy, it returns in another, more rigorous one as the problematic personification that we have found to be the symptom's symptom. In fact, the whole story of Althusser's effort to replace the humanist interpretation of Stalinism with a rigorous Marxist analysis of the "Stalinian deviation" reads like the history of this return. The "cult of personality," the ghostly "undeath" of the Second International, humanism and antihumanism alike, even the consuming/consummating break itself, all these function in the Gothic plots of "Marxism and Humanism" and "Note" as the political and philosophical effects of an aberrant personification, which is always excessively or insufficiently embodied.

The posthumous return of personification in Althusserian theory suggests that the collapse of Soviet Communism in our moment will not be any smoother or simpler than the passage from the dictatorship of the proletariat to the withering-away of the State in and after Stalin's moment. If anything, in the shift to market reforms and democracy, the link between economism and humanism, which Althusser advanced at his "personal risk" in 1972 ("Note," 89), has come into the open. Perhaps we are witnessing its ultimate revenge now that, as in the earlier period, the conditions are overwhelmingly disproportionate to their task. Since the last days of the Union and the first days of the Commonwealth, calls for authoritarian rule—from Gorbachev, the leaders of the unsuccessful August coup, and even the democrat Yeltsin, who in 1991 attempted to impose emergency rule in the Chechen-Ingush Autonomous Republic and has more recently led a war against it—have seemed to threaten a "humanist" return of personality to a historical role.[24] And since this essay was first completed in the spring of 1992, the examples have multiplied. But, at present, we are also witnessing the other side of Althusser's claim that Marxism, when it adopts a humanist/economist ideology, "can, in certain circumstances, be considered as and treated as, *even practised as a bourgeois point of view*" ("Note," 87, Althusser's emphasis).

If Marxism can foster something like capitalism, an article from 1992 in *The New York Review of Books* suggests that, by the same token, in a Communist society, bourgeois economics is limited in how far it can develop. Thus the Russian Republic's current efforts to introduce a free market are being hampered by what might be called survivals from the past. In this transitional phase, a surreal situation exists in which American advertising campaigns are plentiful but commodities scarce, and the resulting contradictions emerge forcefully in one such example the author gives: "[t]he Vidal Sassoon ad for 'shampoo and conditioner in one' that runs on Moscow TV . . .":

---

24. For Gorbachev's request for special powers in his anticrisis plan, see Serge Schmemann, "Gorbachev Orders Republics to Halt Rebellious Moves," *The New York Times*, 10 April 1991, sec. A. The following articles deal with Gorbachev's attempt to stage himself as a charismatic leader, the indispensable man of the hour who alone could stave off a return to the Cold War or a slide into chaos: Benjamin Weiner, "Mikhail the Master Magician," *The New York Times*, 16 June 1991, sec. 3, and Francis X. Clines, "Yeltsin's Foes Back Away from Effort to Topple Him," *The New York Times*, 3 April 1991, sec. A. In "The 'Good Czar' and the Wise Men: A Sad Tale Retold," *The New York Times*, 7 April 1991, sec. 4, Serge Schmemann quotes a glasnost-era journalist, Oleg Popstov, on the desire for rule by personality among Russians. On Yeltsin's autocratic moves, see Serge Schmemann, "Yeltsin Is Telling Russians to Brace for Sharp Reform," *The New York Times*, 29 October 1991, sec. A; Brumberg, 26; and Celestine Bohlen, "Split by Muslim Region Rattles the Yeltsin Camp," *The New York Times*, 11 November 1991, sec. A. Both Brumberg and Bohlen report that the move against the Muslim area of Chechen-Ingush was angrily condemned and rejected by the Russian Parliament, including many members who usually support Yeltsin staunchly. For the arrogation of emergency powers by the leaders of the unsuccessful coup of August 1991, see the "Declaration of Emergency" decree by then Acting President Gennadi I. Yanayev, printed in *The New York Times*, 20 August 1991, sec. A.

The very concept is mystifying in a place where you count yourself lucky to find any shampoo at all; furthermore, to judge by the number of times women have asked me what conditioner is, few understand the time-saving point of the product. The English word "conditioner" used in this ad has been employed in Russian only for "air conditioners."[25]

Hanging on the translation of a single word, the incomprehensibility of this ad in Russian tells us, humorously, that capitalism, like Marxism, requires that the right names be found for things. The present "historical mutation" to a market system will thus take not only hard work on the infrastructure but also, for the most practical of reasons, a great deal of theoretical labor to develop adequate concepts, whose final form cannot be predicted at present. In a world where the future of Marxism seems, at least for now, bleak, this continuing need for theory, insofar as it is also a question of language, might be the transmuted form that Althusser's double legacy takes. This is to say that there is the possibility of an Althusserian return.

---

25. Jamey Gambrell, "Kasha on the Brain," *The New York Review of Books*, 39/8 (23 April 1992): 27.

ELLEN ROONEY

Better Read Than Dead: Althusser and the Fetish of Ideology*

> Who fails here to call to mind our good friend, Dogberry, who informs neighbour Seacoal, that, "To be a well-favoured man is the gift of fortune; but reading and writing comes by Nature."
> —Karl Marx, "The Fetishism of Commodities and the Secret Thereof"

The polemical form of my argument contends that the reception of Louis Althusser's work has fetishized his theory of ideology and virtually overlooked, left unread, his theory and his practice of reading. The essay "Ideology and Ideological State Apparatuses" and the opposition between ideology and science, as it emerges in the course of *Reading "Capital,"*[1] have dominated our response to Althusser's entire oeuvre in a remarkable and unproductive way, while the crucial place of reading has been obscured, even disavowed. The relative neglect of this aspect of Althusser's work is puzzling, not to say perverse, insofar as his theory of reading actually helps to resolve some of the very theoretical and political difficulties that many commentators on his theory of ideology find so troubling. I will argue that the emphasis on the theory of ideology in Althusser's work is in fact a form of resistance to reading as such. The debate about ideology not only takes the place of any debate about reading, but actually enables the relative

---

*This essay was initially written for a 1991 MLA panel, "Ideology III: For Althusser," and I have retained its polemical quality as an objection or question put to the panel's identification of Althusser with a theory of ideology as much as possible. I would like to thank Andrzej Warminski, who organized the panel, and Geraldine Friedman, who chaired it, as well as Jacques Lezra, for bringing it to print. I would also like to thank Khachig Tololyan, Susan Bernstein, Christina Crosby, Mary Ann Doane, Coppélia Kahn, and Karen Newman, for their comments and criticisms.

1. Louis Althusser and Etienne Balibar, *Reading "Capital,"* trans. Ben Brewster (New York: Verso, 1979). All references to Marx's *Capital* in the text are to *Capital: A Critique of Political Economy*, ed. Frederick Engels, trans. Samuel Moore and Edward Aveling (New York: International Publishers, 1967).

YFS 88, *Depositions*, ed. Lezra, © 1995 by Yale University.

silence on the question of reading, and thus has contributed in a crucial way to the consensus (in many circles) that Althusser's work (and/or something called "Althusserianism") is dead.[2] Ironically, or, rather, with what we once called "poetic justice," the refusal to read Althusser's theory of reading seems entwined with a refusal to read his text at all, that is to say, with a stubborn refusal "to abandon the mirror myths of immediate vision and reading, and conceive knowledge as a production," that is, as a product of reading (*RC*, 24). It is, in other words, profoundly ideological.

Marx's account of fetishism in *Capital* provides the best description of the position Althusser's theory of ideology has in the hegemonic reading of his work. (I should say that I read the "Commodities" chapter "after" Althusser, if not "for" Althusser.) To speak schematically, in much contemporary critical work the *correct* theory of ideology stands in for a correct political position vis à vis the exploited, oppressed, and potentially revolutionary classes. (The most immediately relevant "class" is the proletariat, of course, but in a period of "post-Marxisms," any one of the new social movements can serve as a substitute. What is crucial is that the political project or position of the "other" be adequately represented/theorized/known in advance by means of ideology critique; this preference for a theory of ideology over a theoretical practice of reading is certainly not limited to Marxism or Marxists.) The heady pursuit of a "correct" theory of ideology permits a disavowal of the elusiveness of this "correct" political position, simultaneously affirming and denying political engagement and enabling an evasion of the absolutely unavoidable risk entailed in "reading," where reading is recognized as a relation among readers, a productive relation, but one that allows for no theoretical guarantee.[3]

---

2. The observation that "in France today, Althusser is, as Hegel once was, treated like a 'dead dog,'" is fairly commonplace, perhaps especially in the work of those who protest against this dismissal. See Alain Lipietz, "From Althusserianism to 'Regulation Theory,'" in *The Althusserian Legacy,* ed. E. Ann Kaplan and Michael Sprinker (London: Verso, 1993), 134, whose phrase I cite above, and Gregory Elliott, *Althusser: The Detour of Theory* (London: Verso, 1987), 1. Alex Callinicos turns this figure against itself in "What Is Living and What is Dead in the Philosophy of Althusser," in Kaplan and Sprinker, 39–49.

3. I echo Stuart Hall's essay, "The Problem of Ideology—Marxism Without Guarantees" (in *Marx 100 Years On,* ed. B. Matthews [London: Lawrence and Wishart, 1984]), in part because Hall has avoided the temptation to fetishize, even as he takes up the theory of ideology and Althusser, whether in this essay, or in a work like "Signification, Representation, Ideology: Althusser and the Post-Structuralist Debates," *Critical Studies in Mass Communication* 2/2 (June 1985): 19–114. In "Marxism Without Guarantees,"

("Unlike the 'theory of knowledge' of ideological philosophy, I am not trying to pronounce some *de jure* (or *de facto*) *guarantee* which will assure us that we really do know what we know, and that we can relate this harmony to a certain connection between Subject and Object, Consciousness and World" [RC, 69].) To fetishize the theory of ideology, and thus to disavow the theory of reading, is implicitly to seek such a guarantee. The theory of ideology that could render transparent to the critical intelligence any (and every) ideological operation might also protect us from the uncertain work of reading.

To read, for Althusser, is to undertake a political task, that of seeking (producing) alignments and marking exclusions, through close attention to the form of a text's "problematic." Explicitly rejecting what he calls "fetishism," Althusser proposes an account of reading as a guilty, dynamic, flawed, open-ended, historically contingent, and wholly political practice of displacements: reading as antifetishism. Finally, in his model, reading is the activity that keeps "science" alive, where science is understood as the continuous and "endless" project of disrupting ideologies.[4] Insofar as ideology *is* immortal and ideologies are eternally rewritten, all the forms of resistance and displacement must also be constantly repeated, renewed (revolutionized). "A science that repeats itself without discovering anything is a dead science, is no longer a science, but a frozen dogma. A science only lives from its development, i.e., from its discoveries."[5]

Hall explicitly "foreground[s], not so much the theory as the *problem* of ideology" (29), and he proceeds by means of what he calls "rereading" (36) to "establish the *open horizon* of Marxist theorizing—determinacy without guaranteed closures" (43). His seems to me an exemplary instance of taking the force of Althusser's theory of reading and reading it back into the problem of ideology. Etienne Balibar has also been at pains, in "The Non-Contemporaneity of Althusser" (in *The Althusserian Legacy*), to argue that Althusser's theory of ideology offers "absolutely no *guarantee*" that the revolutionary impulse of the exploited classes will triumph over their "normal behavior in the Ideological State Apparatuses" (13). This kind of work is the exception to the fetishizing rule. Another exceptional reading of Althusser that takes reading into account is Michael Sprinker's *Imaginary Relations: Aesthetics and Ideology in the Theory of Historical Materialism* (London: Verso, 1987).

4. As Althusser observes, in his *Essays in Self-Criticism* (trans. Grahame Locke [London: New Left Books, 1976]), theory/science emerges from its ideological prehistory not once, at its inception, but repeatedly, and it "continues endlessly to do so (its prehistory remains always contemporary)" (114). See my discussion in *Seductive Reasoning: Pluralism as the Problematic of Contemporary Literary Theory* (Ithaca: Cornell University Press, 1989), 12–13.

5. Althusser, "Theory, Theoretical Practice and Theoretical Formation: Ideology and Ideological Struggle," in *Philosophy and the Spontaneous Philosophy of the Scien-*

Reading is the only way to produce such discoveries; that is Althusser's point when he argues that "we must completely reorganize the idea we have of knowledge, we must abandon the mirror myths of immediate vision and reading and conceive knowledge as a production" (RC, 24). Knowledge is produced only as an effect of reading practices, and this most emphatically includes knowledge of ideology. Althusser's theory (and his own practice) of reading makes it painfully clear that this is a task that we may very well fail (will repeatedly fail) to complete. The fetishization of a theory of ideology wards off the inevitable failures that reading suffers.[6] For the fetishist, politics takes the form of a correct theory of ideology; politics as a practice of reading—a guilty and double practice that never ends and so never fully succeeds: this Althusserian understanding of politics is obscured.

I will argue that the fetish of ideology (that is, of the theory of ideology) has masked the way in which Althusser's work (especially, in *Reading "Capital,"* and in *Essays in Self-Criticism*) in fact privileges both a rhetoric and a politics of reading; this masking or elision persists, despite the prominence he himself assigns to reading, most dramatically in reference to his reading of Marx. In reading Althusser as a theorist of reading, I am in the most obvious way repeating his own gesture, his reading of Marx as the author of "a theory of history capable of providing us with a new theory of *reading.*"[7] This structure of repetition is in fact essential to Althusser's figure of reading, begin-

---

tists and Other Essays, ed. Gregory Elliott, trans. James H. Kavanagh (London: Verso, 1990), 16–17.

6. Working in a Lacanian idiom, Jane Gallop narrates the consequences of a reading that acknowledges its failures in *Reading Lacan* (Ithaca: Cornell University Press, 1985), where she recounts a reader's report that complained of her willingness to acknowledge a necessarily "insufficient command of the material" (20). She responds by arguing that "Lacan's major statement of ethical purpose and therapeutic goal . . . is that one must assume one's castration. Women have always been considered 'castrated' in psychoanalytic theory. But castration for Lacan is not only sexual; more important, it is also linguistic: we are inevitably bereft of any masterful understanding of language, and can only signify ourselves in a symbolic system that we do not command, that rather, commands us. . . . My assumption of my inadequacy and my attempt to read from that position are thus, to my mind, both Lacanian and feminist" (20). It is also, I would say, Althusserian. This sort of "assumption" is what the fetish of ideology is meant to ward off.

7. For the purposes of this paper, I will leave entirely to the side the question of the correctness of Althusser's reading of Marx; that often Marxological debate is deeply woven into the fetishization of the theory of ideology, but requires its own analysis. However one judges the "accuracy" of Althusser's account of Marx, the question of the disavowal of his theory of reading remains a problem.

ning, as it does, with "guilt," and ending with a warning against the "risk" of "entering a future still charged with dangers and shades, with a virgin conscience."[8] Althusser's theory of reading originates with his rejection of the possibility of "innocent" reading, reading at "first sight," reading without repetition or without guilt. Employing the metaphors of blindness and insight, he proceeds to argue that a structural limit or horizon is essential to the production of any reading whatsoever.[9] This view generates the concept of the "problematic" and with it the metaphor of terrain, and a certain crisis of *form*. It is out of this crisis—and Althusser's insistence on its political force—that reading emerges as a strategy of doubling, of first *and* second readings, or of "symptomatic" reading as a guilty shift in the terrain. Symptomatic reading actively produces "discontinuity," an irreducible gap between problematics or forms, a gap that is nevertheless politically and historically situated and therefore vulnerable to erosion, displacement, and rereading. This discontinuity is specified by the articulation of an "unposed" or "absent" question, the question that the reading (the reader) establishes as unthinkable within the text's own problematic. "Symptomatic" reading is precisely the production of this absent question, which figures the political *and* rhetorical relation—or more accurately, conflict—between a text and its reader, between readers, between positions. To read is to give form to this conflict, to pose the question that gives the problematic its structure. But the symptom is not something that afflicts only the texts of our opponents; our own symptom is visible as our guilt, the guilt that our reading will expose rather than conceal, the guilt that opens the text. Therein lies the very possibility of a politics of reading.

8. *Reading "Capital,"* 198. These are the last words of the appendix to the essay "The Object of Capital," which stands in the place of Jacques Rancière's "Le concept de Critique et la Critique de l'économie politique des *Manuscrits de 1844* au *Capital*" in the English translation of *Lire le Capital*. Althusser's delight in appendices and postscripts signals the problematic of reading in his work.

9. In my "The Problematic of Blindness and Insight: Reading Althusser and de Man" (unpublished), I suggest a deep affinity between the opening gestures in these two bodies of work, although the manner in which de Man plays this tension out in his appropriation of these tropes is quite distinct from Althusser's path, as aporia differs from the unposed question. Although both men begin with the interdependence of blindness and insight and insist on the urgent need to reconceptualize reading, for de Man, to read is to chart the unlimited operation of tropes: "There seems to be no limit to what tropes can get away with" (*Allegories of Reading: Figural Language in Rousseau, Nietzsche, Rilke, and Proust* [New Haven: Yale University Press, 1979], 62). For Althusser, to propose "no limits" is to profess one's innocence; to read is to unmask limits, problematics we can display but never escape.

Althusser never flinches from the acknowledgment, with which he begins *Reading "Capital,"* that "guilt" is the burden of and the grounds for any reading. I propose an analysis that returns the question "what is it to read?" to the Althusserian text.

In *Reading "Capital,"* Althusser argues:

> The Young Marx of the *1844 Manuscripts* read the human essence at sight, immediately, in the transparency of its alienation. *Capital,* on the contrary, exactly measures a distance and an internal dislocation (*décalage*) in the real, inscribed in its *structure,* a distance and a dislocation such as to make their own effects themselves illegible, and the illusion of an immediate reading of them the ultimate apex of their effects: *fetishism.* [17]

Insofar as we seek in Althusser's text a theory of ideology that disavows these dislocating effects—and thus appears to allow us to escape them, either as readers or as political agents—we return to the illusory fetish of "immediate reading" and thus squander the genuinely productive portion of Althusser's (and Marx's) political insight into what reading is. In our embrace of the transparent, we deaden the most lively element of their texts and commit ourselves to a kind of deathly "science," even as we rail against its totalizing illusions. In fact, Althusser suggests that between the "immortality of ideology" (Elliott, 172) and the death of labor-power lies the *unnatural* structure of reading and writing.[10] Inhabiting that structure, a structure of repetition without end, once we have "broken with the religious complicity between

---

10. The word "fetish" is obviously not to be taken for granted. Althusser's reference is to *Capital* and "The Fetishism of Commodities and the Secret Thereof," and Marx is my primary reference as well. But I agree with Emily Apter's suggestion that "Marx's conception of the fetish as socioeconomic hieroglyphic and opaque verbal sign emerge[s] . . . as curiously compatible with Freud's sense of the strangeness of fetish consciousness: a state of mind divided between the reality of noncastration and the fear of it all the same" (*Feminizing the Fetish: Psychoanalysis and Narrative Obsession in Turn-of-the-Century France* [Ithaca: Cornell University Press, 1991], 1), and I find the psychoanalytic term *disavowal* apt for the naturalizing of value that Marx exposes. See also Slavoj Žižek on Marx as the inventor of the symptom and on the "secret of the [commodity] form itself" (*The Sublime Object of Ideology* [London: Verso, 1989]), and Michael Taussig on the process of "defetishizing" and fetishistic "reenchanting" (*The Nervous System* [London: Routledge, 1992]). Fetishism as the persistent naturalization of value, the dogberryish mistaking of reading and writing as things that "com[e] by Nature," and fetishism as a disavowal that simultaneously affirms and denies a perception both seem to work in the fetishism of Althusser's theory of ideology.

Logos and Being; between the Great Book that was, in its very being, the World, and the discourse of the knowledge of the world; between the essence of things and its reading, . . . [we find that] a new conception of *discourse* at last becomes possible" (*RC*, 17). In our readings of Althusser, this new conception of discourse has been obscured by our eagerness to perfect a theory of ideology that strangely revives the old trope of complicity "between Logos and Being," thus helping us to conceal our own. Why does the theory of ideology compel us so?

In Chapter Six of *Capital*, "The Buying and Selling of Labour-Power," Marx observes:

> The owner of labour-power is mortal. If then his appearance in the market is to be continuous, [and the continuous conversion of money into capital assumes this,] the seller of labour-power must perpetuate himself, "in the way every living individual perpetuates himself, by procreation." The labour-power withdrawn from the market by wear and tear and death must be continually replaced by, at the very least, an equal amount of fresh labour-power. Hence the sum of the means of subsistence necessary for the production of labour-power must include the means necessary for the labourer's substitutes, i.e., his children, in order that this race of peculiar commodity owners may perpetuate its appearance in the market. [172]

From the perspective of capital, which is the perspective of *Capital*, death leads to life, that is, it is the inevitable death of the seller of labor-power that makes reproduction or procreation necessary; the natural narrative of the life-cycle is reversed. In this counter-narrative, labor is a commodity, not a use-value, and capital requires a steady supply. One of the conclusions Marx draws from his reflection on the mortality of the laborer is that "the minimum limit of the value of labour-power is determined by the value of the commodities without the daily supply of which the labourer cannot renew his vital energy, [. . . that is,] by the value of those means of subsistence that are physically indispensable" (*Capital*, 173). Death thus imposes twice on the market economy and its laborers. In order to stave off her own death, the owner of that peculiar commodity, labor-power, must never sell it for less than a subsistence wage; and to compensate capital for her nevertheless certain mortality, she must also earn enough to procreate, to reproduce herself physically in the flesh of her children.

In "Ideology and Ideological State Apparatuses," Althusser reiterates Marx's point when he argues that "the ultimate condition of production is . . . the reproduction of the conditions of production."[11] As you doubtless recall, he touches only momentarily on the problem of reproducing the means of production. He quickly moves to his main concern: the reproduction of labor-power as such, and he echoes Marx's remarks in *Capital*, although with a slight shift in emphasis:

> Wages represent only that part of the value produced by the expenditure of labour power which is indispensable for its reproduction: indispensable to the reconstitution of the labour power of the wage earner (the wherewithal to pay for housing, food and clothing, in short to enable the wage-earner to present himself again at the factory gate the next day—and every further day God grants him); and we should add: indispensable for raising and educating the children in whom the proletarian reproduces himself (in n models where n = 0, 1, 2, etc . . .) as labour power. [131]

The erasure of the feminine contribution to this process is far from trivial; the history of Marxist feminist discourse on the family wage, domestic labor, and class itself is the arduous history of rethinking this proletarian and *his* children to the nth power. Ironically (I think), the polemical thrust of Althusser's argument lies in his assertion that the "perpetuation" or "reproduction" of these peculiar commodity owners is not guaranteed by physiological reproduction alone and that it is (has been) a fundamental mistake of Marxist theory to think it is. "It is not enough to ensure for labour power the material conditions of its reproduction if it is to be reproduced *as* labour power" (131, my emphasis).

There is a "surplus" task of reproduction, over and above the indispensable (historic) minimum of calories, health care, and, perhaps, parental leave; this surplus task is carried out "more and more outside production" itself, "by the capitalist education system and by other instances and institutions" (132), including the family, and it goes well beyond "training" the labor force in necessary production skills. As Althusser puts it:

---

11. Althusser, "Ideology and Ideological State Apparatuses," in *Lenin and Philosophy and Other Essays*, trans. Ben Brewster (New York: Monthly Review Press, 1971), 127. He also notes that to stress the process of reproduction is to "ente[r] a domain which is both very familiar (since *Capital, Volume Two*) and uniquely ignored" (127–28), and he complains that "the tenacious obviousnesses (ideological obviousnesses of an empiricist type) of the point of view of production alone . . . are so integrated into our everyday 'consciousness' that it is extremely hard, not to say almost impossible, to raise oneself to the *point of view of reproduction*" (128). This was a long time ago.

> The reproduction of labour power requires not only a reproduction of its skills, but also, at the same time, a reproduction of its submission to the rules of the established order, i.e. a reproduction of submission to the ruling ideology for the workers, and a reproduction of the ability to manipulate the ruling ideology correctly for the agents of exploitation and repression. . . . The reproduction of labour power thus reveals as its *sine qua non* not only the reproduction of its "skills" but also the reproduction of its subjection to the ruling ideology or of the "practice" of that ideology, with the proviso that it is not enough to say "not only but also," for it is clear that *it is in the forms and under the forms of ideological subjection that provision is made for the reproduction of the skills of labour power.* [133, my emphasis]

Althusser argues for the indispensability of ideology as a *form*, first to capitalism as a specific mode of production, but then, in principle, for all social formations; unlike the laborer, ideology will never die, and its "life" is closely bound up with hers. This assertion of the "immortality of ideology" is one of the most frequently commented upon elements of Althusser's work on ideology, whether it is attacked as an irredeemable break with Marx and Marxism, quietism and counter-revolution, antihistoricism, and the sign of a post-Marxist reversion to thinking a generalized consciousness (or subjectivity), or celebrated as an opening that both acknowledges the emphasis Marx (from *The Eighteenth Brumaire* onward) put on ideology, representation, and politics and registers the overdeterminations of social life and social subjects. In either case, commentators have recognized that the argument that places ideology at the center of the problem of reproducing labor-power shifts the internal dynamic of Marxist analysis (in the direction of ideological state apparatuses) and rewrites the relation between Marxism as a theory of exploitation and other forms of social critique: feminism, "minority" discourse, postcoloniality, queer theory. The "outside" of ideology, which is its death, no longer beckons. We face a more intimate enemy, and the recognition of ideology as a permanent form, with potentially new and shifting contents, may leave us with the sense that our task is strangely inchoate.

This analysis of the essential task of ideological reproduction, as it is elaborated in "Ideology and Ideological State Apparatuses" and elsewhere in Althusser's work, seems indispensable to me, for all of the significant critiques it has sustained. Yet, many of his readers (I realize that this phrase itself marks a large if necessary oversimplification: national, disciplinary, and political differences distinguish the various readers of his text), especially readers who are interested in the problems of ideology and the subject, have focused our attention too exclusively on moments in Althusser's text where he literally speaks of ideology, to the detriment of other aspects of his work and, ultimately, to no good purpose even when considered solely in terms of the development of theories of ideology.[12] Perhaps it is the very intimacy and elusiveness of ideology, once it is understood as an unconscious and permanent feature of social practice, that gives it its mesmerizing

12. I have deliberately chosen not to "make an example" of any particular reader of Althusser; the fetishization of the theory of ideology is not a matter of individual readers or of misreading as such, but of a far-reaching problematic that is finally a symptom of the longing for a confident political solidarity, which is in itself positive and only inadvertently (and contingently) bound up with the desire for protection from the risks of reading. I have in mind, broadly speaking, discursive instances such as: "screen theory" and its American counterparts; those elements within feminist and Marxist-feminist discourse that have found ideology a useful way to speak about gender and the Althusserian subject of ideology a plausible figure for woman; all of the accounts of *Reading "Capital"* that stress the epistemological argument without actually acknowledging the operative role that reading as such plays in it; any appropriation of Althusser that detaches the arguments concerning ideology in certain texts from the trope of reading. In most of these instances, if the problematic of "reading" is acknowledge at all, it is only to be subordinated to the ideology/science pair. A glance at two recent anthologies devoted to Althusser's work reveals the subordinate place of reading. In *The Althusserian Legacy*, only Maria Turchetto ("The History of Science and the Science of History," 73–80) puts a sustained and direct emphasis on *Reading "Capital"* and on reading in that text, an emphasis she seems partially to withdraw by insisting on the *"philosopher's* reading" (as distinct from the historian's or the logician's), where she might have also marked the "philosopher's *reading.*" In the same volume, Warren Montag, in "Spinoza and Althusser Against Hermeneutics: Interpretation or Intervention?," addresses reading by a quite different route, but in a very persuasive way. In *Althusser: A Critical Reader* (ed. Gregory Elliott [Oxford: Blackwell, 1994]), Paul Ricoeur's "Althusser's Theory of Ideology" (a selection drawn from *Lectures on Ideology and Utopia*) is a fairly representative piece, which does not cite *Reading "Capital"* or connect the theory of ideology to reading. Even Frances Mulhern, whose essay is entitled "Message in a Bottle: Althusser in Literary Studies," finds little of interest in Althusser's theory of reading, which some would say is the task of literary studies.

I hasten to add two points. I do not mean to suggest that *Reading "Capital"* and its view of reading are the only worthy texts in Althusser's oeuvre. Nor does my regret at the marginalization of *Reading "Capital"* and of reading within it signal a lack of respect for the work that has been pursued under the signs of ideology, epistemology, history, or overdetermination, to name a few. Furthermore, my polemic on behalf of reading is not meant as a covert polemic on behalf of "literature" or "literariness." I do not, in other words, hope to annex Althusser's concept of reading to an already-in-place literary-critical project, as, for example, Derrida's notion of writing has been appropriated by some students of literature as a paradigm for literary criticism. In Althusser's case, as in Derrida's, a familiar term appears in a significantly new problematic and offers possibilities undreamed of in the English department.

power. Certainly, the constant threat of submission/subjection that Althusser's account emphasizes has the potential to call up a fetishistic refusal, a passionate disavowal of complicity. But Althusser's theory of reading, as it emerges in *Reading "Capital,"* responds to the very theoretical and political objections that many commentators on his account of ideology raise, including its traces of scientism and ahistoricism, not to say Stalinism, Althusser's alleged "severance of theory from any real referent" (Elliott, 111), and, perhaps most importantly, the charge that his view of the subject of ideology is "mechanistic" and "inflexible" or leads to a functionalism in which "the 'subject' in history is always wholly subjected to dominant ideology and thus by definition incapable of resistance" (Smith, 21) or any break whatsoever with ideological effects.[13]

The importance of Althusser's account of reading to the problem of ideological reproduction (which is always, in part, a problem of complicity) makes the neglect of this aspect of his work almost incomprehensible, save insofar as reading is seen merely as a protocol in the service of more fundamental categories. But Althusser's theory of reading is not an adjunct to his theory of ideology; his argument about reading—and what he does in his reading practice—establishes the relation between ideology and science; reading precipitates ideology as such: "We have to think (in a completely novel way) the relation between a science and the ideology which gave rise to it. . . . [E]very science, in the relationship it has with the ideology it emerges from, can only be thought as a 'science of the ideology.'"[14]

---

13. Paul Smith, in *Discerning the Subject* (Minneapolis: University of Minnesota Press, 1988), also argues that Althusser conflates the "individual" and the "subject" (19) and ultimately "rejoins Marx in a crude sense of ideology as distortion and of 'subject' as simply *Träger* (support)" (21). All three of these readings seem problematic to me. On the contrary, I agree with Žižek that for Althusser the "'individual' which is interpellated into subject is not conceptually defined, it is simply a hypothetical X which must be presupposed" (101), and I read *Capital* itself as an account of the "taking of forms" in capitalism—a taking of form that always (and will always) require(s) reading and is never a crude matter of distorting the preformed or pristine real.

14. *Reading "Capital,"* 4. Althusser warns in this same passage that "even the theoretically essential and practically decisive distinction between science and ideology gets some protection from this [the "surprises" discovered by the historical investigation of the sciences] against the dogmatist or scientistic temptations which threaten it—since in this work of investigation and conceptualization we have to learn not to make use of this distinction in a way that restores the ideology of the philosophy of the Enlightenment" (45). He of course returns, in a critical second reading of his own text, to these questions in *Essays in Self-Criticism*.

The critical emphasis in readings of Althusser on the theory of ideology dismisses reading as such; as I have suggested, the fetishism of the theory of ideology simultaneously disavows the elusiveness of a correct political position vis à vis the oppressed or potentially revolutionary classes, an elusiveness that is painfully obvious in political practice and insisted upon (and thereby exacerbated rather than soothed) in Althusser's theory of "symptomatic" reading. The search for the correct theory of ideology simultaneously affirms political engagement and allows an evasion of the risks entailed in "reading," the threat that one's reading will simply be disowned or denounced, even (or especially) by one's potential political allies. (Indeed, this is the very fate that Althusser's work has met in some quarters; the threat is originally one of schism.) As Althusser describes it, reading is risky because it is always a relation among readings and readers, a productive and political relation, but productive precisely in that it intervenes in the process of reproduction and thus cannot be guaranteed. The privileging of the theory of ideology—and the ideology/science opposition in *Reading "Capital*—expresses the desire for such a political guarantee, even when the critic may end by dismissing Althusser's efforts in this area (as many have); a science of ideology is invulnerable to the political contempt of the sanctioned Other.

By contrast, for Althusser, to read is to undertake the task of producing political alignments, which require shared readings, which, in turn, are never simply present to be excavated. This is the meaning of his assertion that ideology is immortal—*reading* is an endless process. The fetishization of ideology seeks to ward off the necessary failures that reading suffers; politics takes the form of a correct theory of ideology, and a correct relation to that theory substitutes for (always potentially incorrect) political relations. Politics as a practice of reading—a double and guilty practice that never ends and never fully or finally succeeds—this Althusserian understanding of politics is obscured. In its place we find a *double fetishism: a fetishistic attachment to a theory of ideology and a theory of ideology that is itself fetishistic*, returning to the illusion of a transparent rather than a dislocated text. The theory of ideology thus plays the role of the commodity as Marx describes it in *Capital:* the "social hieroglyphic" whose character is "stamped" upon it and which must thus be *read* as an unpredictable "taking of form" is taken for the state of nature, acquiring the "stability of natural, self-understood forms of social life." The task of reading is elided, for, as Dogberry assures Seacoal, "reading and writing comes by Nature."15

The unnatural character of reading is reiterated at every level of *Reading "Capital."* Althusser argues "that only since Marx have we had to begin to suspect what, in theory at least, *reading* and hence writing *means (veut dire)*" (16). His own texts are in fact frequently figured as "readings," that is, as tentative, contextual, appropriative, interventionist, and unfinished efforts to shift the terrain. The opening words of *Reading "Capital"* provide one such example, insisting that "the following papers were delivered in the course of a seminar on *Capital* held at the École Normale Supérieure early in 1965. They bear the mark of these circumstances: not only in their construction, their rhythm, their didactic or oral style, but also and above all in their discrepancies, the repetitions, hesitations and uncertain steps in their investigations." Such comments appear throughout Althusser's *oeuvre:* "Contradiction and Over-determination" is subtitled "Notes for an Investigation," and the endlessly cited "Ideology and Ideological State Apparatuses" carries the same disclaimer and the following note: "This text is made up of two extracts from an ongoing study. The subtitle 'Notes towards an Investigation' is the author's own. The ideas expounded should not be regarded as more than the introduction to a discussion"; "Freud and Lacan" arrives under the auspices of "friends [who] have correctly criticized me for discussing Lacan in three lines. . . . They have asked me for a few words to justify both the allusion and its object. Here they are—a few words, *where a book is needed*"; "Lenin and Philosophy" begins by mocking the very notion of a "philosophical communication" and ends with an "appendix" (the

---

15. I pursue this argument about the "Commodities" chapter, the "taking of form" and the nature/reading opposition in another essay, "B(u)y Nature" (unpublished). For a summary of the argument around the problematic of ideology and its relation to Marx's understanding of fetishism, see William Pietz, "Fetishism and Materialism," in *Fetishism as Cultural Discourse*, ed. Emily Apter and William Pietz (Ithaca: Cornell University Press, 1993), 119–51, especially 125ff. For a countervailing view, which places fetishism within the problematic of ideology, see Etienne Balibar, "The Vacillation of Ideology," in *Marxism and the Interpretation of Culture*, ed. Cary Nelson and Lawrence Goldberg (Urbana: University of Illinois, 1988). Pietz is the author of a definitive series of essays on the fetish; see "The Problem of the Fetish, I," *Res* 9 (1985): 5–17; "The Problem of the Fetish, IIIa: Bosman's Guinea and the Enlightenment Theory of Fetishism," *Res* 16 (1988): 105–23.

same is true for *For Marx*);[16] "Marxism and Humanism" appends "A Complementary Note on 'Real Humanism'" and the final paragraph of "On the Materialist Dialectic" reads "This could and should be the occasion for new investigations" (*For Marx*, 218). While I am very far from simply accepting these disclaimers and deliberately loosened ends as "true" accounts of either the stylistic or the theoretical mode of Althusser's work (that would be to refuse to *read* his text), to take them seriously is to begin a reading of the degree to which his theory of "what it is to read" shapes his reading practice. Althusser concedes that as the essays of *Reading "Capital"* became a book they might have been subject to some revision:

> We could . . . have gone over them . . . corrected them one against the other, reduced the margin of variation between them, unified their terminology . . . and set out their contents in the systematic framework of a single discourse—in other words, we could have tried to make a *finished* work out of them. [13]

This possibility, the possibility of a systematic "finish," is rejected: "But rather than pretending they are what they should have been, we prefer to present them for what they are: precisely, incomplete texts, the mere beginnings of a *reading*" (*RC*, 13). The finished work is like the death of ideology, an old fetish. And reading is always in its beginning stages, even at its most polished and emphatic.

Althusser is concerned to retain the "various individual protocols" and "peculiar oblique path(s)" (*RC*, 14) of the readings in *Reading "Capital,"* precisely in order to maintain the emphasis on reading as such, on risk, adventure, the new-born, and a certain violence. As he puts it:

> We present them in their immediate form without making any alterations so that the risks and advantages of this adventure are reproduced; so that the reader will be able to find in them new-born the experience of a reading; and so that he in turn will be dragged in the wake of this first reading into a second one which will take us still further. [*RC*, 14]

Reading never actually progresses far from this new-born or beginning moment for Althusser, precisely because a *second* reading—a newly new-born—is always in the process of beginning. (Everything is always

---

16. Althusser, *Lenin and Philosophy and Other Essays*, 195, my emphasis; Althusser, *For Marx*, trans. Ben Brewster (London: Verso, 1979).

a "note toward" or dragging appendices because the end point or last instance is forever receding. In Althusser's view, this is true of Marx's text as well, of course; that observation provoked outrage among some and yawns from others, both "symptomatic" responses from an Althusserian perspective.)

The unfinished quality of every reading is not to be confused with ambiguity. Althusser stresses the open structure of reading as a way of acknowledging the interplay among readers, readers past and readers to come, and with them histories and politics. Hence his view of reading as an endless strategy of *doubling*, a structure of repetition that marks both our historical situatedness (reading is not ahistorical in this account, as the *Essays in Self-Criticism* reiterate) and our political interestedness. To acknowledge this structure is, in fact, to acknowledge ideology; but Althusser makes this point by rejecting the possibility of "innocent reading," reading at first sight, and by embracing "guilty" readings. In *Reading "Capital,"* he argues:

> As there is no such thing as an innocent reading, we must say what reading we are guilty of . . . a philosophical reading of *Capital* is quite the opposite of an innocent reading. It is a guilty reading, but not one that absolves its crime on confessing it. On the contrary, it takes the responsibility for its crime as a "justified crime" and defends it by proving its necessity. It is therefore a special reading which exculpates itself as a reading by posing every guilty reading the very question that unmasks its innocence . . . : *what is it to read?* [15]

The necessity Althusser speaks of is equally a political and a rhetorical one. The necessity of giving a political and a rhetorical, as well as an epistemological answer to the question "What is it to read?" leads him to the rhetoric of blindness (or oversight) and insight. Without the guilt that establishes the necessity of reading, no symptom would ever emerge from a text; guilt is the productive relation, the relation that prevents reading from ever being an explication of what the text "expresses."

Having abandoned the "myth of immediate vision" and the possibility of innocent reading, Althusser must radically revise his epistemological assumptions about reading. The rhetoric of blindness and oversight articulates a structural limit as essential to the production of any reading whatsoever. "Guilt" is one name for this limit, a name that exposes the irreducibility of "positioning," both as "perspective" and as "investment." (The symptom is also such a name.) The "internal dislocation" or structural limit of every reading, the "oversight that concerns vision [and] . . . is a form of vision and hence has a necessary relationship with vision" (*RC*, 21), leads Althusser to the concept of the "problematic," the metaphor of terrain, and a defetishizing reading of symptomaticity. For Althusser, blindness or "oversight" is a consequence of the fundamental and irreducible discontinuities among variously guilty problematics. Thus, he observes:

> What political economy does not see is not a pre-existing object which it could have seen but did not see—but an object which it produced itself in its operation of knowledge and which did not pre-exist it: precisely the production itself. . . . [Political economy] made "a complete change in the terms of the original problem," and thereby produced a new problem, but without knowing it . . . it remained convinced that it was still on the terrain of the old problem, whereas it has "unwittingly changed terrain." Its blindness and its "oversight" lie in this misunderstanding between what it produces and what it sees. [*RC*, 24]

In the metaphor of terrain, the structural limit of reading appears in the *form* of the "problematic." Problematics are inevitably historical, or better, political, forms and as such they constitute the conditions of possibility of any reading, including his own, insofar as they determine "the *forms* in which all problems must be posed, at any given moment."[17] A problematic is thus a position—although not necessarily a consciously (or wittingly) held position—and the discontinuity among problematics is the difference across which "symptomatic" reading, double reading, plays.

Reading thus emerges as an unavoidable practice of first *and* second readings, indeed, as a violent, deliberate, and politically motivated (though never wholly determined) shift in the problematic or terrain. Symptomatic reading actively produces "discontinuity," an irreducible gap between problematics, a gap that is historically situated and therefore always vulnerable to erosion, displacement, and rereading.

---

17. *Reading "Capital,"* 25, my emphasis. See the discussion of "Science and Ideology" in *Essays in Self-Criticism*, 119–25: Marx "*was only able to break with bourgeois ideology in its totality because he took inspiration from the basic ideas of proletarian ideology, and from the first class struggles of the proletariat, in which this ideology became flesh and blood.* This is the 'event' which, behind the rationalist façade of the contrast between 'positive truth' and ideological illusion, gave this contrast its real historical dimension" (121).

The gap precipitates ideology *as a form*, and it is this view of ideology and ideology critique that places Althusser distinctly outside the notion of ideology as false consciousness, without robbing his reading practice of its political edge. The problematic is never simply a theme in Althusser's text; what reading must always disclose is the secret of the form of the problematic, its fetish character, hence the antifetishist gesture at its beginning.[18] This discontinuity that ideologizes and gives form at once is what "science" achieves; it is specified by the articulation of what Althusser calls the "unposed" or "absent" question, the question that the second reading establishes as unthinkable *within* the text's own problematic, on its terrain. This absent question is one that the text *answers*, but never explicitly posits. It is the symptomatically overlooked term in any discourse, or rather, *one* such term—I find no warrant in *Reading "Capital"* for the suggestion that any text produces only one symptom; this would indeed be reading *as* fetishism. (This multiplication [or production] of symptoms is, of course, for some of Althusser's readers, a fatal shortcoming; one response to this shocking possibility is to fetishize the theory of ideology.)

As Althusser puts it in describing Marx reading political economy:

> A correct answer is a correct answer. Any reader in the "first manner" will give Smith and Ricardo a good mark and pass on to other observations. Not Marx. For what we shall call his eye has been attracted by a remarkable property of this answer; it is the correct answer to a question that has just one failing: it was never posed. [22]

What Althusser figures as "his eye" is Marx's problematic, which produces both a reading and a question that are absent in Smith and Ricardo's texts. In the Althusserian practice of symptomatic reading, the *term must be compared with itself* through a double reading that confronts its "non-vision with its vision" in a deliberately defetishizing crisis that exposes the "connection between the field of the visible and the field of the invisible" (*RC*, 20, 21), that refuses to mystify that relation, which is also the relation of reading. As Francis Barker suggests, "the point is not to supply this absence, to make whole what is

---

18. Christina Crosby has pointed out that a thematizing of the problematic is the gesture that defines standpoint theory's epistemology; the shift in terrain that Althusser defines as the task of reading is reified into a subject position and the work of reading is obscured. This is one of the many symptoms of fetishizing the theory of ideology.

lacking [—to fetishize—], but to aggravate its historical significance."[19]

The unposed question figures the irreducible difference of view, of terrain, that is reading, and discloses double reading as a hopelessly political and historical process, one that no text can escape, foreclose, or defend itself against. Symptomatic reading is the production of the absent question that figures the political and rhetorical relation—or, more accurately, conflict—between a text and its reader, between readings and among readers. This is the sense in which a reading may "break" with an ideology and consequently with its own text, even as it clings tightly to it, insisting that "the classical text itself . . . tells us that it is silent: its silence is its own words."[20] If the symptomatic reading exposes both a blindness and its oversight when it utters the unposed question, figuring forth the difference between what a text "produces and what it sees," Althusser stresses that it achieves this insight by means of what "Marx elsewhere calls a 'play on words' (*Wortspiel*)" (RC, 24). This play is the "surprise" of reading as Althusser has read, a surprise that sets the terms of "the form of its *writing*" (RC, 69) and enables us to see ideology finally as a "circle perpetually opened by its closures themselves" (RC, 45) and to undertake to read the secret thereof.

---

19. Francis Barker, *The Tremulous Private Body: Essays on Subjection* (London: Methuen, 1984), 38.

20. *Reading "Capital,"* 22. Althusser was very attentive to words; hence, his insistence that they were weapons and well worth the battles they caused, and his attention to "nuance," to the difference, for example, between an "error" and a "deviation" (*Essays*, 105).

MICHAEL SPRINKER

The Legacies of Althusser

One consequence of the pan-European demise of the hitherto dominant forms of historical Communism is the opportunity provided— indeed, the duty enjoined— to assess its theoretical heritage. If the political dynamic of the Third International was given its ultimate quietus in 1989–92, it is by no means certain that its intellectual resources are equally spent. Much talk circulates about the end of any viable class politics in the advanced industrial societies, at the same time that the brutalities of capitalist accumulation continue unchecked around the globe. At the very moment when traditional mass parties of the working class appear to have forfeited their popular legitimacy (and in most cases have either dissolved or splintered into competing tendencies), the analytical value of social class for comprehending these same political processes remains undiminished.

Among the congeries of theoretical programs typically lumped together under the label "Western Marxism," none has consistently provoked more passionate response *pro et contra* than that associated with the name of Louis Althusser. One could hypothesize a variety of reasons for the extraordinary vehemence with which Althusser's writings have been defended by acolytes and denounced by opponents. In retrospect, it would appear that the principal source for the heat they generated can be located in their novel project to unite two seemingly incompatible tendencies of twentieth-century thought in a singular theoretical program aiming to advance revolutionary politics. Drawing upon the resources of (primarily) French historical epistemology to account for Marxism's emergence out of the classical philosophies of history, Althusser at the same time insisted upon the scientificity of historical materialism, its absolute differentiation from the philosophical ideologies that had preceded it and, in his view, still threatened to impede its development within the official apparatuses of the international labor movement. Repeatedly insisting that he was both a Communist and a philosopher,[1] Althusser was labeled by turns a dogmatist for declining to repudiate Marxism-Leninism, or a relativist for asserting that Marxism stood in continual need of conceptual rectification. From these opposed theoretical indictments, political consequences could be summarily drawn, with Althusser standing accused of unrepentant Stalinism on the one hand, of at first flirting with Maoism while later harboring Eurocommunist sympathies on the other.[2]

No more than Marx's do Althusser's texts exhibit pristine theoretical consistency. Nor have they failed to promote different, often conflicting tendencies over time. The tragic *dénouement* that overtook and abruptly halted Althusser's own development has not prevented the continuation of what may fairly be termed the Althusserian problematic in the human sciences at large, especially in the work of some of those who were intimately associated with the project at the moment when it burst upon the European intellectual scene in the mid-1960s. In what follows, I shall be principally concerned with the itinerary of some of the earliest Althusserians over the thirty years since they participated in the seminar that produced *Reading "Capi-*

---

1. Etienne Balibar put the matter best in remembering his teacher and collaborator at Althusser's funeral: "To be *at the same time* totally a philosopher and totally a Communist, without sacrificing, subordinating, or subjecting either of the two terms to the other—such is Althusser's intellectual singularity, such was his wager and the risk he took" ("Adieu," in Balibar, *Ecrits pour Althusser* [Paris: La Découverte, 1991], 122). Here and throughout, unless otherwise indicated, translations are my own.

2. The most famous arraignment in English of Althusser's supposed Stalinism was the late Edward Thompson's essay, "The Poverty of Theory," in his *The Poverty of Theory and Other Essays* (New York: Monthly Review, 1978), 1–210. Gregory Elliott gives pride of place in the philosopher's development, from the moment of *Reading "Capital"* through the ISAs, to Althusser's Maoism, which was crystallized in an anonymously published text of 1966, "Sur la Révolution Culturelle"; see Elliott, *Althusser: The Detour of Theory* (London: Verso, 1987), 194–97. Elliott argues for a shift towards Eurocommunism during the middle to late 1970s, evident, for example, in the contrast between Althusser's lecture on the Twenty-second Congress of the French Communist Party and Balibar's essay on the dictatorship of the proletariat; see ibid., 289 ff. The charge that Althusserian theory is at once dogmatic and relativistic has also been lodged by Peter Dews in his "Althusser, Structuralism, and the French Epistemological Tradition," in Gregory Elliott, ed., *Althusser: A Critical Reader* (Oxford: Blackwell, 1994), 104–41.

tal." While this preliminary survey of writings by some of Althusser's most famous students cannot pretend to draw up a definitive balance sheet either for their work or for Althusser's significance generally, it does attempt to locate a few of the more promising paths that the Althusserian intervention opened up. By implication, it also passes judgment on several of its less happy outcomes in politics and theory, outcomes for which Althusser cannot be held solely responsible but that his writings did certainly help to license.[3]

ALTHUSSERIAN THESES

The task of philosophy, Althusser famously insisted from 1967 onwards, is to present theses. The specificity of Marxist philosophy consists in proposing materialist theses to counteract the idealist tendencies that perpetually endanger progress in the sciences.[4] No reader of Althusser is likely to miss the self-reflexivity with which this proposition operated on Althusser's own texts, which often read like extended elaborations of a single concept presented in the form of a slogan. Some familiar examples: history is a process without a subject or goals; ideology interpellates individuals as subjects; philosophy is the class struggle in theory; the knowledge of history is no more historical than the knowledge of sugar is sugary.

From among these (and some others I shall enumerate in a moment), we can isolate a number of distinctively Althusserian themes that have achieved general currency (which is not to say they have been widely accepted), and that have, in addition, been subject to develop-

---

3. The longer version of this essay includes a section on Althusser's impact upon history writing, focusing on the work of Jacques Rancière. Space constraints dictated that this discussion be excised from the present text. Omitted altogether—primarily because of the limits of the author's scholarly competence—is the rich and complex work in political economy undertaken by the proponents of Regulation Theory. On their debt to, as well as their divergence from, "high Althusserianism" (viz., the moment of *Pour Marx* and *Lire le Capital*, including the Poulantzas of *Pouvoir politique et classes sociales*), see Alain Lipietz, "From Althusserianism to 'Regulation Theory,'" in E. Ann Kaplan and Michael Sprinker, eds., *The Althusserian Legacy* (London: Verso, 1993), 99–138. Also omitted is any sustained engagement with the most influential Anglophone post-Althusserians, Hindess and Hirst, Laclau and Mouffe, and Wolff and Resnick, who have found in Althusser the charter for their own retreat towards social democracy. The continuing challenge of Althusserianism requires, in my view, sustaining his commitment to Communism on both the theoretical and the political levels.

4. See Louis Althusser, *Philosophy and the Spontaneous Philosophy of the Scientists and Other Essays*, ed. Gregory Elliott, trans. Ben Brewster *et al.* (London: Verso, 1990), 74–77.

ment and refinement in subsequent work. In no particular order of importance, these are:

1. The relative autonomy of the superstructures and the reciprocal action of the superstructures on the base
2. The permanence of ideology
3. The specificity of art in relation to ideology
4. The overdetermination in principle of any historical conjuncture
5. The distinction between objects of knowledge and real objects
6. The nonsubjective nature of historical processes
7. The imbrication of philosophy in politics
8. The ineluctability of class struggle in history

None was original with him. As Althusser himself repeatedly emphasized, all were either explicitly enunciated in or could be extrapolated from the classical texts of Marxism-Leninism. Althusser's accomplishment, to rate it no higher, was to extract these motifs from the tradition and to construct from them a distinctive problematic for historical materialism, one that would enable it to continue producing new knowledges by strictly delimiting its field of investigation. Insistence on the scientificity of historical materialism never had any other goal than this.

The measure of any science's maturity (whether it is "progressive" or "degenerating," in Lakatos's terms), that which distinguishes it from the ideological problematic out of which it is born, is the new knowledges, both theoretical and empirical, it produces. Like any other research program, Althusser's must submit to this test. How have the propositions enumerated above fared in subsequent research?

WE WERE NEVER STRUCTURALISTS, WE WERE SPINOZISTS

On several occasions, Althusser pointed to Spinoza as the key, indeed perhaps the only authentic, antecedent to Marx's materialism. Three features stand out in Althusser's invocation of Spinozist philosophy: 1) "the opacity of the immediate" (which founds a theory of reading to which Althusser will give the Freudian moniker "lecture symptomale"); 2) the absolute distinction between real objects and objects of knowledge; and 3) the notion of a "cause immanent in its effects."[5]

---

5. All are proposed with extraordinary brevity in Louis Althusser and Etienne Balibar, *Reading "Capital,"* trans. Ben Brewster (London: New Left Books, 1970), 16, 40,

These hints—they are no more—have been taken up at length by Etienne Balibar and Pierre Macherey, whose writings on the seventeenth-century philosopher are part of the important contemporary reevaluation of his work in France and elsewhere.[6] Macherey has followed Althusser's lead in commending Spinoza's value over Hegel's for Marxist theory. In particular, Macherey has asserted Spinoza's importance in posing the question of a materialist (i.e., non-Hegelian, nonidealist, nonteleological) dialectic, against the residual tendencies toward evolutionism in the Marxist conception of history.[7]

Balibar's engagement with Spinoza has been for the most part on another front, that of politics and the specific relation philosophy maintains with it. Balibar focuses on "the object or problem that, in a sense, *Spinoza and Marx have in common:* namely the problem of the 'masses,' or better said, of the determining role of the masses in history."[8] He poses this problem most emphatically and perspicaciously in one of his earliest texts on Spinoza, "Spinoza, the Anti-Orwell: The Fear of the Masses":

> In Spinoza the "mass," or to put it better, the masses, become an explicit theoretical object, because in the last analysis it is their different modalities of existence, according to historical conjunctures and according to economies or regimes of passion, that determine the chances of orienting a political practice toward a given solution. [*Masses, Classes, Ideas*, 5]

As in Marx, the concept of the masses cannot be approached without considerable ambivalence. In Spinoza, this takes the form of the simultaneously held conviction that: 1) the crowd or *vulgus* is inher-

---

189, respectively. On the salutary effect of Spinoza's concepts of ideology and causality in avoiding the errors of Hegelian teleology when assessing Marx's theoretical revolution, see Althusser, *Essays in Self-Criticism*, trans. Grahame Lock (London: New Left Books, 1976), 135–41.

6. Among others, Pierre-François Moreau, *Spinoza* (Paris: Editions du Seuil, 1975); Gilles Deleuze, *Spinoza: philosophie pratique* (Paris: Editions de Minuit, 1981); Antonio Negri, *The Savage Anomaly: The Power of Spinoza's Metaphysics and Politics*, trans. Michael Hardt (Minneapolis: University of Minnesota Press, 1991); and Warren Montag, *Spinoza* (forthcoming from Verso).

7. See Pierre Macherey, *Hegel ou Spinoza* (Paris: Maspero, 1979), 259–60. On the recurrent tendency towards evolutionism in Marxist philosophy, from Marx's Preface to *A Contribution to the Critique of Political Economy* (1859) through the texts of the Second International and the official doctrines of the Communist parties, see Etienne Balibar, *La philosophie de Marx* (Paris: La Découverte, 1993), 78–90.

8. Etienne Balibar, *Masses, Classes, Ideas: Studies on Politics and Philosophy Before and After Marx*, trans. James Swenson (New York: Routledge, 1994), xvi.

ently incapable of being governed by reason, since it must always fall prey to superstition and fear (hence, its members could never become citizens in the ideal city posited in the fourth chapter of the *Theological-Political Treatise*); and 2) it is the necessary basis for any democratic politics (which, as is well known, Spinoza advocated in his programmatic prescriptions for the Dutch Republic) (*Masses, Classes, Ideas*, 9). After the disaster (from his point of view) of the Orangist Revolution in 1672, Spinoza would develop this thought further, formulating the core of a most unfashionable—but thoroughly contemporary—politics. Balibar puts the matter thus:

> The constitutive relation between the masses and the state (*multitudo* and *imperium*) is thought in a rigorous way from the outset by Spinoza as an internal contradiction. The argument of the *Political Treatise* is thus the most explicitly dialectical of his writings: exploring the ways to resolve a contradiction means first of all developing its terms. [*Masses, Classes, Ideas*, 19]

Famously, that contradiction, to which Spinoza gives the name democracy, is never resolved. The *Political Treatise* remained unfinished at Spinoza's death, nor does it anywhere set forth the theory of democracy that commentators have ceaselessly attempted to read into it.

If the history of commentary has been consistently frustrated by the *Political Treatise*, this is due less to its incompletion than to its stubborn refusal to indulge in any facile—Spinoza himself would have called it "utopian"—reduction of the contradiction it discovers at the heart of political life. What Balibar elsewhere labels the "political anthropology" of the *Ethics*[9] undergirds a theory of political forms and action that denies in principle any supercession of the dialectic between political power and the masses, or the state and its citizens/subjects. Rather than an end form of historical development, as the liberal tradition would have it, democracy is, rather, a *tendency*, a constitutive aspect of the political process in all regimes. Every conceivable state form is confronted by the necessity to regulate internal conflicts and must thereby "in disengaging from the 'fluctuation of minds' a unique opinion and a choice," project "a union of hearts and minds around the common interest. But from that moment, it becomes thinkable that the multitude [can] govern itself" (*Spinoza et la Politique*, 90). This tendency or inherent potential will persist, even

---

9. See Balibar, *Spinoza et la politique* (Paris: Presses Universitaires de France, 1985), 91–118.

when "the dominant class has been enlarged to the dimensions of the entire people," (ibid.) since the conflict between passion and reason, which on the authority of the *Ethics* determines all human action, is irreducible in principle. In other terms, Spinozist politics issues in the infamous Althusserian thesis on the permanence of ideology.

EVEN A COMMUNIST SOCIETY COULD NOT DO WITHOUT IDEOLOGY

From such a model of sociopolitical life, either optimistic or pessimistic (or, if one prefers, progressive or conservative) conclusions can equally be drawn. The latter interpretation has been forcefully advanced by Aijaz Ahmad, who writes apropos of Althusser's postulating the necessary persistence of ideology under socialism:

> In other words, there is no end to domination and control; even in a classless society, human beings simply cannot be "left to spontaneity," nor can they *live* the relations of knowledge (which come only through theoretical practice and are not, in any case, *lived*). This entrapment of humankind in ideology, now and forever, is eerily close to Foucault's notion of the power of discourse.[10]

Leaving aside the unwarranted conflation of Foucault and Althusser with so-called "discourse theory"—as is well known, ideological conditioning in Althusser and subject formation in Foucault are never purely intradiscursive—principally at stake here are differing conceptions of a future classless society. The passage from "Marxism and Humanism" on which Ahmad is commenting continues as follows:

> It is in ideology that the classless society *lives* the inadequacy/adequacy of the relation between it and the world, it is in it and by it that it transforms men's "consciousness," that is, their attitudes and behaviour so as to raise them to the level of their tasks and the conditions of their existence.[11]

Althusser maintains, with perfect justice, that no one is born a communist, not even if one is born into a communist society. The social relations of production, indeed all social relations, must be constantly reproduced, in the family, in schools, in the workplace, in political

10. Aijaz Ahmad, *In Theory: Classes, Nations, Literatures* (London: Verso, 1992), 327n34; cf. Perry Anderson, *Considerations on Western Marxism* (London: New Left Books, 1976), 84–85.
11. Althusser, *For Marx*, trans. Ben Brewster (London: New Left Books, 1977), 235.

meetings, in short, at the myriad sites and institutions where social life is carried on. Eliminating the fundamental antagonism between classes will not render society transparent to immediate inspection—although it will remove those massive sources of mystification associated with the wage and commodity forms. The role of ideology in a classless society will be formally the same as that which it plays in class-divided societies: namely, to produce subjects who understand and affirm the social relations governing life in that society. That a constitutive feature of communist ideology is the liberation of its members from material exploitation—"from each according to his ability, to each according to his need"—does not render this principle any less ideological in an Althusserian sense. The lessons of communist ideology will, *ex hypothesi*, be more readily accepted in a classless society than under capitalism; they will remain lessons to be learned and constantly repeated for all that.

One needs to recall the general context in which Althusser wrote his early essays and to bear constantly in mind the object of his critique. His assertion of the permanence of ideology is at one with his general critique of economism and reformism, viz., of Stalinism and of the parliamentary road to socialism proclaimed by the PCF during the 1960s. Transforming the relations of production—e.g., Stalin's famous assertion that class struggle had been banished from the Soviet Union when private ownership of the means of production was eliminated—does not by itself guarantee ideological cohesion. Stalinist state terror was, among other things, a sign that political and ideological struggle in a postcapitalist society remained bitter and widespread long after the fundamental material conditions giving rise to and sustaining it had been removed. Nor would a "peaceful transition to socialism" abolish at a stroke the forms of capitalist domination. This characteristic error of social democracy was relentlessly attacked by Lenin, who insisted on the necessity for a revolutionary transformation of the state apparatus, hence, of a society's political and ideological structures. When the Twenty-second Congress of the French Communist Party eliminated the phrase "dictatorship of the proletariat" from its statutes, Balibar argued strenuously—if in the end unsuccessfully—that to do so was to abandon the ultimate project of socialist transformation by accepting capitalist society's terms and many of its underlying conditions of existence.[12]

12. See Balibar, *On the Dictatorship of the Proletariat*, trans. Grahame Locke (London: New Left Books, 1977).

Reformism thus mirrors economism: both rely on the mistaken notion that production relations are expressed without contradiction in politics and ideology; change the one and everything else follows—forever. Althusser and Balibar rightly challenge this view, insisting upon the perpetual necessity for ideological struggle, even beyond the historical rupture of socialist revolution. With the experience of three quarters of a century of socialist economic experiments in a variety of historical situations to guide us, we are in a position to recognize Althusser's and Balibar's superior theoretical insight on this point.

THE MOTOR OF HISTORY

I shall discuss Balibar's important writings on the Marxist concept of ideology below. For now, though, I wish to rejoin his exegesis of Spinoza's political theory, which, as we have seen, turns decisively on the latter's understanding of the masses in all its contradictory complexity. In one respect, Spinoza's Enlightenment progeny (whom Balibar is generally at pains to criticize)[13] were not wrong to discern in his political prognostics the precursor of that *communauté des lumières* which they postulated as the goal of their own ideological struggle. Observations like the following from the *Theological-Political Treatise* disclose the unmistakable utopianism motivating Spinoza's political thought: "For it is almost impossible that the majority of a people, especially if it is a large one, should agree in an irrational design. And, moreover, the basis and aim of democracy is to avoid the desires as irrational and to bring men as far as possible under the control of reason, so that they may live in peace and harmony."[14] Provoked in the first instance by an acute consciousness of the many forms of superstition and intolerance that have historically dominated politics—and were spectacularly evident in the social upheavals of seventeenth-century Europe—Spinoza's thought nevertheless aims at what his psychology and anthropology pronounce to be by definition impossible. Balibar's concluding judgment is to the point:

> If we admit with Spinoza . . . that communication is structured by relations of ignorance and of knowledge, of superstition, of ideological antagonism, in which are invested human desire and which express an activity of bodies themselves, we must also admit with him that

13. See, for example, *Masses, Classes, Ideas*, 32.
14. Cited in Frederick Copleston, S.J., *A History of Philosophy*, vol. 4, "Descartes to Leibniz" (Westminster, Maryland: Newman Press, 1965), 256.

knowledge is a practice, and that the struggle for knowledge (philosophy) is a political practice. In the absence of this practice, the tendentially democratic processes of decision described by the *Political Treatise* would remain unintelligible. We understand thereby why the essential aspect of Spinozist democracy is from the outset liberty of communication. We understand also how the theory of the "body politic" is neither a simple physics of power, nor a psychology of the submission of the masses, nor the means of formalizing a juridical order, but the search for a strategy of collective liberation, for which the password is: *to be the greatest number possible to think the most possible* [thoughts] (*Ethics*, V, 10). [*Spinoza et la politique*, 117–18; Balibar's emphasis]

Epistemology and ontology—the focus of Althusser's and Macherey's promotion of him—aside, Spinoza opens the door to a concept of politics that, if it found no resonance in the dominant theory of his own time, would become increasingly the norm a century after his death and continues to demarcate the horizon of Left strategic thought two hundred years later. No socialist politics worthy of the name can dispense with the projection of a future society in which all humankind will enjoy equally the freedom of thought and expression postulated in Spinozist democracy. At the same time, this very freedom must perforce create conditions for conflict and internal upheaval—held in the *Political Treatise* to be the most potent cause of the dissolution of existing regimes[15]—that would threaten the order that enables it.

Marxist political theory has never ceased dreaming of a realm of freedom in which social conflict has been abolished, where classes having been eliminated, and where the hitherto ineluctable struggles of history will be deprived of their nurturing conditions. Spinoza, too, dreamed this dream, nowhere more explicitly than in the *Political Treatise*. Balibar identifies its contours, and comments:

> The "best regime," by definition, is thus that which realizes the strongest correlation between the security of individuals and the stability of institutions. . . . If this correlation could be total, that is to say, if the

---

15. See *Spinoza et la politique*, where it is argued that the "*illegal actions* of individuals," motivated by the tendency to "interpret the sovereign's decisions according to one's whim," provoke the "*arbitrary power* [of the sovereign to] tyrannical degeneration," which in turn, "at the point when the 'delirious' State threatens the incompressible minimum of individuality of the men who compose it," will result "finally in *the indignation of the multitude*, which destroys it [viz., the State]" (82–83).

form of the State no more "threatened" the security of individuals than the activity of individuals placed institutions in danger, one would have a perfect body politic, which one could call free or rational (*Political Treatise*, V, 6; VIII, 7). But also, in a certain way, there would no longer be either history or politics. . . . [*Spinoza et la politique*, 80–81; the final ellipsis is Balibar's]

As Spinoza himself opined, and as Balibar and Althusser have consistently reaffirmed, such a society is, strictly speaking, an illusion. Althusser's famous interdiction, licensed, he insisted, by historical materialism, of an ideology-free communist society (and, by implication, one liberated from politics as well), accords with a famous pronouncement of Marx and Engels, who said of communism that it would usher in, not the end of history, but of humankind's prehistory. To reverse the valence of Oscar Wilde's famous *mot*, among the pleasures of socialism will be that many of one's evenings will be taken up by meetings.

THE CLASS STRUGGLE IN THEORY

Balibar's most recent book[16] is an introduction to Marxist philosophy that undertakes "to defend a somewhat paradoxical thesis: whatever one may have thought, *there is not and there never will be a Marxist philosophy;* for this very reason, *Marx's importance for philosophy* is greater than ever" (*La philosophie de Marx*, 3). This thesis is glossed in the following pages, wherein Balibar argues that all of Marx's works are engaged in philosophical labor: they mobilize and elaborate theoretical concepts in a ceaseless process of philosophical critique. At the same time, these works precisely put into question the traditional conception of philosophy from Plato to Hegel, not excluding the materialists from Epicurus to Feuerbach (ibid., 5–8). Taking his cue from the *Theses on Feuerbach*, Balibar maintains that in order to realize "what was always his highest ambition: emancipation, liberation," Marx understood the necessity to effect "a definitive exit [*sortie, Ausgang*] from philosophy" (18). But however much he sought to make a "revolution against philosophy," he found himself "installed not only at the heart of philosophy, but of its most speculative movement, that which

---

16. With the exception of four previously published essays, *Lieux et noms de la vérité* (Paris: Editions de l'Aube, 1994). It contains an interesting text on Hobbes's and Spinoza's differing conceptions of knowledge, "L'Institution de la vérité: Hobbes et Spinoza."

endeavors to *think its proper limits*, if only to abolish them, to establish itself in discovering them" (21).

Balibar's account of Marx's philosophical problematic is far from intraphilosophical; that is to say, the Hegelian ring of the preceding sentence notwithstanding, Marx came to occupy a unique position in relation to philosophy for determinate material, historical reasons. The biographical facts are well known and need not be rehearsed here. Balibar draws attention to the significance of the term "revolution" in the *Theses*, locating its origins in the radical democratic tendencies of 1789 (whose most notable representative was Babeuf), its contemporary incarnation in Marx's lifetime in the communists. Far from a pure idea, "a speculative conception, that of an ideal or experimental city," communism signifies "a social movement whose demands represent simply the consequent application of the principle of the [French] Revolution: measuring the realization of liberty by that of equality and reciprocally, in order to end in fraternity" (22). Famously, from the 1840s onwards, Marx equated this social movement with the real existence of the proletariat. His theoretical itinerary, his production of new philosophical concepts, was only possible because of bourgeois society's evolution, which culminated in the emergence of the proletariat as a class. As Althusser once observed: "It was by *moving* to take up absolutely new, proletarian class positions that Marx realized the possibilities of the theoretical conjunction from which the science of history was born."[17]

What, from the point of view of philosophy itself, was Marx's major philosophical innovation? In Balibar's account, it consisted in Marx's absolutely novel conjugation of two types of human activity classically counterposed in the tradition from Aristotle on down:

> Here, then, is the basis of Marx's materialism in *The German Ideology* (which is effectively a *new* materialism): not a simple inversion of the hierarchy, a "theoretical workerism" I should dare to call it (for which he has been reproached by Hannah Arendt and others), that is to say not a primacy accorded to *poiesis* over *praxis* by virtue of its direct relation with matter, but the identification of the two, the revolutionary thesis according to which *praxis* passes constantly into *poiesis*, and reciprocally. There is no effective liberty that is not at the same time a

---

17. Althusser, "On the Evolution of the Young Marx," in *Essays in Self-Criticism*, 157.

material transformation, that is not historically inscribed in *exteriority*; but neither is there any labor that is not a transformation of the self, as if human beings could change their conditions of existence while conserving an invariant "essence." [*La philosophie de Marx*, 40–41]

The further consequence of this conceptual innovation is to alter the very notion of theory itself, which is now necessarily "identified with a 'production of consciousness.' More exactly, with *one of the terms* of the historical contradiction to which the production of consciousness gives rise. This term is precisely ideology . . ." (ibid., 41). Rejecting Althusser's so-called "first definition of philosophy"—which held philosophy to be the "theory of theoretical practice," hence, on a par with the empirical sciences—Balibar programmatically situates philosophy squarely within ideology. Small wonder that philosophers have hitherto only interpreted the world in various ways. But how might they (help to) change it?

The idealist temptation to imagine that thought will revolutionize reality cannot easily be banished from philosophy. Balibar himself succumbs to it on occasion.[18] Marx's signal achievement was not merely to recognize—and denounce—idealism in its many forms, but to account for its existence—indeed, its persistence. The error of the *philosophes* was to stigmatize ideology as pure illusion, to locate its origins in the deceptions of priests and kings, a view aptly summarized in Diderot's famous slogan. By contrast, Marx insisted on: a) the universality of ideology; and b) its origin in the material conditions of human existence.

Balibar follows a widespread tradition within Marxism (whose most notable contemporary representative is Alfred Sohn-Rethel) in characterizing the fundamental division in society as that between manual and mental labor. Those whom Marx openly calls "ideologues" are among the most important agents for sustaining this basic

---

18. For example, in an unpublished paper delivered at the colloquium on "Cultural Diversities: On Democracy, Community, and Citizenship," sponsored by the Bohen Foundation in New York City, February 1994, in which he proposes that "a practical transformation in the 'real' structure of politics is necessarily reflected, or expressed, in the use of such notions as Universality, Community, Rights, etc., albeit this transformation is not always immediately 'conscious,' which can produce distortions and blockages. To help becoming aware of this complex relation is where theoreticians, or philosophers, can be useful."

social division and thus for reproducing the domination of owners over producers. In the "bourgeois public sphere," ideologues promulgate the illusion that the rule of the dominant class is determined solely by the power of their ideas, an illusion generated not out of cynical lucidity, but because of their objective social position, as Balibar argues in *La philosophie de Marx* (50). Intellectuals—to give this group a more familiar, currently fashionable name—are no more exempt from the objective processes that create ideology than are the classes whom they either represent or help to dominate.

How, then, can there be such a thing as Marxist philosophy? Balibar takes up this challenge in a seemingly paradoxical way. Recalling the imbrication of philosophy in ideology—"ideology designates for philosophy the very element of its formation"—he then refers once more to the youthful Marx's counterposing of ideology with the revolutionary practice of the proletariat, which latter Marx "exalted to the level of an absolute." To follow Marx down this path, however, requires

> holding *at once* two antithetical positions: philosophy will be "Marxist" as long as, for it, the question of truth is put in play in the analysis of the fictions of universality that it autonomously produces; but it must from the outset be "Marxist" *against* Marx, making the denegation of ideology in Marx the first object of its critique. [*La philosophie de Marx*, 117]

Philosophical discourse is rational—it is concerned with adjudicating between truth and falsehood in competing accounts of the world— but Marxist philosophy is not a rationalism. It is, rather, to use the Althusserian term, a practice, i.e., a transformation of preexisting materials into a new product. Its materials are the ideologies that crowd the social world and compete for hegemony in the thoughts and actions of the masses, in particular those elaborated by the ruling class's ideologues. Marxist philosophy is just another instance of the class struggle, carried out on the terrain proper to philosophy, namely, theory. Its ultimate success or failure cannot be decoupled from other instances of class struggle in a given conjuncture. At the same time, even in the darkest periods—the counter-revolutionary moment of the Holy Alliance, the aftermath of 1848, the white terror that followed upon the Bolshevik seizure of power—its singular vocation persists. In the words of another distinguished contemporary Marxist philosopher, that vocation is to assist in "the building of a movement for socialism—in which socialism wins a cultural-intellectual hegemony, so that it becomes the enlightened common-sense of our age."[19]

IDEOLOGY HAS NO HISTORY

In the Anglophone world, Althusser's most enduring, and also his most ambiguous, legacy has been the *rifondazione* of cultural studies for which his writings provided the ostensible charter. Even among those who would now repudiate nearly every aspect of their Althusserian past, the occult force of Althusser's various indications concerning ideology persists.[20] Two closely related topics will concern us here: 1) What is the distinctively Althusserian contribution to the Marxist theory of ideology? 2) How are art and ideology at once intimately connected and yet analytically distinct in Althusserian theory? I shall approach the first through Balibar's essays on "the vacillation of ideology," and the second by taking up Macherey's writings on literature.

Althusser once provocatively remarked that ". . . *The German Ideology* does offer us, after the *1844 Manuscripts*, an explicit theory of ideology, but . . . it is not Marxist. . . ."[21] Balibar elaborates on this seemingly scandalous assertion by showing how the concept of ideology, while it is definitive for historical materialism, nonetheless exhibits a curious textual history in Marx and Engels: "Omnipresent in the writings of 1845–1846, reduced to a few peripheral appearances in the period 1847–1852, ideology is almost nowhere to be found after that until its full-blown restoration in the 1870s, chiefly from the *Anti-Dühring* on" (*Masses, Classes, Ideas*, 88). In the earlier texts—those primarily authored by Marx—the concept of ideology marks the site at which historical materialism stakes its claim to theoretical originality, its absolute break from all the philosophies of history that have preceded it:

> Historical materialism is primarily a program of analysis of the process of the formation and real production of idealist representations of history and politics—in short of the process of idealization . . . historical

---

19. Roy Bhaskar, *Reclaiming Reality: A Critical Introduction to Contemporary Philosophy* (London: Verso, 1989), 1.
20. See Francis Mulhern's evocation of the fate that befell Althusserian motifs when they migrated into British cultural studies during the 1970s and 1980s, in his "Message in a Bottle: Althusser in Literary Studies," in *Althusser: A Critical Reader*, 167–72.
21. Althusser, *Lenin and Philosophy and Other Essays*, trans. Ben Brewster (New York: Monthly Review, 1971), 158; the second ellipsis is Althusser's.

materialism is constituted to the extent to which it can prove that the idealization of history is itself the necessary result of a specific history. [Ibid., 91]

So much is uncontroversial; it has never ceased being repeated in the Marxist tradition. But the canonical interpretation presents a difficulty, one that has haunted Marxist theory from the late Engels to the young Lukács to the mature Sartre and beyond: to wit, from what position can the ideological character of ideology be recognized (and criticized)? Marx's answer, explicit in *The German Ideology*, strongly implied in the *Manifesto*, is in one sense straightforward: only from the standpoint of the proletariat can ideology be recognized as such. But what is the proletariat for Marx? An apparently naive question, it discloses, when one attempts to answer it by closely examining Marx's texts, a constitutive aporia in the concept. On the one hand, the proletariat is that class which, by virtue of its position in the social relations of production, stands opposed to the bourgeoisie and struggles against the hegemony of bourgeois ideology to establish its own dominance in society. On the other hand, it is not a class at all, but the bearer of universal values that are, *stricto sensu*, beyond all ideology. "Because the proletariat is the act of practical negation of all ideology, there is no such thing as a proletarian ideology," Balibar abruptly observes (ibid., 95). This is the position that undergirds the historical (and theoretical) claims of *The German Ideology*. To sustain it, Marx must evacuate all historical or political specificity from the proletariat. Balibar explicates Marx's view, but only in order to put it into question.

As we have seen, the withering away of the state in the classless society of the future does not imply a corresponding disappearance of ideology as such—all Marx's and Engels's indications to the contrary notwithstanding. But how can this be known? Isn't it a symptom of Althusser's and Balibar's own dogmatism that they insist on the permanence of ideology, even in communist society? Their prediction of an ideologically saturated classless society is, one could say, scarcely less "ideological" than the contrary proposition it vehemently denies. Similar in this respect, the two positions are nonetheless not symmetrical; they posit alternative, incompatible concepts of ideology.

In projecting a time when there will be no more ideology, the former implies that this time is already upon us, that the revolutionary practice of the proletariat unites politics with truth. From the Erfurt Program through the post-Leninist parties of the Third International, this belief has provided the rationale for the major organizational forms of the working class to proclaim their theoretical rectitude (and thus their effective immunity from "external" critique) and to maintain their monopoly over political strategy. By contrast, Althusser and Balibar have written the charter for Communist dissidents (the former continuously from within the party; the latter at first within, now outside it) by defining ideology, not as the opposite of truth or an object of pure theoretical investigation, but as the condition of the emergence of knowledge. Following Lenin, who defined Marxism as "the concrete analysis of a concrete situation," Balibar designates truth as "a *conjunctural fact* and an *effect* of the conjuncture" insofar as it "contradicts the 'dominant' forms or criteria of universality, that is, it embodies a practical criticism of ideology" (*Masses, Classes, Ideas*, 170). Truth, or what might be better termed correct theory, is inextricably bound up with the ideological, with those forms of practical activity, of beliefs and their institutional rituals, that govern all our lives and constitute our fundamental relation to social reality. Knowledge emerges out of the real struggles within ideology, or, to be more precise, in the conflict between ideologies that is the irreducible condition of social life.

This conflict has, historically speaking, two elements: class struggles and mass movements, which Balibar avers always "remain relatively *heterogeneous* [to each other]" (ibid., 173), at the same time that they repeatedly coalesce in, more or less, decisive conjunctures. These latter are, strictly speaking, unpredictable, and yet their results are not simply random or without lessons for subsequent practice. The fundamental structure in which the two elements are combined is characterized thus:

> To parody Kant, it could be said that without the mass movements the class struggle is empty (which is to say, it remains full of dominant ideology). However, without the class struggle [for which read organizational forms] the mass movements are blind (which is to say, they give rise to counterrevolution, even fascism, as much as to revolution). But there is no pre-established correspondence between these two forms, no universal "schematism." The true is then produced as the critical effect of the unpredictable that obliges the class struggle to *go back over* and correct its own representations (and its own myths). [172][22]

---

22. Balibar's note to this passage refers the reader to "Althusser's thesis of the 'overdetermination' and 'underdetermination' of contradictions" in the programmatic essay, "Contradiction and Overdetermination" (*Masses, Classes, Ideas*, 240, n19).

Pace Marx, Engels, and a long tradition of their inheritors (not excluding Althusser in some of his writings), there can be no Marxist theory of ideology, indeed no Marxist science of society as such. The work of revolution, so Balibar implies here, does not result from controlled theoretical prediction but from contingent practices whose field of action is constantly being reconfigured. Revolutionary politics is less a science than an art.

ART IS NOT RANKED AMONG THE IDEOLOGIES

Pierre Macherey's *A Theory of Literary Production*[23] extends the Althusserian project of "lecture symptomale" onto the terrain of literary art. Specifically, it poses a series of questions implicit in the science/ideology problematic that forms the core of Althusser's work: what kind of knowledge does literature (or art) produce; what is the precise relation between literature and ideology; and, correlatively, what is the status of literary criticism in the science/ideology relation? Macherey will adhere strictly to the canons of historical materialism, which hold that literature is a production of ideology; at the same time he will attempt to define literature's specific mode of material existence, that which distinguishes it from other ideological forms. His project aims to bridge the gap between formalism and Marxism, both at the level of theory and in exemplary analyses of literary texts. The essence of his conceptual innovation is conveniently summarized near the end of the book's lengthy theoretical overture, "Some Elementary Concepts":

> What we are seeking is analogous to that relationship which Marx acknowledges when he insists on seeing the material relations as being derived from the social infrastructure behind ideological phenomena, not in order to explain these phenomena as emanations from the infrastructure, which would amount to saying that the ideological is the economic in another form: whence the possibility of reducing the ideological to the economic. [*A Theory of Literary Production*, 92–93]

As Macherey goes on to explain (in a passage to which we shall return), the symmetry between Marx's conception of ideology and the concept of literature proposed here can be expressed as a proportion: Ideology/Economy = Text/History. On both sides of the equation, the first

---

23. Macherey, *A Theory of Literary Production*, trans. Geoffrey Wall (London: Routledge & Kegan Paul, 1978).

term does not simply or directly express the second; and yet neither can they be completely divorced from each other. A noneconomistic theory of ideology derived from Marx (via Althusser) implies an antimimetic theory of aesthetic representation.

Macherey proceeds in an entirely orthodox Althusserian fashion, inaugurating his project to establish the conceptual foundations for literary science by delimiting its terms and defining its boundaries in relation to the ideological problematic with which it seeks to break. The latter is characterized as critical appreciation, the aim of which is to cultivate literary or aesthetic judgment, to produce educated subjects possessed of discriminating taste. To this still powerful model for reading and criticism, Macherey opposes the notion that the purpose of literary criticism is to produce knowledge, which involves, rather than a judgment concerning a text's aesthetic value, explanation of its "conditions and possibilities" (*A Theory of Literary Production*, 3). The "science of literary production" that Macherey proposes has, in the first instance, to produce its object; as in any science, the domain of investigation is never simply given. At stake here is the Althusserian offensive against empiricism, in this context the rejection of any concept of the text as immediately available to inspection. Against the far from moribund belief that texts are enclosed, self-sufficient, fully explicit, and the correlative (positivist) conviction that interpretation requires only that a reader approach the text without prejudice or prior conviction, Macherey asserts the irreducible complexity or unevenness of literary texts, what he terms in his essay on Balzac's *Les Paysans* their "disparate" nature. Texts for Macherey are necessarily and in principle overdetermined in their structure, hence also in their effects.

Flirting with the terminology of Russian Formalism and the later Bakhtin, Macherey attributes two principal properties to literature: autonomy and parody. What is it that literary texts parody? Macherey suggests three objects: ordinary language, previous literary forms, and ideology (*A Theory of Literary Production*, 52–53; 59). What distinguishes his conception of literature from formalism in the strict sense of that term is his locating the ultimate determination of literary texts in the third of these domains. The specificity of a given text emerges from posing questions to it on two distinct levels. On the one hand are those elements "properly interior to the work," what Macherey terms "a question of structure," or what traditional criticism would recognize as the work's themes. On the other hand are features that, while not purely external to the work, nonetheless demand inquiry that goes beyond the work's own statements. These involve the work's position in "ideological history" as this is "present in the work in so far as the emergence of the work required this history, which is its only principle of reality and also supplies its means of expression" (93–94). How is this internalization of ideology realized? Macherey points directly here to his analysis of Jules Verne, but a somewhat clearer idea of the characteristic procedures involved can be obtained from his account of Lenin's essays on Tolstoy.

One might legitimately ask: of what value are Lenin's occasional pieces on art, not only for us, but for Lenin himself? These articles, written between 1908 and 1911, would seem on the face of it to be a distraction for a professional revolutionary whose immediate task was to comprehend the failure of the revolution of 1905. Macherey faces this objection head-on at the outset:

> Lenin's contribution to Marxist aesthetics was intimately connected with the elaboration of a scientific socialism. The literary articles were to play their part in this larger enterprise. In certain determinate circumstances, then, Lenin discovered a novel function for literary criticism within a general theoretical activity. . . . The general principle of Lenin's critical method is that the literary work only makes sense if considered in its relation to a determinate historical period. It derives its distinctive characteristics from this period, but it can also be used to illuminate the period. [107]

In assessing the possible paths forward for Russian revolutionary strategy, Lenin drew upon the historical lessons to be learned from Tolstoy's representation of the Tsarist social formation. "Art," Althusser says, "does not give us a *knowledge* in the *strict sense* . . . , but what it gives us does nevertheless maintain a certain *specific relationship* with knowledge" (*Lenin and Philosophy*, 222). Macherey's project attempts to delineate what this "specific relationship" of art to knowledge could be.

How, in Macherey's account, does Lenin proceed? The first task is to identify Tolstoy's historical period, viz., the material (including the ideological) conditions that produced Tolstoy's texts and in which they intervened. This spanned the years 1861–1905, the era in which, after the abolition of serfdom, the Russian peasantry emerged from feudalism and that witnessed, simultaneously, the birth of capitalism in Russia (*A Theory of Literary Production*, 108–10). Second, Lenin explores the complex ideological identifications that defined Tolstoy's relation to this period. In the first instance, Tolstoy's social origins dictate his "spontaneous" representation of the landed aristocracy. But secondly, as a consequence of the "social mobility" he could achieve as a writer, he programmatically recommended an ideology "not 'naturally' his own, by looking to the peasant" (113–14). Tolstoy's work thus presents a series of ideological contradictions that establish a double relation: on the one hand to history (the real), on the other to ideology (the representation of the real) (115). The theoretical problem, Macherey recognizes, is to determine the way in which this double relation is made to appear in Tolstoy's texts.

The key to Lenin's analyses lies in his metaphors: mirror, reflection, expression (118). Contrary to what a too-hasty reading would conclude, these do not indicate his commitment to a naive theory of mimesis; rather, they point to that mechanism of figuration which Freud termed "considerations of representability" (*Rücksicht auf Darstellbarkeit*). Macherey writes:

> The secret of the mirror is to be sought in the form of its reflections; how does it show historical reality, by what paradox does it make visible its own blindness without actually seeing itself? . . . The work of Tolstoy is itself an assemblage. And, just as Freud has established that a dream has to be deconstructed into its constitutive elements before it can be interpreted, Lenin states that the literary text must be studied in the same way—not in the pursuit of a factitious totality, but according to its real and necessary discontinuity. [122]

But isolating the elements is only the first step. Macherey will argue that the object of scientific investigation in Tolstoy's texts is no individual, historically discrete ideology, nor any single social class. Scientific criticism investigates the structure or system of the text that produces a determinate contradiction. The contradiction produced in and by the text opens the door to the historical truth that the text, because of its own ideological limitations, cannot state openly.

IS IT SIMPLE TO BE A MARXIST IN PHILOSOPHY?

Macherey is not principally a theoretician of literature. Yet for an English-speaking audience, this is how he must perforce appear. His only two books, and the majority of his essays, to have been translated into English either develop theoretical positions on literature or engage in practical criticism of literary texts. The most recent of these, *The Object of Literature*, reopens the theoretical problematic inaugurated by *A Theory of Literary Production:* What is the object to be studied, analyzed, explained in a yet-to-be-constructed science of literature? This early project was indicted for its unremitting formalism, while the Macherey of the 1970s was held to have succumbed to the opposite error of functionalist reductionism. Doubtless, both charges will resurface in response to *The Object of Literature.* Warrant for each can be adduced. We could turn, for example, to the formalist Macherey who appears virtually without adornment in his essay on Céline:

> We must abandon the attempt to look behind literature's statements for the other discourse of which it is the distorted and deformed expression, and which constitutes its authentic meaning. For if literature does deal with truth, the truth in question has no value other than that conferred upon it by literature. It is the truth of its style. Literature establishes a real stylistics of depth rather than a metaphysics, and stylistics is in itself a partial substitute for philosophy.[24]

Or we could consider the following lapidary observation from the programmatic essay that brings the book to a close: "In the final instance, all literary texts have as their object—and this seems to be their real 'philosophy'—the non-adhesion of language to language, the gap that constantly divides what we say from what we say about it and what we think about it." From Roman Jakobson to Roland Barthes, the specificity of literary language has been the mark of that "literariness" which Macherey has elsewhere been at great pains to deny is even a proper category for articulating literature's objectivity.

But these are not Macherey's only words. In another place he could write of literature and language (in collaboration with Etienne Balibar):

> The objectivity of literature is its necessary place within the determinate processes and reproduction of the contradictory linguistic practices of the common tongue, in which the effectivity of the ideology of bourgeois education is realised.
>
> This siting of the problem abolishes the old idealist question, "What is literature?," which is not a question about its objective determinance, but a question about its universal essence, human and artistic. It abolishes it because it shows us directly the material function of literature, inserted within a process which literature cannot determine even though it is indispensable to it.[25]

24. Macherey, *The Object of Literature,* trans. David Macey (Cambridge: Cambridge University Press, 1995), 132.
25. Balibar and Macherey, "On Literature as an Ideological Form," trans. Ian McLeod et al., *Oxford Literary Review* 3/1 (1978): reprinted in *Untying the Text: A Post-*

Plainly it is possible to construe Macherey's pronouncements on literary language as other than formalist, viz., in the materialist spirit in which he certainly intended them. There is indeed such a thing as "literary language," distinct from and yet derivative of ordinary language. Its existence issues less from the intrinsic properties of literary texts, than from a system of social stratification that trains certain readers to identify (and identify with) literature, while consigning others to the lower ranks of mere users of the *lingua franca*. There is no inherent contradiction between the ostensible formalism of the early (and also the more recent) Macherey and the sociological criticism Macherey produced in the mid-1970s. The task of formal analysis is to expose the contradictions in a text's linguistic practices that sociological research demonstrates to be constitutive of literature as an ideological apparatus.

Compatible, then, with these two earlier Machereys, *The Object of Literature* nevertheless stages the literary problematic somewhat differently. It brings together in a single speculative project the philosophical and the literary, as if Macherey had sought here to unite the two poles of his *oeuvre*. These essays all concern the ways in which literature and philosophy, representations and concepts, are intimately entwined in a range of texts from Sade and Mme de Staël to Queneau and Foucault. The relationship between these two domains is conveniently summarized in the following passage from the essay on Hugo:

> By comparing texts borrowed from Marx or Tocqueville with texts written by Sue or Hugo, and by demonstrating that comparable schemas of representation are at work in them, we are not attempting to deny the originality of their content by arguing that, ultimately, everything is mere literature; the point is to call attention to that content by showing how fictional texts can, in their own way, not only convey but produce forms of speculation which are directly expressive of a determinate historical reality. They allow us both to understand it and to imagine it. [*The Object of Literature*, 109]

The concept of literature adumbrated here is in line both with the so-called "formalist Macherey" and with the much-vilified passage from Althusser's "Letter on Art" that surely inspired it. Literature is not

---

Structuralist Reader, ed. Robert Young (London: Routledge & Kegan Paul, 1981), 86. The French original of this text was published as the introduction to Renée Balibar, *Les français fictifs* (Paris: Hachette, 1974).

history (or science or philosophy), but it stands in a quite particular relation to the historical materials out of which it produces its specific mode of existence.

What is the nature of that relation? Macherey remains an utterly impenitent Althusserian on this point, which he puts most directly near the end of *The Object of Literature:*

> The problematical thought which runs through all literary texts is rather like the philosophical consciousness of a historical period. The role of literature is to say what a period thinks of itself. The age of literature, from Sade to Céline, does project an ideological message which demands to be believed on the basis of the actual evidence. If taken literally, the message seems to be patently inconsistent and incoherent. It projects an outline sketch of its own limits, and that sketch is inseparable from the introduction of a relativist perspective. What, from this point of view, is the philosophical contribution of literature? It makes it possible to relocate all the discourses of philosophy, in its accredited forms, within the historical element which makes them the results of chance and circumstances, the products of a pathetic and magnificent throw of the dice. [234]

No one trained in the history of philosophy is likely to miss the way in which a certain Hegelianism has been turned on its head in this passage. According to Macherey, it is not philosophy that paints its grey on grey at the end of an epoch, but literature that exhibits the self-consciousness of an age. In a much-cited—if seldom understood—observation, Hegel opined that art "is and remains for us a thing of the past."[26] Macherey takes Hegel's point and gives it a characteristically Althusserian twist. Art is a thing of the past in the same way that historical science can be said to expose to view the ideological (and other) structures of a social form on its way to extinction. The literature of the bourgeois epoch—in Macherey's view there has never been any other—brings that epoch's ideological contradictions into plain view. We are not so far here from Marx's and Engels's celebration of Balzac, except that, as Macherey remarks elsewhere, it is not only generic realism that is capable of laying bare the contradictions of capitalist society: "The idea of reflection correctly understood teaches us that a product can very well be objective, i.e., determined by material reality, without being exact, i.e., conforming to this reality or to our idea of

---

26. G. W. F. Hegel, *Aesthetics: Lectures on Fine Art*, trans. T. M. Knox (Oxford: Clarendon Press, 1975), 11.

reality: Kafka is no less objective than Thomas Mann, even if he is differently so."[27]

If there ever was a functionalist Macherey—a description I hope to have shown is open to challenge—he would appear to have been given his quietus in *The Object of Literature*. The ambiguities and contradictions that admittedly adhere to the term "Althusserian" (evident in the first instance in Althusser's writings themselves) cannot, for all that, disguise the fact that the research program launched in *For Marx* and *Reading "Capital"* has been continued on a variety of fronts by his first students and collaborators. That program, which insisted on, among other things, the necessity for any science to produce its object of investigation, is carried forward in *The Object of Literature*, with results that will ultimately be judged not by this book alone, but by the future research that it inspires. I shall hazard the prediction that this project is unlikely to be without issue.

27. Macherey, "The Problem of Reflection," *Sub-stance* 15 (1976): 15.

Contributors

ETIENNE BALIBAR's many publications since his contribution to *Reading "Capital"* include *Spinoza et la politique* (1990), *Les Frontières de la démocratie* (1992), and *La Philosophie de Marx* (1993). The most recent translations of his work into English are *Masses, Classes, Ideas: Studies on Politics and Philosophy before and after Marx* (1994) and *Race, Nation, Class: Ambiguous Identities* (1991; written with Immanuel Wallerstein).

JUDITH BUTLER, Professor of Rhetoric and Comparative Literature at the University of California at Berkeley, is author, most recently, of *Bodies that Matter: On the Discursive Limits of "Sex"* (1993) and of *Gender Trouble: Feminism and the Subversion of Identity* (1990).

ROGER CELESTIN is Associate Professor of French and Comparative Literature at the University of Connecticut, Storrs, and the author of *From Cannibals to Radicals: Figures and Limits of Exoticism* (University of Minnesota Press, 1995).

GERALDINE FRIEDMAN is Associate Professor of English at Purdue University. She is the author of a forthcoming book entitled *The Insistence of History: Revolution in Burke, Wordsworth, Keats, and Baudelaire* (Stanford University Press, 1996). Her essays on British Romanticism and Baudelaire have appeared in *PMLA, English Literary History, Studies in Romanticism,* and *Texas Studies in Literature and Language*

JACQUES LEZRA is Assistant Professor of English at the University of Wisconsin, Madison. He is the translator and editor of *Visión y ceguera*, the Spanish edition of Paul de Man's *Blindness and Insight*, and has published articles on Freud, Foucault, Shakespeare,

CONTRIBUTORS 227

and Elizabethan rhetoric. He is completing work on a book that treats the genealogy of the event.

PIERRE MACHEREY's publications include *Comte, la philosophie et les sciences* (1989), *Hegel ou Spinoza* (1979), and *A Theory of Literary Production* (1966; English translation, 1978). His *The Object of Literature* (1995) has just appeared in translation, and a collection of his work is forthcoming from Verso.

WARREN MONTAG is Associate Professor of English at Occidental College. His most recent publication is *The Unthinkable Swift* (Verso, 1994). He is editing a collection of essays by Pierre Macherey, forthcoming from Verso.

THOMAS PEPPER teaches in the Department of Foreign Languages and Literatures at the University of Miami, Coral Gables, and at the Søren Kierkegaard Research Centre at the University of Copenhagen. He has published essays on Adorno, Celan, Derrida and Heidegger, and Merleau-Ponty and Lacan, and his *Singularities: Essays Before the End* will appear in 1996 from Cambridge University Press. He is currently working on a monograph on marriage and the feminine in Kierkegaard.

JEAN-MARC POISSON is a Dissertator in the Department of French and Italian at the University of Wisconsin, Madison. His most recent publications include a translation of Yves Bertrand's *Théories contemporaines de l'éducation*. He is also the translator for *Domitor*, an international journal for the study and promotion of early cinema.

ELLEN ROONEY is the Director of the Pembroke Center for Teaching and Research on Women and Associate Professor of English and Modern Culture and Media at Brown University. She is the author of *Seductive Reasoning: Pluralism as the Problematic of Contemporary Literary Theory*.

MICHAEL SPRINKER is Professor of English and Comparative Literature at the State University of New York, Stony Brook, where he teaches literary theory, modern European literature, and the history and literature of the British Empire. His most recent book is *History and Ideology in Proust*, published by Cambridge University Press.

ANDRZEJ WARMINSKI is Professor of Comparative Literature at the University of California, Irvine, and the author of *Readings in Interpretation: Hölderlin, Hegel, Heidegger*. His book of "material readings" is forthcoming.

French in Action–
The Capretz Method, Second Edition

The first fully integrated multimedia course that effectively combines video, audio, and text to train students to use real, unsimplified French in the dynamic context of actual communication.

Now in its second edition, *French in Action*'s innovative approach helps teachers and students at over 2,000 institutions to listen, watch, and get involved!

"The best method ever devised for teaching French."
—Alan Astro, Trinity University

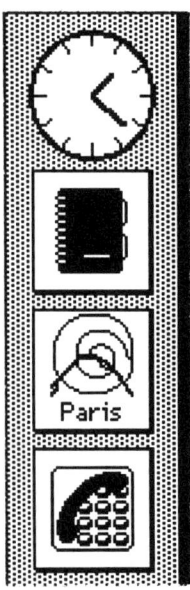

For the language lab

A la rencontre de Philippe
Athena Language Learning Project
Gilberte Furstenberg, creator

An interactive videodisc program to improve intermediate students' comprehension of spoken French.

Coming in Spring 1996

Ecritures de femmes
Nouvelles Cartographies
Mary Ann Caws, Mary Jean Green, Marianne Hirsch, & Ronnie Scharfman

A new intermediate level anthology and reader for French studies.

Yale University Press
Call 800 987–7323 • yupmkt@yalevm.cis.yale.edu

Funding for *French in Action* and *Philippe* is provided by the Annenberg/CPB Project.

The following issues are available through **Yale University Press,** Customer Service Department, P.O. Box 209040, New Haven, CT 06520-9040.

69 The Lesson of Paul de Man (1985) $17.00
73 Everyday Life (1987) $17.00
75 The Politics of Tradition: Placing Women in French Literature (1988) $17.00
Special Issue: After the Age of Suspicion: The French Novel Today (1989) $17.00
76 Autour de Racine: Studies in Intertextuality (1989) $17.00
77 Reading the Archive: On Texts and Institutions (1990) $17.00
78 On Bataille (1990) $17.00
79 Literature and the Ethical Question (1991) $17.00
Special Issue: Contexts: Style and Value in Medieval Art and Literature (1991) $17.00
80 Baroque Topographies: Literature/History/Philosophy (1992) $17.00
81 On Leiris (1992) $17.00
82 Post/Colonial Conditions Vol. 1 (1993) $17.00
83 Post/Colonial Conditions Vol. 2 (1993) $17.00
84 Boundaries: Writing and Drawing (1993) $17.00
85 Discourses of Jewish Identity in 20th-Century France (1994) $17.00
86 Corps Mystique, Corps Sacré (1994) $17.00
87 Another Look, Another Woman (1995) $17.00

Special subscription rates are available on a calendar year basis (2 issues per year):
Individual subscriptions $26.00
Institutional subscriptions $30.00

ORDER FORM Yale University Press, P.O. Box 209040, New Haven, CT 06520-9040
I would like to purchase the following individual issues:
_____
_____

For individual issue, please add postage and handling:
Single issue, United States $2.75   Each additional issue $.50
Single issue, foreign countries $5.00 Each additional issue $1.00
Connecticut residents please add sales tax of 6%

Payment of $_____ is enclosed (including sales tax if applicable).

Mastercard no. _____

4-digit bank no. _____ Expiration date _____

VISA no. _____ Expiration date _____

Signature _____

SHIP TO _____
_____
_____

See the next page for ordering other back issues. Yale French Studies is also available through Xerox University Microfilms, 300 North Zeeb Road, Ann Arbor, MI 48106.

The following issues are still available through the **Yale French Studies Office,** P.O. Box 208251, New Haven, CT 06520-8251.

19/20 Contemporary Art $3.50	43 The Child's Part $5.00	Fiction: Space, Landscape, Decor $6.00
33 Shakespeare $3.50	44 Paul Valéry $5.00	58 In Memory of Jacques Ehrmann $6.00
35 Sade $3.50	45 Language as Action $5.00	
38 The Classical Line $3.50	46 From Stage to Street $3.50	59 Rethinking History $6.00
39 Literature and Revolution $3.50	47 Image & Symbol in the Renaissance $3.50	61 Toward a Theory of Description $6.00
41 Game, Play, Literature $5.00	52 Graphesis $5.00	62 Feminist Readings: French Texts/American Contexts $6.00
	53 African Literature $3.50	
42 Zola $5.00	54 Mallarmé $5.00	
	57 Locus in Modern French	

Add for postage & handling

Single issue, United States $3.00 (Priority Mail)   Each additional issue $1.25
Single issue, United States $1.80 (Third Class)   Each additional issue $ .50
Single issue, foreign countries $2.50 (Book Rate)   Each additional issue $1.50

YALE FRENCH STUDIES, P.O. Box 208251, New Haven, Connecticut 06520-8251
A check made payable to YFS is enclosed. Please send me the following issue(s):

Issue no.   Title   Price
_____
_____

                                                           Postage & handling _____
                                                                       Total _____

Name _____

Number/Street _____

City _____ State _____ Zip _____

The following issues are now available through Kraus Reprint Company, Route 100, Millwood, N. Y. 10546.

1 Critical Bibliography of Existentialism	17 The Art of the Cinema
2 Modern Poets	18 Passion & the Intellect, or Malraux
3 Criticism & Creation	21 Poetry Since the Liberation
4 Literature & Ideas	22 French Education
5 The Modern Theatre	24 Midnight Novelists
6 France and World Literature	25 Albert Camus
7 André Gide	26 The Myth of Napoleon
8 What's Novel in the Novel	27 Women Writers
9 Symbolism	28 Rousseau
10 French-American Literature Relationships	29 The New Dramatists
11 Eros, Variations...	30 Sartre
12 God & the Writer	31 Surrealism
13 Romanticism Revisited	32 Paris in Literature
14 Motley: Today's French Theater	34 Proust
15 Social & Political France	48 French Freud
16 Foray through Existentialism	51 Approaches to Medieval Romance

36/37 Structuralism has been reprinted by Doubleday as an Anchor Book.
55/56 Literature and Psychoanalysis has been reprinted by Johns Hopkins University Press, and can be ordered through Customer Service, Johns Hopkins University Press, Baltimore, MD 21218.